POWER AND GLORY

POWER AND GLORY

Elizabeth II and the Rebirth of Royalty

ALEXANDER LARMAN

ST. MARTIN'S PRESS
NEW YORK

First published in the United States by St. Martin's Press, an imprint of
St. Martin's Publishing Group

POWER AND GLORY. Copyright © 2024 by Alexander Larman.
All rights reserved. Printed in the United States of America. For information,
address St. Martin's Publishing Group, 120 Broadway, New York, NY 10271.

www.stmartins.com

The Library of Congress Cataloging-in-Publication Data is available upon request.

ISBN 978-1-250-28959-9 (hardcover)
ISBN 978-1-250-28960-5 (ebook)

Our books may be purchased in bulk for promotional, educational, or
business use. Please contact your local bookseller or the Macmillan Corporate and
Premium Sales Department at 1-800-221-7945, extension 5442, or
by email at MacmillanSpecialMarkets@macmillan.com.

Originally published in the United Kingdom by Weidenfeld & Nicolson, an imprint of
The Orion Publishing Group Ltd

First U.S. Edition: 2024

10 9 8 7 6 5 4 3 2 1

For my daughter Rose, the greatest queen any father could wish to have

Kings are pretty cheap these days.

Ernest Bevin, 10 September 1946

Above all things our royalty is to be reverenced, and if you begin to poke about it you cannot reverence it . . . Its mystery is its life. We must not let in daylight upon magic.

Walter Bagehot, *The English Constitution*

Behold, my desire is, that the Almighty would answer me, and that mine adversary had written a book.

Job, 31:35

Contents

Dramatis Personae

Royalty and their circle

George VI, King of the United Kingdom, the Dominions of the
    Commonwealth, and Emperor of India
Queen Elizabeth, his wife
Princess Elizabeth, their elder daughter; queen 1952-2022
Princess Margaret, their younger daughter
Prince Philip, Duke of Edinburgh, husband to Princess Elizabeth
Prince Charles, son to Philip and Elizabeth
Princess Anne, daughter to Philip and Elizabeth
Edward, Duke of Windsor, former king, now international
    playboy; known as 'David' to his family and familiars
Wallis Windsor, his wife
Queen Mary, the royal mother
Prince Henry, Duke of Gloucester, her third son
Mary, Princess Royal, Countess of Harewood, her daughter
Lord Mountbatten, Edward's cousin and Philip's uncle
Lord Brabourne, his son-in-law
Patricia Mountbatten, Philip's cousin
Bessie Merryman, Wallis's aunt
May Elphinstone, Queen Elizabeth's sister
David Bowes-Lyon, Queen Elizabeth's brother, 'a vicious little
    fellow'
Sir Alan 'Tommy' Lascelles, private secretary to George VI
    1945-52; private secretary to Elizabeth II 1952-53
Sir Edward Ford, assistant private secretary to George VI 1946-52

Martin Charteris, private secretary to Princess Elizabeth 1950–52;
    assistant private secretary to Elizabeth II 1952–53
Marion 'Crawfie' Crawford, former governess to the princesses
Major George Buthlay, her husband
Peter Townsend, equerry to George VI
Dermot Morrah, journalist and royal speechwriter
Owen Morshead, royal librarian and archivist
John Gibson, footman to Prince Charles
Lady Anne Glenconner, lady-in-waiting
[Albert] George 'A. G.' Allen, solicitor to the Duke of Windsor
Sir Walter Monckton, lawyer and counsellor to George VI and the
    Duke of Windsor
Kenneth de Courcy, confidant to the Duke and Duchess of
    Windsor
Godfrey Thomas, former royal courtier
Charles Murphy, ghostwriter for the Duke of Windsor
F. J. Dadd, secretary to the Duke of Windsor
Mike Parker, equerry to Prince Philip
Lord Beaverbrook, newspaper magnate and friend to the Duke of
    Windsor
Viscount Ednam, Earl of Dudley, and Laura, Countess of Dudley,
    friends of the Duke of Windsor
Joan Martin, Wallis's maid
Anne Seagrim, secretary to the Duke of Windsor

Politicians

Clement Attlee, Prime Minister 1945–51; Leader of the Opposition
    1951–55
Herbert Morrison, Deputy Leader of the Labour Party 1945–56
Hugh Dalton, Chancellor of the Exchequer 1945–47
Ernest Bevin, Foreign Secretary 1945–51
James Chuter-Ede, Home Secretary 1945–51
Arthur Creech Jones, Secretary of State to the Colonies 1946–50
Harold Laski, Labour politician

Tom Driberg, Labour politician

William Jowitt, Lord Chancellor

Winston Churchill, Leader of the Opposition 1945-51; Prime
  Minister 1951-55

Anthony Eden, de facto Deputy Prime Minister 1951-55

Robert 'Bob' Boothby, Conservative politician

Henry 'Chips' Channon, Conservative politician and diarist

Harold Nicolson, Conservative politician and diarist

Leo Amery, Conservative politician

Rab Butler, Conservative politician

Jock Colville, private secretary to Princess Elizabeth 1947-49;
  private secretary to Churchill 1951-55

Lord Halifax, British ambassador to the United States 1940-46

Archibald Clark Kerr, 1st Baron Inverchapel, British ambassador
  to the United States 1946-48

Duff Cooper, British ambassador to France 1944-48

Ramsay MacDonald, former prime minister

Alexander Cadogan, Permanent Under-Secretary for Foreign
  Affairs 1938-46

John Martin, private secretary to Churchill 1941-45

Sir Pierson Dixon, private secretary to Bevin 1945-48

Edward Holman, assistant ambassador to France

Sir Edward Baring, high commissioner to South Africa

Sir William Murphy, ambassador to the Bahamas

John Wheeler-Bennett, British representative in Germany

Clement Davies, Leader of the Liberal Party 1945-56

Harry S. Truman, American president 1945-53

James F. Byrnes, US Secretary of State 1945-47

George Marshall, US Secretary of State 1947-49

Admiral William Leahy, Truman's chief of staff

Robert Coe, US diplomat to the United Kingdom

Jan Smuts, Prime Minister of South Africa 1939-48

Norman Robertson, Canadian high commissioner

Joseph Stalin, Leader of the Soviet Union 1924-53

Society - high

Clementine Churchill, wife to Winston

Diana Cooper, wife to Duff

Susan Mary Alsop, socialite

Osla Benning, Canadian debutante

Cecil Beaton, society photographer and diarist

John Reith, Director General of the BBC 1927-38

Herman and Katherine Rogers, friends of Wallis

Osbert Sitwell, writer and wit

Noël Coward, playwright and actor

Peter Coats, companion to Chips Channon

Kathleen Kennedy, daughter of American ambassador Jack
    Kennedy

Cecil Roberts, friend to the Duke and Duchess of Windsor

Henry Luce, publisher and founder of *Life* magazine

Dan Longwell, editor of *Life* magazine

John Gordon, *Sunday Express* editor

Norman Hartnell, royal couturier

Cyril Garbett, Archbishop of York

Commander Sir Morton Stuart, Manipulative Surgeon to the King

Sir Thomas Dunhill, Serjeant Surgeon to the King

Professor James Learmonth, Regius Professor in Clinical Surgery

Clement Price Thomas, a leading chest surgeon

Lord Moran, physician to Churchill

Lady Astor, friend to Queen Elizabeth

D'Arcy Osborne, diplomat and friend to Queen Elizabeth

James 'Jimmy' Donahue Jr, socialite, playboy and friend to the
    Duke and Duchess of Windsor

Ella Maxwell, American gossip columnist and hostess

Earl of Athlone, friend to the Duke of Windsor

Rowland Baring, 2nd Earl of Cromer, friend to the Duke of
    Windsor

Oscar Nemon, sculptor to the great and good

Edmund Hillary, mountaineer
Michael Ramsey, Bishop of Durham

Society – low

John Capstick, chief inspector at Scotland Yard
Leslie Holmes, convicted thief
John Dean, butler to Lord Mountbatten
James Cameron, *Daily Express* journalist
Marietta Fitzgerald, American journalist
Bruce and Beatrice Blackmar Gould, co-editors of *Ladies' Home
    Journal*
Dorothy Black, ghostwriter for Crawfie
Vera M. Brunt, outraged by Crawfie
Colm Brogan, *Daily Express* journalist
Kenneth H. Smith, president of the Book Publishers'
    Representatives Association
R. M. MacColl, *Daily Express* journalist

Introduction

When I sat down to write *The Crown in Crisis* in late 2018, it was without any intention of the book turning into the first instalment in a trilogy. Indeed, in all its drama and richness, the abdication saga seemed like a perfectly self-contained story. Yet by the time I had finished, I was desperate to continue the narrative, which concluded with the exiled former Edward VIII heading into Europe under cover of night. It was a particular thrill while writing its sequel, *The Windsors at War*, to be able to draw upon a vast amount of rare and unseen material, which gave insight into everything from the fractious relationship between King George VI and his disobedient brother, the Duke of Windsor, to the extent to which leading courtiers' Nazi sympathies permeated Buckingham Palace at the beginning of World War II.

Yet when I finished *Windsors*, I was caught in a dilemma. It seemed clear that the logical next step was to finish the story of the era that I had begun, and that I needed to write a third and final book that would begin with VE Day and follow the story up until the coronation of Elizabeth II. But my fear was that it would be anticlimactic compared to the other two. Those books had been steeped in grand, operatic themes of betrayal, power and a family being torn apart by war and treachery. If this one could offer nothing more dramatic than a royal wedding, the slow death of a king, and a coronation, was it really worth the effort?

It will be for readers to judge for themselves as to whether I have succeeded, but *Power and Glory* proved every bit as thrilling and revelatory to research and write as the earlier books, exploding any belief that I had that this period was somehow less eventful.

The focus this time lies with three separate protagonists: the young Princess Elizabeth, whose marriage and family life is coloured by the increasing knowledge that she will be taking on an awesome weight of responsibility; George VI, whose fragile health was dealt a terminal blow by the strain that the war placed upon him and his country; and, naturally, the Duke of Windsor, seeking to pursue his own agenda and damn the consequences.

I have attempted to be fair towards the duke, as in my other books, but the man does not make it easy for even the most generous of biographers to portray him in a warm and sympathetic light. In 2022, I stayed at a hotel in Paris that he and Wallis used to frequent, and, unable to sleep, wondered what the chances were of a spectral visit from an outraged Edward, chastising me for his presentation in these books. Had I been taken to task by his apparition, I hope that I should have had the presence of mind - shortly before telephoning the concierge and asking for bell, book and candle - to reply that nothing I have said about him in the trilogy is based on anything other than meticulously documented fact: usually, and most damningly, his own entitled words. Unlike fine wine, he does not improve with age.

If the duke supplies much of *Power and Glory*'s high drama (and, at times, comic relief), it is his brother's story that constitutes its tragic arc. George VI was the monarch who never wanted the responsibility of the role, and it is testament to his belief in duty that he committed himself to its onerous burdens, even as it became increasingly clear that the strain was having a terminal effect upon his health. I have attempted to present the monarch as a rounded character, neither sanctifying him nor belittling him, but I hope that my portrayal of him as someone whose greatest strengths were domestic rather than regal is one that firmly anchors the book as a deeply human story.

If the book has a heroine, however, it can only be the future Elizabeth II. She made only fleeting appearances in *The Crown in Crisis* and *The Windsors at War*, but I am finally able to give her the full measure that she deserves, bringing her to life in both private and public spheres. If my first book was a ticking-clock suspense thriller set against the backdrop of something thought constitutionally unprecedented, and the second a wartime saga that explored a dysfunctional, squabbling family tested to its limits, so this one too has a simple story at its heart: it is an account of a close and loving father-and-daughter relationship, albeit one where the father is dying and the daughter is facing upheaval and change on an unimaginable scale.

Both of my earlier books were intended, to a large extent, as black comedies of manners. *Power and Glory* is different. While writing about the Duke of Windsor's misdemeanours never ceased to amuse - or shock - me, I was struck by how often I would attempt to finish chapters of this book and be unable to type because I was weeping so copiously. Even now, certain lines - 'I felt that I had lost something very precious'; 'my whole life whether it be long or short shall be devoted to your service' - still have a Pavlovian effect upon me.

I was writing *Power and Glory* when I learnt of the queen's death on 8 September 2022, and like everyone else in Britain, I felt as if one of the aspects of my life that had been forever constant was removed from me. Yet amid the millions of words written about her in the subsequent days, by sources sympathetic, hostile or otherwise, there was one central point universally acknowledged: in both her remarkable longevity and her lifelong dedication to service, she was a monarch *sans pareil*. It is therefore appropriate that *Power and Glory* should depict the end of one era, and of one Britain, and the birth of a new one. This book may be a tragedy, and a requiem for a lost nation, but it is also a paean of praise to the woman who redefined the country in her image.

It may, or may not, come as a surprise to my readers to learn that I am not a monarchist. Unlike some of my historian peers, I have always attempted to look at the royal family with clinical detachment, rather than from the perspective of a fully paid-up admirer of what strikes me as a deeply flawed and anachronistic institution. Certainly, the ludicrous indulgence offered to the Duke of Windsor - a man who should have gone to prison during World War II for treason, and ideally remained there - shows the worst aspects of 'the Firm' and the *noblesse oblige* offered to its members, regardless of their activities. Yet the virtues they exemplified at their best were real, too: courage, generosity, compassion and a dedication to serving their country rather than themselves. When I finished writing this book, I had to restrain an urge to leap onto a table and shout, 'God Save the Queen!' If I am a republican, I am a very, very flawed one indeed. But if this conclusion to the trilogy engenders a similar urge in a single reader, I will proudly consider my duties as a historian and biographer fulfilled.

Alexander Larman
Oxford, June 2023

Prologue

'My Whole Life Shall Be Devoted to Your Service'

Sir Alan 'Tommy' Lascelles, private secretary to George VI, was a man who prided himself on his unflappability. After all, during his decades of royal service, he had done everything from act as a reluctant counsellor to the Prince of Wales - later Edward VIII cum Duke of Windsor - to being the king's confidant, right-hand man and general major-domo. If Tommy didn't know about something taking place in the royal household, the chances were that it was either irrelevant or mere conjecture. Yet in April 1947, something of international import had occurred that had disturbed his composure. A speech had been written that would be crucial to the future of the monarchy and was due to be broadcast in a matter of a few days. And not only had it been vetoed by the king as not being good enough, it was currently lost.

As Lascelles careered up and down the White Train, an air-conditioned train that housed both the royal family and a gaggle of courtiers, journalists and staff on their state trip to South Africa, desperately searching for the missing draft, he was able to think about the successes and failures of the royal tour; the first that had taken place since 1939, when the king and queen had visited Canada and the United States in a successful attempt to drum up support for the world war that everyone believed was imminent.

Then, the affection with which the royal couple had been greeted was only matched by the outpouring of national pride that awaited them when they returned home. Yet now, despite the similarly warm welcome that the pair and their daughters, Elizabeth and Margaret, had received in this outpost of the Commonwealth, the trip had not recaptured past glories. The king, especially, was worn down, querulous and increasingly resembling a relic of a bygone era. It was vital that the speech that would be broadcast at the end of the tour should restore international faith in the monarchy. The speech, Lascelles reflected, that had not only been dismissed by the king as inadequate, but was now nowhere to be seen.

It also did not help that Princess Elizabeth, who would be delivering the speech, was herself something of an unknown quantity. She was, of course, familiar to her future subjects thanks to such high-profile events as her appearance alongside her parents on the Buckingham Palace balcony on VE Day, smiling and rejoicing in her country's deliverance and triumph; while rumours of her nascent relationship with a young Greek-born naval officer, Philip Mountbatten, had been dominating newspaper headlines for weeks, if not months, before she departed on the South African trip earlier in 1947. Yet, wholly intentionally, Lascelles and her family had kept her away from public view while she was still young. It was only now, as she turned twenty-one, that the appropriate moment had come to introduce her on the world stage. And the means of doing so had to be perfect.

In any case, Lascelles took comfort from one small measure of relief. The speech would not be recorded live, partly for reasons of timing - Elizabeth would have been broadcasting in the darkness - and also because the speaker was exhausted. Her coming-of-age would be celebrated among well-meaning strangers rather than among her family, all of whom were coping with the myriad responsibilities that any royal tour of this nature demanded. She was particularly concerned about her father, King George VI, whose health appeared to be suffering. That the South African tour had been intended, in part, as a break for him, a chance to ease off the enormous responsibilities that his now decade-long reign had involved, seemed little more than a cruel joke.

Yet Elizabeth's address to the Commonwealth was the symbolic conclusion of the trip. It was intended not only for the inhabitants of the country she was currently in, but as a reminder to the people of Britain that they were not forgotten, and that the woman who would one day be their queen took her future responsibilities as seriously as her father did – and considerably more so than her uncle, the Duke of Windsor, ever had. Crafting the speech was an awesome responsibility, but thankfully, there was a man at hand who seemed to be up to the task.

Dermot Morrah was one of those men who had succeeded in several different areas of life, and had done so with a wry assurance that belied any arrogance in his achievements. In addition to being an accomplished mathematician and a fellow of All Souls College, Oxford, he was also a *Times* leader writer, and well respected for his ability to summarise complex, even contradictory sentiments in a pithy phrase or aphorism. It was as a result of these pieces that he came to the attention of Lascelles, who drew upon Morrah's erudition and literary accomplishment to polish, and occasionally write, many of George VI's public speeches and statements. It seemed only natural that he would be called upon to do the same for his daughter.

It was a shame, then, that when the king was shown the draft that Morrah had prepared of Elizabeth's pivotal speech, he sighed in disdain. It read, he felt, like a second-rate rote series of blandishments; the BBC radio correspondent Frank Gillard later suggested that George believed Morrah had produced something that was 'too pompous and full of platitudes'.[1] Although Lascelles had been initially impressed, raving to its creator that 'I cannot recall [a draft] that has so completely satisfied me and left me feeling no single word should be altered', it became clear that some tweaks and reworking were essential in order for the broadcast to feel as if it was coming from a twenty-one-year-old woman rather than a fifty-one-year-old man.

Not for the first time, Lascelles turned to the task himself, and attempted to take Morrah's high allusions and Oxbridge learning in a more comprehensible, to say nothing of accessible, direction. As it stood, the speech seemed almost comically ill-suited to the princess. Its allusions to Rupert Brooke and William Pitt were typical of its author, and its implicit gestures of support to Smuts in South Africa and to Mountbatten's efforts in India, as partition approached, were political in the extreme, rather than personal. Yet these things could not be helped; after all, royal speeches were more notable for being made at all than for any revelatory content within them.

However, Lascelles had remarked to Morrah of the original draft that 'it has the trumpet-ring of the other Elizabeth's Tilbury speech* combined with the immortal simplicity of Victoria's "I will be good"',[2] and so now he had to make good on his own praise. Finally, to his inordinate relief, he found the missing draft lurking under bottles of spirits in the dining car, and the two could set to work afresh. The speech needed to combine the general themes that any traditional speech of this nature had to contain - much talk of duty, honour, tradition and service - with something altogether different, which would reflect the character of the young woman who would be delivering it. It was a demanding brief, but the two men believed they could master it.

At last, after Lascelles had lavished 'much care' upon the redraft, he handed it to Elizabeth, and waited for her reaction with considerable trepidation. She finished reading it, looked up at him and said, simply, 'It has made me cry.' A relieved Lascelles responded, 'Good, said I, for if it makes you cry now, it will make 200 million other people cry when they hear you deliver it, and that is what we want.'[3] He was correct. Countless millions more, at the time and since, have shared her sentiments.

Despite the princess's admiration, the content was not yet felt to

---

* In which Elizabeth I declared in 1588, rallying her troops before the anticipated invasion of the Spanish Armada, that 'I know I have the body but of a weak and feeble woman, but I have the heart and stomach of a king, and of a king of England too.'

be perfect. On Sunday 20 April, the king, queen and Elizabeth sat down together in the garden of the Victoria Falls Hotel and minutely tweaked the speech, line by line, to make it feel like an authentic and heartfelt broadcast by a young woman, rather than the dry-as-dust harrumphing of two middle-aged men. It had to come across as authentic and natural, but it also had to say something profound; this was the only chance that Elizabeth would ever get to make a first impression on the world, and she could not afford to blow it, for the continued stability and future of the monarchy. Yet all of them knew that they were, by now, working with material that had been much improved through careful and judicious editing and rewriting.

At last, when the trio were satisfied that the speech was as good as it possibly could be, Elizabeth began to rehearse the broadcast under Gillard's tutelage. He regarded her as 'composed, confident and extremely cooperative', and fully aware of the gravity of what she had to do. After they had ensured that she was word, even letter, perfect, the speech was recorded and filmed in the garden, with the future queen's sole audience the local wildlife. It was an inauspicious beginning to the most significant seven minutes of her life so far, but as she began to speak, any nerves or doubts she might have had fell away.

On 21 April 1947, Elizabeth's voice could be heard on every radio set in Britain and the Commonwealth. As many as 200 million people tuned in to listen to her. She spoke clearly, if with an understandable hint of nerves in her voice, as she set out what would be her credo for her life. Those who had been given advance sight of the speech had been advised that it would be the most significant public statement she would ever have made.

Yet as she began, declaring, 'On my twenty-first birthday I welcome the opportunity to speak to all the peoples of the British Commonwealth and Empire, wherever they live, whatever race they come from, and whatever language they speak', some of those most intimately involved with the broadcast could be forgiven for breathing a sigh of relief that it was taking place at all. Nonetheless,

those who were listening eagerly at home might have been disappointed by its first half. Much of it was almost boilerplate in its sentiments, a legacy of the surviving Morrah draft - 'it is a great help
to know that there are multitudes of friends all round the world
who are thinking of me and who wish me well'; 'that is the great
privilege belonging to our place in the world-wide commonwealth
- that there are homes ready to welcome us in every continent
of the earth' - and her audience might have wondered if it was
entirely the work of its young speaker, despite the fluency with
which she delivered it.

And then, suddenly, it shifted from the universal to the personal,
and became desperately affecting. Acknowledging the sacrifices
and havoc wrought by war - 'these years of danger and glory' -
Elizabeth looked forward to a happier and better world. 'If we all
go forward together with an unwavering faith, a high courage, and
a quiet heart, we shall be able to make of this ancient commonwealth, which we all love so dearly, an even grander thing - more
free, more prosperous, more happy and a more powerful influence
for good in the world - than it has been in the greatest days of our
forefathers.'

Yet she knew that this required her to make her own commitment, and one that implicitly renewed her family's vows to their
country. 'To accomplish that we must give nothing less than the
whole of ourselves. There is a motto which has been borne by
many of my ancestors - a noble motto, "I serve".' She then made a
promise - or, as she put it, a 'solemn act of dedication' - that would
define her life and subsequent reign, and might be the most famous
single public statement she ever made.

I declare before you all that my whole life whether it be long
or short shall be devoted to your service and the service of
our great imperial family to which we all belong. But I shall
not have strength to carry out this resolution alone unless
you join in it with me, as I now invite you to do: I know that
your support will be unfailingly given. God help me to make

good my vow, and God bless all of you who are willing to share in it.[4]

It was simple, and hugely powerful. It expressed the family's belief in public service more effectively than any longer or drier speech could have done. For the princess to make such a binding declaration, knowing that it established a standard she would be held to for the rest of her life, was a truly regal act. It was little wonder that Lascelles would proudly say of her to his wife that 'she has come on in the most surprising way, and all in the right direction . . . [She has] a perfectly natural power of enjoying herself without any trace of shyness, and a good, healthy sense of fun.'

He was particularly impressed by the way that, despite being an 'extremely businesslike' young woman, and being unafraid to tell the king and queen off if they needed to be disciplined, she retained 'an astonishing solicitude for people's comfort'. Whatever the disappointments and trials of the tour had been, the princess was not among them; Lascelles even stated that 'the most satisfactory feature of the whole visit is the remarkable development of Princess Elizabeth'.*[5]

Reaction in Britain to the speech was unanimously positive. Elizabeth's grandmother, Queen Mary - not a woman given to frivolous displays of emotion - wrote in her diary, 'Of course I wept',[6] and the man who would later become her first prime minister, Winston Churchill, had a similar reaction, confessing his deep emotion at the prospect of this young woman one day being queen. It had been a triumph. Yet at a time when the monarchy - and Britain - faced existential crisis, from both within and without, one speech, no matter how well conceived and delivered, would not be enough to save the institution. Everyone who cared about the royal family looked to a woman in her twenties to safeguard its future. It was an awesome responsibility for anyone, and the fear of those who

---

* Lascelles was not uncondescending amid the praise; he still described the twenty-one-year-old princess as 'a child of her years'.

knew and loved Elizabeth was that she would not be up to it. After all, it would take someone truly remarkable and extraordinary to cope with such a responsibility.

Still, cometh the hour, cometh the woman.

Chapter One

'The Most Terrible Thing Ever Discovered'

On the evening of 8 May 1945, the nineteen-year-old Princess Elizabeth, dressed in her Auxiliary Territorial Service uniform, stood next to her mother, father and sister and gazed out at an innumerable crowd from the balcony of Buckingham Palace.* The noise was deafening. A great shout of 'We want the king!' yelled in unison by tens, if not hundreds, of thousands of voices was all that could be heard, followed by a vigorous rendition of 'For He's a Jolly Good Fellow' whenever the assembly's wish was granted.

Yet although the attention and volume were overwhelming, there was also a dizzying sense of escape and catharsis that meant that what would have been an otherwise overwhelming ordeal for a young woman became a stirring, even thrilling, moment of unity with the people who she would one day reign over. As she gazed down at the ecstatic men and women who were celebrating the end of World War II, she felt, for perhaps the first time, that there was no barrier between them and her.

Her younger sister, Margaret, then fourteen years old, was more impatient for excitement and drama than the rest of her family. She petitioned their parents that she and Elizabeth should be allowed to go out into the crowd and mingle with the revellers. Under normal circumstances, such a request would have been refused

---

* Which, after the bomb damage wrought on it earlier in the war, had to be surveyed to make sure that it could stand the (far from considerable) weight of the royal family, as well as the stouter proportions of the prime minister, who had joined them earlier that day.

on grounds of both propriety and simple security, but, exhilarated and conscious of the unique occasion, the king granted them both leave. He later wrote indulgently in his diary that 'Poor darlings, they have never had any fun yet.'[1]

The girls headed out, accompanied by an honour guard of sorts that included their former nanny, Marion 'Crawfie' Crawford, their French tutor, Marie-Antoinette de Bellaigue, and, for their necessary protection, some Guards officers, along with a royal equerry. Elizabeth had not had an opportunity to change out of her uniform, and, conscious of not wishing to seem too conspicuous, pulled her cap over her eyes. One of her fellow officers, a stickler for propriety even amid the celebrations, insisted that she remain properly dressed while wearing such attire, and made her adjust it into its correct form.

The group wandered freely around the neighbouring streets, heading over to Piccadilly and Park Lane, visiting the Dorchester and Ritz hotels and finally returning to the palace through Green Park. For the average teenage girl, such a journey would have been unexceptional in the extreme, but for Elizabeth, and especially, Margaret - who had often chafed at the bit when it came to protocol and restriction - the moments of being let off the leash were as glorious, in their own way, as the wider victory that was being hailed. As Elizabeth later said, '[There were] lines of people linking arms and walking down Whitehall and all of us were swept up by tides of happiness and relief.'[2]

As the communal excitement gripped them, initial ideas of decorum were forgotten, and the princesses joined their countrymen in wild and ecstatic dances, kicking their legs up to 'The Lambeth Walk' and the Hokey Cokey. Then, in a moment of untrammelled giddiness, they raced back to the palace and stood outside, looking up at their parents and shouting, 'We want the king!' with the rest of the crowd. What Crawfie later described as 'almost hysterical relief'[3] was shown by everyone in London, and indeed the country, at that moment. Princess Margaret would later describe her own impressions of the evening in a televised interview: 'Suddenly the lights came on and lit up the poor old battle-scarred palace . . . my mother was wearing a white dress with a tiara . . . and it all sparkled and there was a great roar from the crowd, which was very exciting. VE Day was a wonderful sunburst of glory.'

The next morning, the country awoke, happily, to a collective hangover. The princesses were desperate to take advantage of their new-found freedom, and so, with the king's permission, headed out once again into the great crowds still gathered in central London. As Elizabeth wrote in her diary, 'Out in crowd again - Trafalgar Square, Piccadilly, Pall Mall, walked simply miles. Saw parents on balcony at 12.30 a.m. - ate, partied, bed 3 a.m.!'[4] This time, they were unable to retain their anonymity; a headline in *The Times* read, 'Big Crowds at the Palace. Royal Family on the Balcony. Princesses Join the Throng.'

A visit to the bombed-out districts of the East End was a more sobering experience for both princesses, as they saw the devastation that the previous years of war had caused. As they had been largely sequestered in the safety of Windsor Castle since the outbreak of the conflict, they had been spared the omnipresent experiences of death and destruction that their subjects had become all too familiar with over the last half-decade. It was no wonder that Margaret was driven to remark, in dismay, 'It was a nasty shock to live in a town again.'[5]

The party had been brief, exhilarating and wonderful. But as the broken country could not be mended by dancing and singing, transformation had to come. Churchill might have been cheered to the skies by the people when he appeared on the balcony next to the royal family, flashing his signature 'V for Victory' sign to the applauding masses, but two months later, he and the Conservative Party would be ousted from power, replaced by Clement Attlee's transformative Labour government in a landslide election.

Britain was impoverished, exhausted and in dire need of change. The people looked to the politicians for everyday reassurance, but it was the monarchy from which they sought inspiration. The unspoken agreement was that the royals would hold themselves above the populace, and pledge themselves to a higher standard of personal conduct and dignity. In exchange, they would be both adored and trusted. It was a deal, and one that required both parties to play their part. But in the new world order that now existed, with old certainties swept away with the rubble of cities, it remained deeply uncertain as to what was going to come next.

'We listened to the King's [victory] broadcast. It was really too embarrassing: he ought to talk better by now: the contrast to Winston's eloquence and that of [the] Dominion PMs is shocking.' The politician and bon viveur Henry 'Chips' Channon remained in a caustic humour with George VI after VE Day, despite being in the embrace of the playwright Terence Rattigan. Nor did he reserve his contempt for the king. On the same day, he wrote, 'I have no patience with the present Sovereigns [sic], both are bores and dull', although he allowed, gracelessly, that '[they] do their job well enough, I suppose'. Although Channon made it to the palace to see the celebrations on VE Day ('the enthusiasm extreme, but little rowdiness'),[6] he anticipated that in the post-war settlement, there would be a mixed public reaction to 'Their Majesties'.

Shortly afterwards, he was present at St Paul's on Sunday 13 May for a service of thanksgiving, where he observed the royal duo. Never one to say anything pleasant if something caustic would do instead, he commented that although the king and queen looked 'young and smiling', and that George VI had 'the Windsor gift of appearing half his age',* the king seemed 'drawn and tired' and the queen's appearance was 'appalling – her bosom is big and her bottom immense'.[7] Although Channon was cheerfully vile about the couple,† he was also able to observe how, at the opening of

_____

* Which would have made him look approximately twenty-five; Rattigan, by way of contrast, was thirty-three at the time, and Channon himself was forty-eight.

† He may also have been surprised to discover that the queen agreed with him, although not in the specifics that he described. On 18 September 1945, she wrote to Queen Mary to lament that '[We] have aged a lot, and look rather haggard & ravaged! & one's clothes are so awful!'

Parliament, the king made a long speech with only one pause, on the word 'imperishable', and that Churchill demanded that there be 'three cheers for the King and Queen'. Channon noted that 'people were too embarrassed to cheer lustily, but there was a rather embarrassed, well-bred response'.[8]

Peace in Europe had been secured, and hopes were high of similarly imminent resolution in Japan. But domestic matters were harder to come to terms with. The king himself wrote in his diary on 22 May that 'I have found it difficult to rejoice and relax as there is still so much hard work ahead to deal with.'[9] The war had been an all-consuming and exhausting affair, demanding more from him than any man could have reasonably given. But at least throughout most of its duration he had had Churchill by his side, combining the offices of counsellor, friend and, on occasion, surrogate father. Nonetheless, as he observed on 28 May, 'Parliament is 10 years older, no one under the age of 30 has ever voted, and the House of Commons needs rejuvenating. Country before Party has been the [Coalition's] watchword. But now what?'[10]

He soon had his answer. When the prime minister was relieved of power on 5 July, the king responded both petulantly and angrily, as if it had been a personal betrayal. In their last audience as monarch and premier, he denounced his people's ingratitude 'after the way they had been led in the war'.[11] Even as Lascelles and Churchill attempted to reassure him that the country's desire for change had to be respected,* and Lord Mountbatten, a man whose own political sympathies were closer to Labour than the Conservatives, suggested that the king might even be able to influence political developments in a way that he had seldom been able to before, there was still the innate sense that the shift in the country's post-war political and social temperature could yet have unforeseeable repercussions.

---

* Churchill suggested that '[the people] are perfectly entitled to vote as they please. This is democracy. This is what we've been fighting for.'

George VI feared the coming of socialism.* He wrote in his diary on 20 June that 'Dr Harold Laski's† statements that Mr Attlee cannot go to the Meeting in Berlin except as an observer show that Mr Attlee is not the real leader of the Labour Party. Laski as chairman of the Executive Committee of the Labour Party appears to be the real leader & can tell Attlee what he is to do.'[12] Nonetheless, he also wished for a decisive result, writing, 'A small majority to either Party would be useless. I must have a Government to run the country & the war against Japan.'[13] His daughters may have sung and danced around London incognito, but it was clear that their father was not in a similarly jocular humour. He desperately needed a holiday from what could only be onerous responsibilities. But no such remedy was possible.

The relationship between the king and his new premier, meanwhile, did not begin amicably; as, in fairness, his association with Churchill had not. Attlee might have served with distinction as deputy prime minister in the wartime Government of National Unity, but even after the Labour government had been elected in a landslide victory, there was still some doubt as to his suitability to be prime minister, mostly sown by his right-hand man, Herbert Morrison. As Laski put it, 'Nature intended for [Attlee] to be a second lieutenant.'[14] On 25 July 1945, when Attlee was supposed to head to Buckingham Palace to accept the king's invitation to form a government, Morrison informed him that he would not be able to do so until there was another election within the Labour Party for a new leader: the implication being, naturally, that Morrison himself (who had unsuccessfully stood for the leadership in 1935) should now take up his position.

Attlee may have written in his autobiography - in lines that did not make the final version - that 'the idea [of Morrison as prime minister] was fantastic and certainly out of harmony with the

---

* On 29 June, he wrote angrily in his diary that 'The Socialists are playing a dirty game in intimidating electors in various districts.'

† Laski was a political theorist and economist whose views tended towards the Marxist.

feeling of the Party'.[15] Nonetheless, when he did arrive at Buckingham Palace that evening, sent on his way by his lieutenant Ernest
Bevin ('Clem, you go to the Palace straight away'), his first official meeting* with the king was an underwhelming one. Lost for
anything more insightful to say, the new premier blurted out, 'I've
won the election!' The king, who had said an emotional farewell
to Churchill only a few minutes earlier that evening,† replied, 'I
know. I heard it on the six o'clock news.' Taking pity on the bewildered Attlee, who seemed uncertain as to whether he really was
prime minister, he added, 'You look more surprised than I feel.'[16]

Following up on Mountbatten's suggestion that he might seize
the advantage and be more interventionist with the new government, the king overruled Attlee's suggestion that Hugh Dalton
should be his new Foreign Secretary, putting forward Bevin instead. The reasons for this appointment were at least partly personal: Dalton's father, John, had been tutor to a young George V,
and his Old Etonian son's socialist beliefs were felt to be a betrayal
of this once-close relationship between the Daltons and the royal
family – so much so that Hugh was scornfully referred to by
George V as 'your anarchist son'; there was also the matter of a
thoughtless disposal of gifts that John Dalton had been given by
the former king.‡ Attlee, who may or may not have known of this

---

* They had met privately before, in 1938, but the conversation between the
two had been limited to a discussion about the most efficient way to clean one's
pipe; Attlee expressed interest in the king's self-cleaning pipe device.

† There has been a suggestion by the writer Robert Rhodes James that
Churchill, desperate to remain in power to announce the defeat of the
Japanese, wished to attend the Potsdam Conference and so toyed with the
unconstitutional idea of delaying his resignation as premier for over a week.
The influence of the king, via Lascelles, Anthony Eden and the former chief
whip David Margesson, led to his changing his mind.

‡ Nor was there any love lost between subject and monarch. In his diaries,
Hugh Dalton refers to the 'inanimate' monarch, which may either have been
a dig at the king's speaking difficulties or simply a reflection of the contempt
that his sovereign displayed towards him, and wrote of how, after the election
result, 'the King hadn't much to say, but seemed quite resigned'.

association, agreed, and the meeting ended. Afterwards, the king quipped to Lascelles that 'I gather they call the new Prime Minister Clem. "Clam" would be more appropriate.'[17]

The king's disappointment at the ousting of Churchill was mirrored by his uncertainty as to what kind of prime minister he now had. Although a Labour victory in the election had been anticipated in the polls for some considerable time, neither Churchill nor 'Clam' seemed to have expected it, and certainly not in the magnitude that had resulted. The monarch wrote in his diary that Attlee 'was very surprised his Party had won & had no time to meet or discuss with his colleagues any of the Offices of State'.[18] In the spirit of determined optimism, he observed, 'I hoped that our relations would be cordial & that I would always be ready to do my best to help him.'[19] After the premier left Buckingham Palace, he arrived, shell-shocked, at a victory party at Central Hall in Westminster. In a daze, he murmured, 'I have just left the Palace.' As cheers and celebrations echoed around him, he was able to observe, with characteristic understatement, that 'it had been quite an exciting day'.[20] For the king, by way of contrast, it had been 'a long and trying'[21] one.

This final confirmation that Britain now had a transformative socialist government, with a Labour prime minister for the first time since Ramsay MacDonald a decade before, confirmed that the old order had indeed changed, and had yielded its place to modernity. It was now up to the royal family to see how far they could adjust to the new Britain, or whether they would come to be regarded with the polite curiosity that bygones of an earlier era usually merited.

'The Japs have rejected the joint ultimatum, so I suppose they will shortly get what is coming to them.'[22] So Lascelles reflected in his diary on 27 July. He was proved correct soon enough. Yet before this could take place, there was another, equally pressing matter. The king wished to meet the new president of the United States, Harry S. Truman, for the first time, and the president's presence at the Potsdam peace conference in Europe meant that such an encounter could be easily arranged.

Memories of the late Franklin D. Roosevelt were still fresh, and the close and affectionate relationship that had grown up between the king and Roosevelt - first sparked by the time that the two had spent in Roosevelt's holiday home, Hyde Park, in 1939[23] - was one that had been invaluable for the successful prosecution of the joint war effort. Truman and the monarch would be hard pressed to recapture such a degree of personal affinity, but circumstances meant that the audience had to be arranged swiftly.

Truman had become vice president at the beginning of 1945, in the expectation that Roosevelt was unlikely to survive his fourth term, and so his presidency had begun in the most stressful circumstances imaginable. He informed reporters on his first day that 'Boys, if you ever pray, pray for me now. I don't know if you fellas ever had a load of hay fall on you, but when they told me what happened yesterday, I felt like the moon, the stars, and all the planets had fallen on me.'[24] Although victory in Europe was assured, the issue of Japan remained urgent. Yet as Lascelles had so grimly forecast, a reckoning lay at hand. In the midst of the Potsdam conference, Truman wrote in his diary on 25 July 1945 that 'We have discovered the most terrible bomb in the history of the world. It may be the fire destruction prophesied in the Euphrates Valley Era, after Noah and his fabulous Ark.'

Truman was wholly aware of the potential of what the theoretical physicist J. Robert Oppenheimer had discovered; he had known about it since April that year, and now the moment of its implementation lay at hand. He wrote that 'This weapon is to be used against Japan between now and August 10th. I have told the Sec[retary] of War, Mr [Henry] Stimson, to use so that military objectives and soldiers and sailors are the target and not women and children ... the target will be a purely military one and we will issue a warning statement asking the [Japanese] to surrender and save lives. I'm sure they will not do that, but we will have given them the chance. It is certainly a good thing for the world that Hitler's crowd or Stalin's did not discover the atomic bomb. It seems to me to be the most terrible thing ever discovered, but it can be made the most useful.'

It was around a week after Truman wrote this that he met the king for the first time. The last time an American president had visited Britain was in 1918, when Woodrow Wilson had made a three-day trip to the country shortly after Christmas, and so the encounter between the two men, which took place off the Plymouth coast, on HMS *Renown*, was epochal. The king had been informed of the successful tests of the atomic bomb, which had been conducted in the New Mexico desert on 16 July, and so he was determined to meet the man who at that time held more power than anyone else on earth, perhaps more than anyone who had ever lived. Oppenheimer may have breathed, 'I am become death, destroyer of worlds', but it was the bespectacled, businesslike man who clambered aboard the *Renown* on 2 August 1945 who had a greater claim to such a title. In his presence, even the king seemed insignificant.

Truman arrived with James F. Byrnes, US Secretary of State, and Admiral William Leahy, the president's chief of staff. His first words, referring to the recent election, were 'You've had a revolution', to which the king pointedly replied, 'Oh no! We don't have those here.'[25] Lascelles noted in his diary that the lunch they had was a 'cheerful' meal, but that the 'chatterbox' Byrnes was highly impolitic. '[He] made me and [Lord Halifax, the British ambassador to the United States] gasp by talking about the "T. A." or "heavy water" atomic bombs, with the stewards still in the room. As this is so secret a matter in this country that only about six people have ever heard of it, this seemed somewhat indiscreet, even for an American.'[26] The king tactfully intervened. 'I think, Mr President, that we should discuss this interesting subject over our coffee on deck.'[27] Lascelles regarded the existence of the atomic bomb with fear. 'The expense of producing it is fantastic . . . [While] attention may be diverted to its potentialities for good, as a source of heat, power etc. . . . on the whole, I would rather that it had never been invented at all.'

Lascelles was not present for the conversation between the king and the 'good, resolute . . . grave [and] humorous' Truman, of whom he gained a 'favourable impression', but was pleased that 'they seemed to get on very well'. During their meeting, monarch and president discussed the necessity of the use of the atomic bomb, and their fears that an emboldened Stalin was growing too powerful. Both men agreed that they would have to use their combined influence at the forthcoming Foreign Secretaries' Conference in London to prevent the possibility of an Eastern Europe controlled by Russia.

The king wrote in his diary that '[The president] admitted he had learnt a great deal & understood European difficulties from a new standpoint . . . [Truman] was horrified at the devastation of Berlin by our combined bombing . . . he could see that the Big Powers would have to combine for all time to prevent another war.'[28] Although neither man discussed the possibility of the two topics of their conversation being combined, the implication - Stalin in possession of a nuclear weapon - was a terrifying one, and best avoided if they were not to spoil what Truman later approvingly described as a 'nice and appetising' lunch of soup, fish, lamb and ice cream.

Not everyone present was convinced that the atomic bomb was as deadly a weapon as Truman seemed to suggest it was. Leahy, a figure once described as the 'second most powerful man in the world' for his influence over America's foreign policy in World War II, was impressed at how well briefed the king was over his country's nuclear capabilities, but inclined to belittle the bomb's efficacy. 'It sounds like a professor's dream to me', he sniffed. His host responded suavely, and not without humour, 'Would you like to lay a little bet on that, Admiral?'

After the king and his entourage paid a reciprocal visit to the American vessel USS *Augusta*, Truman and the others departed. Lascelles summed it up as a 'memorable and historic meeting, and [I] have no doubt it did a lot of good'. Although the king's relationship with Truman showed no immediate signs of blossoming into the genuine friendship that had developed with Roosevelt, there was nevertheless a welcome sense that the two men shared the same ambitions. Lascelles wrote, not without complacency, that 'Our visitors were obviously well pleased by the encounter, and could not have been more friendly.'[29] Subsequent events would prove that Truman's largesse was not as unconditional as it appeared.

Four days later, on 6 August 1945, the conversation bore fruit, as the Americans dropped the atomic bomb on Hiroshima. Before he had been driven from power, Churchill had already prepared a statement about the weapon's effects. Its time had now arrived. Compared to Attlee's dry words ('the problems of the release of energy by atomic fission have been solved and an atomic bomb has been dropped on Japan by the United States Air Force'), the former premier was able to explain the use of the deadliest weapon ever invented in both practical and near-poetic terms: he almost seemed to imagine himself a modern Prometheus, telling humanity about this new source of fire. 'It is now for Japan to realise in the glare of the first atomic bomb which has smitten her, what the consequences will be of an indefinite continuance of this terrible means of maintaining a rule of law in the world. This revelation of the secrets of nature, long mercifully withheld from man, should arouse the most solemn reflections in the mind and conscience of every human being capable of comprehension. We must indeed pray that these awe-striking agencies will be made to conduce to peace among the nations, and that instead of wreaking measureless havoc upon the entire globe, they may become a perennial fountain of world prosperity.'[30]

The immediate reaction in Britain was something between incomprehension and unease. After hearing the news, the Conservative politician Harold Nicolson wrote of how '[the bomb] is to be used eventually for domestic purposes',[31] but he was also amused to be called up by the press the next day and asked whether he had had advance knowledge of the weapon, due to having prophesied its invention in his 1932 novel *Public Faces*. In that book, he had written of a single bomb, 'no bigger than an ink-stand', that would be able to destroy New York 'by the discharge of its electrons'. His wife, Vita 'Viti' Sackville-West, was 'thrilled' by its detonation; Nicolson wrote, 'she thinks, and rightly, that it will mean a whole new era'.[32]

Lascelles was more measured. Writing on 7 August, he noted how the bomb's detonation had overruled all other news ('the newspapers today scarcely mention any other subject'), and agreed with both Churchill and Viti that its use would alter society irrevocably, probably for ever. 'The introduction into human history of this particular form of energy may be the most important event since Noah's ark. Its implications, for good and for evil, are unpredictable and alarming.'[33] He believed that it was important for the king to address what had occurred when he spoke at the state opening of Parliament the following week, observing, 'it struck me that it would be all wrong for the King to make no mention . . . of the atomic bomb and its immense potentialities for good and evil . . . As most people, all over the world, are talking and thinking of little else, the omission would surely seem strange.'[34]

When another bomb was dropped on Nagasaki on 9 August, it became clear that Japan would surrender, and therefore bring World War II to an end. VJ Day on 15 August would therefore do double duty, serving also as the day for the king to open Parliament: a fitting use of expensive resources in these straitened times. Yet behind the scenes, there was panic. While VE Day had been anticipated for a considerable time, there was no speech for the king to deliver for VJ Day, and Lascelles, beset by tiredness and a 'jaded brain', was barely in a fit state to write one. He asked Churchill for advice, but was surprised and irritated that the former premier's suggestions were 'tired, disappointing and uninspiring'. In the end, he worked with the Cabinet Secretary, Sir Edward Bridges, to produce something that would meet with the king's approval.

On VJ Day, Lascelles saw to it that there would be at least some pageantry and pomp. The king and queen travelled to Parliament in an open carriage driven by four horses, refusing to have it closed despite intermittent showers, and Lascelles later wrote approvingly that '[the day] was restored to something of its pristine splendour by the revival of a carriage procession so the holiday crowds got their money's worth'. Channon dropped his usual sneering to praise the queen for looking 'dignified and gracious' in her outfit of aquamarine blue, though he could not help remark that 'the many new socialists looked dazed and dazzled'.[35] The speech that the king delivered was boilerplate, announcing his government's plans for nationalisation, and Lascelles called it 'only interesting in that it foreshadowed no legislation beyond what everybody had already anticipated'.[36]

The king did allude to the unparalleled means of power that had ended the war - 'The devastating new weapon which science has now placed in the hands of humanity should bring home to all the lesson that the nations of the world must abolish recourse to war or perish by mutual destruction'[37] - but he reserved his stronger feelings for a radio broadcast that he made that evening from Buckingham Palace, which he delivered in what Churchill called a 'pin-drop silence'. It struck an altogether different tone, both from the formality of how he had spoken in the House of Commons, and from the triumphalism of his VE Day broadcast and appearances three months before. Then, all had been optimistic and exultant. Now, with the country suffering and struggling, fine words alone were not enough.

He asked his listeners to thank God for the defeat of a 'strong and relentless enemy', and that Britain, and other countries, could now concentrate on '[turning] their industry, skill, and science to repairing its frightful devastation and to building prosperity and happiness'. Yet even as he could say, finally, 'the war is over', he knew that its consequences would linger indefinitely. 'There is not one of us who has experienced this terrible war who does not real-ise that we shall feel its inevitable consequences long after we have all forgotten our rejoicings of today . . . Relief from past dangers must not blind us to the demands of the future.'

The king knew that his purpose was to lead, and to inspire. So it was that, using language that Churchill might have approved of, he stated, 'In many anxious times in our long history the unconquerable spirit of our peoples has served us well, bringing us to safety out of great peril . . . I doubt if anything in all that has gone before has matched the enduring courage and the quiet determination which you have shown during these last six years.' It was exhortation he offered now, not congratulation. 'Great as are the deeds that you have done, there must be no falling off from this high endeavour. We have spent freely of all that we had: now we shall have to work hard to restore what has been lost, and to establish peace on the unshakable foundations, not alone of material strength, but also of moral authority.'

He strove to reassure - '[once] the curse of war may be lifted from the world . . . states and peoples, great and small, may dwell together through long periods of tranquillity in brighter and better days than we ourselves have known' - but also suggested that the wartime spirit had to endure. The battles had been won; now the peace had to be successful too. 'The world has come to look for certain things, for certain qualities from the peoples of the Commonwealth and Empire. We have our part to play in restoring the shattered fabric of civilisation. It is a proud and difficult part, and if you carry on in the years to come as you have done so splendidly in the war, you and your children can look forward to the future, not with fear, but with high hopes of a surer happiness for all.' He concluded his speech by saying, 'It is to this great task that I call you now, and I know that I shall not call in vain. In the meantime, from the bottom of my heart I thank my Peoples for all they have done, not only for themselves but for mankind.'[38]

As he concluded his broadcast, the previously silent crowd listening in the streets began to cheer and sob hysterically. Lascelles was delighted, writing in his diary that the king 'has never yet spoken so fluently and forcefully'.[39] The king, queen and princesses once again appeared on the Buckingham Palace balcony, and, as on VE Day, were received with adulation and ecstasy. Yet as the queen wrote to her friend Lady Helen Graham earlier that day, 'one can hardly take it in . . . I do pray that the sacrifices & comradeship &

love which people have felt for each other will not fade.'[40]

It was a victory. Yet everyone involved in it knew that nothing could be taken for granted. As the king exhorted his people to take joy in one another, and to rebuild ties of community and family that had been fractured, if not destroyed altogether, by the previous six years, he knew that there was a member of his own family he could no longer avoid seeing, much as he might have wished to.

Chapter Two

'I Never Saw a Man So Bored'

Two decades after the end of World War II, the Duke of Windsor was invited by the *New York Daily News* to write an autobiographical account of how he felt his participation in the events of the war had gone. There were many potential angles he could have taken, most of them incriminating, but he erred on the safer side of conceit instead. He wrote that 'I'd thought that my performance as a colonial governor, and the spirit in which I had gone about my duties, would have persuaded the sceptics in Britain of my desire to stay on in my country's service, and that I had fairly earned my passage back.'

His country did not see it like this. Initial overtures to his supporters had been unsuccessful, not least because his tenure as governor to the Bahamas between 1940 and 1945 had been dogged by endless controversy, whether it was his friendship with the Nazi-sympathising mogul Axel Wenner-Gren, the (unsolved) murder of the islands' wealthiest resident, Sir Harry Oakes, or the continued racial tensions, which the duke did little, if anything, to assuage. Nonetheless, he retained his usual Candide-like levels of optimism. 'I was resolved, in any case, to make one more hard try at drumming up interest in the Palace and in Whitehall for putting me to work somewhere in the British Diplomatic Service, in the absence of any marked enthusiasm for making a place for me in Britain.'[1]

The duke had ostentatiously quit his governorship in April 1945, and had left Nassau in early May that year for New York. However, he and Wallis were unable to return to Europe until September because of an absence of any civilian transport across the Atlantic. Once, they would not have been subject to such restrictions, but now, humiliatingly, they were shown that they were private citizens, and unpopular ones at that. They based themselves at the Waldorf Towers in New York, with brief trips to Newport and New Brunswick, and, bored and underemployed, the duke occupied himself with thinking about world affairs, and what his place was likely to be in the new post-war order.

He was unafraid to speak his mind, a characteristic that had endeared him to few, but that remained a consistent feature of his life. After the death of President Roosevelt on 12 April 1945, he and Wallis offered the usual formal condolences, but he wrote to his friend Kenneth de Courcy to criticise the late president for his intervention in the war, without which he believed the conflict could have been resolved without the loss of life that subsequently ensued. Edward had form in this regard. Not only had he sighed to the journalist Frank Grimes in the Bahamas that the war could have been avoided without 'Roosevelt and the Jews', before stating that 'if I'd been king, there'd have been no war',[2] but he had complained to Jock Balfour, the British minister in Washington, that 'if Hitler had been differently handled, war might have been avoided'.[3]

Even when he was granted an audience with Truman in early August - shortly after the president's return from visiting George VI - he found himself unimpressed. He had expected a vigorous reformer, but instead he was faced with a man who he described as being 'in a state of utter gloom' and moaning bleakly that the Japanese had refused to accept his ultimatum. 'I now have no alternative than to drop an atomic bomb on Tokyo',[4] the duke reported Truman saying, and he left the meeting disappointed, believing that the United States had inherited yet another president who had no clear understanding of international affairs. Clearly, what the country needed was the duke's wisdom and counsel.

By the middle of 1945, however, Edward had begun to make Job seem upbeat. He did not see a permanent future for Wallis and himself in America, unless some deputation of business leaders and politicians would offer him the sinecure that he believed he deserved. Yet he looked to Europe without any greater enthusiasm. Hitler, who he later privately described to his friend Lord Kinross as 'not such a bad chap',[5] was dead and Germany, which he had once believed was a crucible of progress, was in chaos. In France, de Gaulle was in the ascendancy, but the duke lamented that he was 'not the leader he is portrayed . . . he would do a lot better if, instead of trying to lift France's prestige abroad by assuming high-hat attitudes, he concentrated upon exhorting the people to get on with the job of reconstruction'; a state of affairs made more difficult by his having 'the Communists around his neck'.[6]

Nor was Edward wanted in France. The civil servant and diplomat Oliver Harvey wearily stated, 'I confess I regard without enthusiasm his intention of returning to Paris. His friends there turned out to be for the most part collaborators and he will expect to live there in luxury amid general poverty.' There was a sense of buck-passing when Harvey noted that 'he is also a close friend of the Ambassador which will not make it easier for the latter'.[7] Nevertheless, the couple eventually arrived in France in early September, after the duke high-handedly informed the prime minister ('dear Attlee') that 'we are planning to visit France in September for the purposes of attending to our interests in that country'. Once *in situ*, he set about making a nuisance of himself there.*

In the same letter, sent on 3 August, the duke announced that 'it is also my intention to go to Great Britain when I am in Europe, and I therefore look forward to an opportunity of seeing you again'.[8] His attitude towards the Attlee government and Labour was a mercurial one. On the one hand, he loathed anything that smacked of communism, and denounced the 1945 election victory to his friend Duncan Stewart as 'discouraging and a great surprise'. Although he joked to his solicitor, A. G. Allen, that 'tradition precluded any political comment on his part', he painted himself as a lounge-bar

---

* A despairing contemporary note suggests that Bevin 'sees no alternative to allowing the Duke and Duchess to visit France as proposed'.

Cassandra when he said of the result that 'I must admit to a sense of disappointment – not so much for Great Britain herself, who is well able to control the extent and tempo of new political and economical experiments with sanity and moderation, but as regards the effect of the British Socialist victory in [the United States] and on the continent of Europe, where the spread of Communism was the greatest danger confronting us and must now be a certainty.'[9]

Publicly and privately, then, the duke stood against socialism in all its forms, regarding it as little more than a back door into communism. However, he was also a pragmatist. If he wanted to be treated with any favour by the new administration, he would have to charm them into submission. His subsequent ghostwriter, Charles Murphy, later wrote that 'he had been encouraged to believe that he would have better luck with the Labour Government than he had had with the departed Tories ... he hoped that his popularity with the British working man was still untarnished, and that the Socialists still cherished his words of compassion for the Welsh miners* on the eve of the abdication'.[10] He retained his popularity with the working man, many of whom refused to judge him for his marriage to Wallis – and who were unaware of his complex political sympathies – and so he resolved to return to Britain, and see what he could accomplish.

Lascelles reported the news of the second coming of the duke with laconic exasperation on 12 August. 'The King, wonderful to relate, had a letter from the Duke of Windsor ("Dear Bertie ... Yours, David" – the first so begun and ended for many a long day') in which he announced his intention of taking his Duchess to Antibes next month, and subsequently paying a short visit to this country, *en garçon*.'† The tidings were less of a surprise than they might have been, because Edward had already informed Duff

---

* As king, he had witnessed the depressed mining conditions in South Wales in November 1936, and had remarked, 'these works brought all these people here ... something must be done to get them at work again'. His words were not backed up with action.

† Meaning 'as a bachelor'. The absence of Wallis was unlamented.

Cooper, the British ambassador to France, Attlee ('who showed me the letter, which he was not at all pleased to get') and Queen Mary of his intention to return. Lascelles scorned this as his 'usual propensity for doing everything in the order exactly opposite to that which normal people would follow'.[11]

The king had no especial desire to see his brother, who he had not been in the same room with since 1939. He received Allen in order to ascertain what his client's plans were, and generally steeled himself for such an encounter. He sent Edward a non-committal telegram saying, 'I hope to have a rest at Balmoral, but trust that there will be a chance of our meeting while you are in England.'[12] Although Lascelles had informed Churchill's private secretary, John Martin, the year before that 'HM would not be sorry if his brother did not come to England for the next ten years',[13] the monarch's attitude had mellowed since the end of the war, as had Queen Mary's. After she had refused to receive the duke on his previous visit to the country, she was now able to say that 'I need scarcely assure you what a joy it will be to me to see you once again after all these years, for I have missed you very much indeed.' For a woman not given to emotional outpourings, this was tantamount to the fatted calf being slaughtered.*

Nonetheless, as the king wrote to his mother on 23 September, 'it seems to me that when he does come here . . . we must take the line that he cannot live here . . . we have told him that we are not prepared to meet "her" and they cannot live in this country without even meeting us'. After the usual run-through of the duke's perceived objections to returning to Britain (taxation, Wallis's dislike for the royal family and vice versa, her essential obsolescence), the king sighed that 'he seems to think that when he gave up his work for which he was trained, he could "live" it down and return here as a private individual and all would be well'. He concluded

---

* This did not extend to Wallis. Queen Mary wrote to her friend the Countess of Athlone to say, 'I hope he does not bother me too much about receiving her - as nothing has happened since to alter my views about that unfortunate marriage.'

that 'he has to consider others beside himself, and I doubt whether even now he realises the irrevocable step he took nine years ago and the ghastly shock he gave this country'.[14]

The duke's subsequent return to Britain was, superficially, an amicable and peaceable one,* even if he was unable to obtain the preferment that he had sought, either from his family or from the government. It might not have helped his case that after the indifferent start to their relationship,† Attlee and the king had found common ground. Lascelles reported that the prime minister had visited Balmoral on 26 September, and that the visit had been a success, with the king getting on 'very well' with his premier, despite the queen being laid up with a chill. The private secretary wrote of Attlee, with some respect, that 'I find him excellent company when he thaws out; like most men with no natural presence, he seems to be fighting a continual rear-guard action against his physical insignificance, though his mental stature is good enough.'[15]

Naturally, they had discussed the impending visit of the duke, and Attlee had indicated to the king that he shared his scepticism about the desirability of Edward being given any kind of job.‡ The monarch wrote to his mother that the premier 'agrees with me that [Edward] cannot live here permanently owing to his wife & he is not prepared to offer D. any job here or anywhere'. When he met his brother, along with Queen Mary, on 5 October, it was a pleasant, if pointed, encounter. The king later wrote in his diary that '[Edward] was looking very well & talked a great deal about America. After dinner he broached the subject of his wife. He asked Mama if she would receive her. After some moments in a strong silence she replied that she could never do so, as nothing had happened to alter the circumstances which had led to his Abdication.

---

* See *The Windsors at War*, Epilogue, for further details.
† The king had written in his diary of 3 August, 'We discussed many matters of the moment. I find I have to tell him many things.'
‡ In a letter of 23 August, Attlee had referred to the duke's 'long and successful administration as Governor of the Bahamas during the war', perhaps with tongue slightly in cheek.

He could see this was final . . . we discussed the whole matter very thoroughly & quietly. He was very happily married and he knew he had done the right thing, as he felt he could never have done the King's job properly without her. I told him frankly that he had profoundly shocked everyone here & in the Empire, he would not listen to his friends, family or advisers, & he had not thought out the consequences of his behaviour.'[16]

Another account, relayed to Channon by the Polish diplomat Alic Poklewski, was more vivid. The duke had begun the evening by saying 'in his strong American accent', 'No point beating about the bush – will you receive my wife or not?' Upon being told that this was impossible, he replied, 'Then you cannot expect me to receive my sisters-in-law.'[17]

The greatest note of scepticism from the family had been struck by the queen. She had written to 'Dearest Mama', Queen Mary, shortly before the duke's arrival to hope that the visit went well, 'for whatever the sad events of the past, it is very hard for a mother to be parted from her son'. Her truer feelings about her brother-in-law could be discerned from her remarks that 'I do trust that . . . he won't have any press conferences. He ought to say that his visit is private and refuse to see the press, for it is most indiscreet to start something which the family have avoided so successfully here.'[18]

Needless to say, the duke held a press conference upon his arrival, albeit without the hoopla that such an event would once have attracted, and the queen's unease was justified. Channon commented that 'the fact is that the Queen* lives in the eighteenth century – the King in the nineteenth and the Duke in the twenty-first . . . none of them is in time with the present age'.[19] The modernistic man also did not help himself in his dealings with Queen Mary.† She later commented to the royal librarian, Owen Morshead, that although her son had been 'very nice . . . quite like old

---

* In this case, Queen Mary.
† Channon reported that she was 'always agitated' during her son's stay, but that they parted on 'friendly terms', with her kissing him goodbye.

times, very well informed, knew everything that was going on', he once again offered a not-so-enigmatic variation on the usual theme, namely the family's treatment of Wallis. 'Still persisting about my receiving his wife, when he <u>promised</u> he'd never mention the subject to me again.' Typically, the duke's parting words to his mother were 'Well, goodbye - and don't forget, I'm a married man now.' She commented sardonically to Morshead, 'Don't forget, indeed; as if one ever could!'[20]

After the duke's departure, Lascelles, who had had a lengthy interview with him on 9 October in which he had tried to make him see sense about his future role within the royal family, commented that 'he has come, and gone, without a breach of the peace. I feel rather as one did on hearing the all clear after a prolonged air raid.' This was kinder than a remark of the socialite Lady Diana Cooper's that he reported, namely that, after seeing the Windsors in Paris, she thought they were 'both looking as thin as if just out of Belsen . . . she grown a little more common, and he more pointless, dull and insipid'. Lascelles's tut-tutting - 'hard words from an old friend'[21] - did not obscure the obvious satisfaction that he took in repeating her insults.

The duke's visit to Britain had been a success, in that it had made future dealings with his family more harmonious. For the next few years, he was able to travel to and from his home country with far less hoo-ha than hitherto. He cemented his reconciliation with his mother by telling her on 13 October, 'it really was wonderful to be with you again after so many years and to find you so young and well', although he was unable to restrain himself in his sign-off. 'The only thing I have regretted all these years is not seeing more of you, regarding which for the future I can only ask you to remember that I am no longer a bachelor.'[22] Her reply was suitably tactful. 'It was the greatest pleasure to me to see you again after all these long years, looking so well & young, and so full of energy - and so nice to have had those long talks on so many subjects in which both of us are interested.'[23]

When he wrote to his brother upon his return to Paris, the duke began and ended with the usual endearments ('Dear Bertie ... Yours ever, David') and praised the king for all that he had undertaken 'after the strain of the last six years of total war'. He acknowledged that certain issues - namely Wallis, although her name was unmentioned - had to be left alone, and then pressed on with his greater aim: securing some kind of future role for himself.

During his time in Britain, he had insisted on an audience with Bevin, and suggested a suitable post: ambassador-at-large to the United States. Although Lord Halifax currently occupied the ambassadorial position, the duke did not see any contradiction in terms between their overlapping but distinct roles. Halifax would continue to attend to the drudgery and official business; Edward, meanwhile, would concentrate on having fun.

He was, of course, too diplomatic to describe it thus. In an article he wrote many years later for the *New York Daily News*, he outlined what he saw as the major requirements of the role. 'I would concentrate on the public relations aspect. Such a job would require my bringing Americans and visiting Britons together, providing a good table and a comfortable library for informal talks and helping along what Winston Churchill called the "mixing-up process".'[24] To Bevin, he added the sweetener that his presence would not be required in Washington full time. After all, the whole point of such a roving role was to allow him to travel the world - first class, naturally - and for the bill to be picked up by someone else.

Bevin's dealings with the duke had previously been limited to seeing him at a remove, so he approached him with neither reverence nor contempt. Instead, he viewed the proposition on its merits and drawbacks. On the one hand, if the duke was a roving ambassador, he would undoubtedly raise the profile of post-war Britain overseas. Amid the greyness and exhaustion of his country, he would convey a sense of glamour and excitement. On the other, it was unconscionable that the British taxpayer would subsidise a wealthy man's life of leisure for the rest of his working days. Bevin sent the memorandum of his conversation to Attlee without com-ment, and there the matter had to rest.

The duke was, however, happy to go over the Foreign Secre-tary's head in pursuit of his ambitions, and so made a similar sug-gestion to the king. He wrote that 'it is only natural that I should want to place my experience at the disposal of any organisation that could use it rather than retire to a life of complete leisure. My desire therefore to offer my services to you and British inter-ests is sincere and genuine.' With a potential allusion to Wallis ('I suggested the field of Anglo-American relations'), he outlined his credentials for a newly created post. 'I am convinced that there can be no lasting peace for mankind unless the two countries preserve a common approach to international politics . . . I have made many useful contacts [in America] and I believe a number of converts among convinced isolationists . . . It is a difficult and subtle subject and one that requires a realistic approach as well as a thorough knowledge of the two peoples and their ever-changing political reactions.'[25]

The king replied shortly afterwards with an amicable, if distant, letter,* in which he acknowledged how good it had been to see his brother, and that he was relieved that the duke planned to take up permanent residence in America 'in order to lead the kind of useful life which is in your mind'. He concluded, 'I fully realise that you and I are placed in a most unique position & we must work out a plan which will make the situation as easy & workable as possible for both of us. I want you to know that I shall do everything in my power to help you in your plan for the future & I do hope & trust that this idea of yours will work out successfully for all concerned.'

This was not a platitude. The monarch had consulted Churchill – 'He was not very helpful as to his future. He thought diplomatic status was unnecessary for any job in America; he could do more privately to improve the 2 countries relations'[26] – and although the king suggested that he was prepared to help, even to the extent of

---

* Lascelles called it 'quite a good letter', with just an ounce of condescension.

sending a letter of support to President Truman – a suggestion of Lascelles' – he remained sceptical about the idea of creating any kind of formal post, especially one that he noted 'would appear to be invented for you alone'.[27] The situation appeared irresolvable.

The duke was, however, cheered by a meeting that he had with Churchill in Paris on 14 November. The former prime minister may have been bored, or wishing to make mischief, but he promised to offer his assistance and counsel, even if Wallis commented to her aunt that '[he] is more helpful now that he is out of power'.[28] The duke was more effusive when he wrote to Churchill to thank him the next day. 'We were also very interested to hear your views regarding our future and the plan by which I could be most usefully employed in the service of my country, and wish to thank you for your efforts on our behalf with the present powers in Great Britain.'[29]

On the same day, Edward also replied to his brother, buoyed by Churchill's support. He was robust ('while I appreciate your suggestion of writing to the President to inform him of the project under discussion, I do not understand the difficulty of actually creating an official post for me which would appear to have been invented for me alone') and self-assured: 'As it is agreed my position is unique, why should a unique post not be created for me?' He went on to suggest that Churchill – for whom the king retained a unique degree of respect* – would explain 'how I could be appointed to work in America "within the ambit of the British Embassy in Washington" . . . Most of my activities would, of course, be of a private and personal nature, but any efforts of mine would be fruitless and the American press puzzled and derisively critical were my return to America not accompanied by an official statement from the Foreign Office that I was accredited to the British Embassy in the form Winston suggests.'

---

* Although the relationship between the king and Attlee swiftly became an amicable one, the king never came to the head of the Buckingham Palace stairs to meet him for their weekly audiences; a concession only offered to Churchill. He wrote on 22 November of the former premier, who he had invited to dinner, 'how refreshing to have a friend to talk to for a change'.

As so often with the duke, the rationale for his behaviour was financial, rather than ideological. If he was allowed to return to America under diplomatic auspices, he would be saved the bother of having to pay income tax. Otherwise, he faced an embarrassing and financially ruinous situation, and although he did not hint to the king that he would be forced into acts that might embarrass the royal family - such as, for instance, writing a revelatory memoir - he nevertheless ended the letter with a warning. 'I hope that you will make arrangements for me along these lines in the same spirit that I am willing to respect your feelings with regard to my living in Great Britain. Be assured that I appreciate your interest in my future activities, but it is not so easy to embark upon a fresh venture at the age of fifty-one, and it is important to start off on the right foot.'[30]

The duke and duchess found their present existence disappointing. He had complained to his brother that 'Life in France is really quite impossible for a foreigner who has no official job, and conditions are bound to deteriorate during the coming winter months . . . The electric current is switched off for long periods throughout the twenty-four hours and heating is a serious problem.'[31] But this was not all that vexed him.

They had returned to Paris in September, and Wallis had initially amused herself by trying to re-create the social whirl that she had fondly imagined the city wished to return to. But many of their former friends had left, or avoided the entreaties of a pair who had been mired in scandal and gossip, even if the duke's wartime activities were yet to become public knowledge.* Their English friends were largely prevented from travelling due to currency restrictions, and their home in the Boulevard Suchet would have to be given up in April 1946.

It was not a settled or happy time. When they had arrived, one ambassadorial functionary, Edward Holman, had had an audience

---

* For further details about this, see *The Windsors at War,* Epilogue.

with the duke. He described him as 'much older ... [but] quite natural and full of charm', and as loquacious as ever ('It was with great difficulty that I got in a word edgewise'). Holman warned the duke to behave himself, avoid dealing in black market goods and not give the French press an opportunity to write scandalous stories about him and Wallis - 'he might like to receive the Press officially and thus be finished with them once and for all', he wrote optimistically - and Edward concurred, even suggesting that his main preoccupation was 'the growing menace of Soviet Russia, which in his opinion was creating alarm in America too'.[32]

Edward wrote many years later in the *New York Daily News* that 'of all the world's unemployed, none can be more practiced in the art of weaving a tolerable existence from loose ends than a former King in a foreign land', and that 'I got to be rather good at it'.[33] This was wishful thinking. At the time, he and Wallis drifted around the city, searching for a purpose but frustrated by bureaucracy. He growled to Queen Mary that 'One is obliged to spend hours of each day pursuing functionaries in often fruitless attempts to cut one's way through the lanes of red tape with which the simplest operations are bound!'[34]

An insight into Edward's *régime de vivre* can be gleaned from a letter from the socialite - and mistress to Duff Cooper - Susan Mary Alsop to her friend Marietta Tree. She called him 'pitiful', and wrote that although he looked 'young and undissipated', 'I never saw a man so bored'. He described his day to her, asking, 'How do you manage to remain so cheerful in this ghastly place?' Even the duke's sternest detractors could hardly fail to find it poignant. 'I got up late and then I went with the Duchess and watched her buy a hat, and then on the way home I had the car drop me off in the Bois to watch some of your soldiers playing football and then I had planned to take a walk, but it was so cold that I could hardly bear it. In fact I was so afraid that I would be struck with cold in the way people are struck with heat so I came straight home ... When I got home the Duchess was having her French lesson so I had no one to talk to.' As Alsop said, 'I thought this description of a day was pretty sad from a man who used to be Edward VIII by the Grace of God of Great Britain, Ireland and the British Dominions beyond the Seas, King, Defender of the Faith and Emperor of India.'[35]

Diana Cooper, who was by now desperately weary of her former friend, summed up her feelings about him in an interview with *W* magazine over thirty years later. 'He had such an awful life in Paris. He couldn't speak French, he didn't enjoy nightclubs and he had very few friends he could talk with. If only I had been Mrs Simpson, I would have bought him the most lovely house in Virginia. He was *violently* pro-American and he would have enjoyed it so much.'[36] Had the duke been offered the quasi-ambassadorial post he longed for, he would undoubtedly have headed to America and left behind Paris for ever. But the French did not ask him to pay tax, and the Americans would, and so he and Wallis remained in limbo.

In Britain, the duke's activities were discussed far more often than he might have imagined. Lascelles wrote on 8 November that Churchill had proposed 'an ingenious expedient whereby the Duke can be settled in USA on some quasi-diplomatic basis',[37] but a wider problem was what could be done about his present behaviour. Duff Cooper had written to the private secretary on 8 November to say that Edward was being 'a bit of a nuisance, "talking big" to various French officials whom he meets at dinner, and telling them how to run their own country, which naturally they don't like'. Lascelles saw this as par for the course. 'He was always given to holding forth, and indeed, as long ago as 1926, showed increasing signs of becoming a hearth-rug bore; with increasing years, he may be developing George IV's tendency to arrogate to himself capabilities, and performances, which are actually beyond him.'[38] He did not mention that this included an ambassadorial role,* but the implication remained clear.

---

* It had in fact been discussed as recently as 5 October as to whether the duke might be made ambassador to Argentina – something he requested when he dined with his mother and brother, according to Poklewski – but it was believed that his Nazi connections and the general unsuitability of Wallis made such an appointment impossible.

On 30 November, Bevin and Lascelles met at the Foreign Office to attempt to discuss the possibilities of a position for the duke. Bevin was sceptical about the idea of any American ambassador being prepared to work alongside him, and saw Churchill's solution of the so-called 'silken thread' as being impractical.* As he asked, 'What would be his personal relationship with an ex-King, either on the same plane as himself or under his orders?' The Foreign Secretary then suggested that the major problem was that 'if any sort of diplomatic status, however carefully camouflaged, were given to the Duke of Windsor, the Americans would immediately say that the chief reason for it was to get the Windsors immunity from taxation'. As Lascelles pointed out, 'the Americans would not be far wrong'.

It was a sign of British inability to deal with the duke that Churchill's cousin Shane Leslie – a committed advocate of Irish Home Rule – was now asked to step into the breach and receive Edward at Castle Leslie, 'to study the Irish background of Anglo-American relations' with a view to his taking some role in Ireland, if he so wished. Lascelles denounced this 'bazaar [sic] rumour' as 'a good judgement of the D of W's irresponsibility and lack of political and personal judgement . . . It is a crazy idea, the execution of which would certainly do him harm, besides infuriating the Ulstermen – and, if he had any contact with de Valera, many people in this country.' Even Churchill considered this 'a most dangerous plan, which ought to be stopped at all costs'.[39]

The king, fearing chaos, now tried to make a case for his brother being given some kind of semi-formal role in America, with the assistance of Lascelles and the lawyer and politician Walter Monckton; the private secretary even wrote on 6 December that 'we have

---

* Churchill's wish that Edward head to the United States was tempered with caution. He wrote to George VI, mindful of the drawbacks of an out-of-control duke, to say, 'there might be serious disadvantages in utterly casting off the Duke of Windsor and his wife from all official contact with Great Britain, and leaving him in a disturbed and distressed state of mind to make his own life in the United States'.

contrived a rational solution of the Windsors' move to the USA'.[40]
On the same day, the king had an interview with Bevin, who
suggested that Edward should go to the USA with all the embassy
facilities but with no 'diplomatic status'. As the monarch wrote in
his diary, 'He said it work [sic] with Halifax but he would not like
to make it a condition for future ambassadors.'[41]

As Wallis complained to her aunt that 'we are always waiting results of the Duke's visit to London which though won't be anything
grand (if anything at all) would be better than having nothing to do
for the moment', they were visited by Monckton. He attempted
to provide good cheer and reassurance, but without any actual
grounds for so doing: the king had briefed him to tell Edward that
he could do no more than he had already done. After Monckton's
visit, the duke wrote to him testily to reiterate his disappointment
at not being offered the post he sought, saying, 'My retiring nature
should be sufficient guarantee that I possess the goodwill, tact and
experience of State affairs to prevent any infringement on the important and exalted post of British Ambassador in Washington.'[42]

It did not. As Wallis and Edward fell into dejected inertia ('the
Duke thinks everything is dull after the American parties . . . [he] is
for pulling up all stakes here as there is really nothing for him to do
and no men who would be congenial to him',[43] she told her aunt),
the problem of what to do with them only got worse. The paradox
was best expressed by Duff Cooper, who informed Lascelles on 20
December that 'any form of outward liaison between the Duke of
Windsor and our Embassy in Washington would be impracticable',
but, as the private secretary noted, this was set against Cooper's
anxiety 'to get the Duke out of his own bishopric, Paris'.[44]

Eventually, a solution of sorts was arrived upon. The duke
would visit Britain early in 1946, and the matter could be discussed
again then. It was difficult, but at least it meant that the issue could
be forgotten about over Christmas, which for the royal family was
a jolly house party at Sandringham, in Norfolk: seventy-eight-year-
old Queen Mary was said to be 'youthful, skittish and generally
rejuvenated . . . really full of fun and giggles. She dances given any

chance at all, coming out shooting (with stick <u>and</u> umbrella) and generally contributes to any jolly fun.'[45] If 1945 had been a year of both triumph and sorrow, the former had outweighed the latter. As Lascelles mused, closing his diary for the year, '1945 [may], as I wrote to the King today, prove to have been the most exacting year of his whole reign. It has been a tough year for me too.' Still, there was one abiding consolation. 'But we beat the Boche.'[46] One enemy was defeated. But other adversaries would emerge.

Chapter Three

'I Believe She Loves and Will Marry Him'

On New Year's Day 1946, Queen Elizabeth remarked to her friend, the diplomat D'Arcy Osborne, 'It is rather a sad thought, but both my daughters have never set foot outside these Islands! For some years before the war they were not only too small but dictators strutted in Europe, & for six years they lived under fairly warlike conditions here, so that when people are kind to each other again, I can see that they will be off & away to travel & see for themselves.' Her optimism was, however, tempered with regret. 'Indeed, they have hardly even met a foreigner! It is too extraordinary & wrong.'[1]

As the year began, her daughter Princess Elizabeth was nineteen, and the possessor of several impressive-sounding titles: counsellor of state, honorary colonel, veteran of the Auxiliary Territorial Service and, of course, first in line to the throne. She had spent the months after the end of the war as a good public servant, whether she was addressing the Welsh Girl Guides, opening the library of the Royal College of Nursing or travelling to Ulster with her parents; her first overseas flight, albeit within the confines of the British Isles. She was offered an honorary degree from Cambridge University - the first woman to be so recognised - but Lascelles turned it down on her behalf, perhaps with an air of righteous disdain.*

Marion Crawford wrote, accurately, in *The Little Princesses* that

---

* He was happy for her to accept an honorary bachelor's degree in music from London University, however, convincing the queen of the idea on 23 May 1945.

'peace turned out to be not very peaceful'. Crawfie described the existence that Princess Elizabeth now led, and it was an exhausting one. 'At ten o'clock . . . Lilibet would ring for her lady-in-waiting and deal with her own correspondence and see her dressmaker. Most afternoons she would either open some bazaar or visit factories and hospitals.' She mused that 'I felt now that my job was to provide a little light relief for Lilibet. Her days were so full of functions and duties that cannot have been other than oppressive for a girl of nineteen.'[2]

Life for the princess may have been taken up with the unadventurous and the unexciting, but, as Crawfie commented, the idea 'that the heiress to the throne would stay unmarried was unthinkable'.[3] Elizabeth was the most eligible woman in Europe in 1945. It was universally assumed that she would be queen before very long, and her father's weariness suggested that this time could come far sooner than many would have been comfortable with. But the idea that she could fall deeply in love with a man who might be both politically and personally awkward was anathema to many. Except, that is, to someone largely responsible for facilitating a match between a woman who enjoyed every conceivable advantage a human being could have, and a man who, twenty-four years previously, had been born on the dining room table of a Corfu villa named Mon Repos: my rest.

Prince Andrew of Greece and Princess Alice of Battenberg had made little secret of their desire for a son. They had had four daughters, Margarita, Theodora, Cecilie and Sophie, and therefore the unorthodox arrival of their fifth and last child, Philip, on 10 June 1921 was a welcome distraction from the rigours of the Greco-Turkish War, which was then approaching its final phase. Turkish victory was finally declared on 11 October 1922, and the results were punitive for the family: Philip's uncle and the commander of the Greek military forces, King Constantine I, had already been forced to abdicate, on 27 September 1922, and Prince Andrew was arrested and accused of disobeying orders and abandoning his post in the face of the enemy. It was believed that he would be executed, unless a *deus ex machina* appeared, and fast.

This happened in part due to Princess Alice's diplomatic efforts. Her younger brother, the energetic Louis 'Dickie' Mountbatten, secured an audience with George V and with the prime minister, Andrew Bonar Law. He emotively described his brother-in-law's predicament, which now included his being banished from his homeland for life by a hastily convened revolutionary court. Impressed by the urgency of the situation, the king, premier and Foreign Secretary Lord Curzon saw to it, with the aid of the naval attaché Commander Gerald Talbot, that Prince Andrew and his family would be evacuated from Greece, travelling aboard HMS *Calypso*.

It was a narrow escape for the family, and subsequently Princess Alice would write that her family owed 'a deep debt of gratitude to HM the King for the promptitude and efficacy of his action'. Even as her husband complained of 'the monstrosity of the crime'[4] that had been visited upon his family, they were, for the time being, safe, and bound for France, where Prince Philip would spend his early years. He would later dismiss the idea that he was somehow traumatised by what had happened, saying, 'I was barely a year old when the family went into exile, so I don't think I suffered the same disorientation.'[5] They lived in Saint-Cloud, a suburb of Paris, but in order to give Philip the education his father believed a European prince merited, he was sent to boarding school in England at the age of nine, in Cheam. He shone in sport but was an undistinguished student academically, who received the comment 'Could do better if he tried'[6] in one school report.

He may, by this stage, have had other distractions. His sisters all married in a relatively short period, between December 1930 and August 1931; a reflection of some of the troubles the family faced at this time. In 1930, his mother was diagnosed with paranoid schizophrenia after claiming to see visions of Christ, and was placed in the Bellevue sanatorium in Kreuzlingen in Switzerland, run by a disciple of Sigmund Freud, Ludwig Binswanger. Her institutionalisation all but tore the family apart. Her husband did not divorce her, undoubtedly because of the scandal it would have caused, but instead began a new life in Monte Carlo. He would die of a heart attack there on 3 December 1944, at the age of sixty-two.

Their daughters married various leading German noblemen - which would become deeply problematic in due course - but Philip was too young to be so attached. He found himself living an itinerant existence that included a brief stay at a German boarding school, Schule Schloss Salem, and then a longer and more formative experience at Gordonstoun, a Scottish school established by Kurt Hahn, the founder of Salem. The young 'Philip of Greece', as he styled himself, was one of Gordonstoun's first pupils, and enjoyed the school's vigorous regime of personal improvement through exercise and hard work, under Hahn's enlightened tutelage.

Yet away from the blissful days of school, Philip's life was a difficult and often tragic one. His sister Cecilie died in a plane crash on 16 November 1937, at the age of twenty-six, along with her husband, Georg Donatus, their two eldest children and her unborn son. Their other child, Princess Johanna, would die of meningitis in June 1939. His uncle and guardian, George Mountbatten, Marquess of Milford Haven, perished of bone cancer in April 1938, and the man who had acted as a surrogate father was now removed from his life, leaving him, as the historian and biographer Philip Ziegler described it, 'stateless, nameless and not far from penniless'.[7] It was a restless, rootless existence, but one that was redeemed by two factors. The first was the presence of his other uncle, Lord Dickie, a charismatic if somewhat rakish figure who took care to guide his nephew, and the second was the outbreak of World War II.

While his surviving sisters' husbands fought on the German side, Philip, under Mountbatten's tutelage, had a distinguished career in the Royal Navy, eventually rising to become first lieutenant of HMS *Wallace* in October 1942, at the age of twenty-one. It was later said of him by Lord Charteris, his future private secretary, that 'he was a very gallant officer',[8] and this was borne out by the fact that he was mentioned in dispatches for his service at the

Battle of Cape Matapan in 1941, and was also awarded the Greek War Cross for his participation in the latter event. He certainly had, by any definition of the term, 'a good war', and ended it a splendidly whiskered and dashing twenty-four-year-old man of action. Yet it was his involvement with Princess Elizabeth that would see him transformed from an itinerant European aristocrat into one of the most famous men in the world.

His first recorded meeting with the royal family occurred when he was a small child and took tea with Queen Mary: she called him 'a nice little boy with very blue eyes'.[9] He was unlikely to have met his future wife on this occasion, as she would have been little more than an infant, but they were certainly both present at the wedding of the Duke and Duchess of Kent on 29 November 1934 – he would have been thirteen and she eight – and then subsequently at the coronation of King George VI on 12 May 1937.

Yet the first time the two would have enjoyed any degree of intimacy was on 22 July 1939, a few weeks before the outbreak of war, while Philip was a student at the Royal Naval College at Dartmouth. The ever-ambitious Mountbatten ensured that the pair met for tea that day on the royal yacht, the *Victoria and Albert*; he later noted in his diary that '[Philip] was a great success with the children.'[10] As Ziegler wrote, with diligent understatement, 'it is hard to believe no thought crossed [Mountbatten's] mind that an admirable husband for the future Queen Elizabeth might be readily available'.[11]

Crawfie described Philip as 'a fair-haired boy, rather like a Viking, with a sharp face and piercing blue eyes . . . good-looking, though rather offhand in his manner', and one whom 'Elizabeth never took her eyes off'. Yet general focus at this stage was on the princess, rather than the young prince. Crawfie wrote that Philip was 'quite polite to her, but did not pay her any special attention',[12] and it is likely that the eighteen-year-old naval cadet did not have any pressing inclinations towards the thirteen-year-old princess, to say nothing of the nine-year-old Margaret, who her governess noted was much teased by the prince.

Nonetheless, it has now become a given among the sentimental that it was on this day that the beginnings of romance began between the two. Certainly, the rumours were widespread enough for Channon to write of Philip in his diary on 11 January 1942 that 'he is to be our Prince Consort, and that is why he is serving in our navy'. Channon, never one to pass up an opportunity for personal comment, declared that he is 'an absolute "charmer" aged only 20. He is about the best-looking boy I have ever seen, fair, a touch languid but with good manners.' Typically, the politician described himself as 'impressed and attracted'.*[13] There was a correspondence between the young prince and princess at this time, but it remains unclear as to whether these letters were anything other than formal pleasantries. In any case, Philip enjoyed a reputation as a ladies' man; Queen Alexandra of Yugoslavia recorded in her memoirs that 'the fascination of Philip had spread like influenza, I knew, through a whole string of girls'.[14] One particular dalliance was with the Canadian debutante Osla Benning, who was possessed of 'dark hair, alabaster white skin, an exquisite figure and a gentle loving nature'.†[15] It amounted to little, however: there was a greater potential prize, for both the prince and his uncle, than Benning.

Nearly two years later, in December 1943, a more productive opportunity for Philip and Elizabeth to renew their acquaintance arrived. To celebrate the news that the tide of war seemed, at last, to be changing in the Allies' favour, the king and queen held a small dance party for selected guests, and offered them the chance to watch the annual family pantomime. Although ill health frustrated Philip's presence at the dance, the queen was pleased at how the

---

* Naturally, Channon also wrote, 'I deplore such a marriage . . . he and Princess Elizabeth are too interrelated.'

† She was also conspicuously naïve in sexual matters. One biographer recorded how 'she caused a mild sensation in a nightclub when she complained loudly that it was very inconsiderate of her boyfriend always to carry his torch in his pocket as it was so uncomfortable when dancing'. History does not recall whether this boyfriend was Prince Philip.

event had gone - 'I fear that they are all starved of colour and beautiful things to look at, in these days'[16] - and he managed to rouse himself from his sickbed (at Claridge's, naturally) and attend the pantomime at Windsor Castle, laughing heartily from his front-row seat.

He remained on hand all over Christmas; Princess Elizabeth later described to Crawfie how 'we had a very gay time, with a film, dinner parties and dancing to the gramophone',[17] and Lascelles wrote, with a hint of a splutter, that 'they frisked and capered away till near 1 a.m.'.[18] Princess Margaret later said of Philip and the other guests, '[they went mad] and we danced and danced and danced . . . [it was] the best night of all'.[19]

The dynamic between the young Elizabeth and Philip had subtly altered. Crawfie later wrote, indiscreetly, that 'Lilibet came to me, looking rather pink' and expressed her excitement at the presence of the person the governess described as 'greatly changed . . . it was a grave and charming young man who sat there, with nothing of the rather bumptious boy I had first known about him now'.[20]

'I hope my behaviour did not get out of hand', Prince Philip wrote, suavely, to the queen in a thank-you letter on 31 December 1943. He felt sufficiently at ease to describe Windsor Castle as one of his favourite places, along with Mountbatten's home of Broadlands in Hampshire and the Kents' residence of Coppins in Buckinghamshire, and noted that its inclusion 'may give you some small idea of how much I appreciated the few days you were kind enough to let me spend with you'.[21] It was an impeccably polite letter, but the favourable reference to Windsor - and to spending time with its occupants - was no coincidence. It does not take a cynic to see the hand of Mountbatten in Philip's correspondence. His uncle was subsequently described by Lord Charteris as 'a shrewd operator and intriguer, always going round corners, never straight at it . . . he was ruthless in his approach to the royals'.[22] The opportunity to match his nephew with the queen-to-be was too tempting for Mountbatten not to scheme towards.

The success of the party was commonly enough known by the

beginning of 1944 for Channon to write in his diary on 16 February that 'I do know that a marriage may well be arranged one day between Princess Elizabeth and Prince Philip of Greece.'[23] A few days earlier, Channon had panted that Philip was 'le bel' and that 'he is the most handsome boy I have ever seen, and has immense engaging charm and insinuating manners'.[24] It was not just London's most inveterate gossip who had heard the rumour. On 6 March, Queen Mary wrote to the king to say that she had heard that the King of Greece thought the match was a respectable one, and added her own conditional approval of Philip, pronouncing him 'in some ways, very suitable'.[25] It helped that she was an admirer of what she called his 'brilliantly successful' naval career; gallantry and valour would endear anyone to her.[26]

The king liked him, and had done so since at least 1941, when he had seen him in October; he had written to Philip's grandmother, Victoria Milford Haven, to say 'what a charming boy he is, & I am glad he is remaining on in my Navy'.[27] Nothing had changed over the following years. Replying to his mother, he said approvingly that 'he is intelligent, has a good sense of humour, and thinks about things in the right way', but wondered whether it might be a safer bet for his daughter to marry an Englishman - especially one with a less controversial family background than a man whose sisters had married Nazis - and gently suggested that Elizabeth - still not eighteen - was not quite ready to contemplate marriage. '[She is] too young for that now, as she has never met any young men of her own age . . . P had better not think any more about it at present.'[28]

Despite this, as the rumours of an engagement spread, there were tensions. Harold Nicolson, with some exaggeration, described the family as 'horrified' at the prospect of a union between Philip and Elizabeth, and Lascelles suggested that 'they felt he was rough, ill mannered, uneducated and would probably not be faithful'.[29] He also wrote in his diary on 2 April 1944 that he had been told by the king that Prince Philip had asked his uncle, George of Greece, whether he thought he stood a serious chance of being able to marry the princess: the idea was thought impractical for many reasons, partly because of her youth and relative inexperience of the world, and partly because of Philip's nationality. It was therefore not wildly surprising that on 23 August, Mountbatten made his intentions clear, sounding out both Philip and the King of Greece as to whether the prince would be prepared to take British citizenship. Mountbatten's stated reason – an implausible one – was that after the death of the Duke of Kent,* George VI had a paucity of male relatives, and that if Philip became a naturalised citizen, 'he should be an additional asset to the British Royal Family and a great help to them in carrying out their royal functions'.[30]

Mountbatten had already paved the way for such an assimilation. On 20 February 1944, he had written to the king to extol Philip's essential Englishness, and, by extension, to play down his Greek heritage. 'Personally I hope you can persuade him to stay in your Navy & not go mixing himself up in Greek affairs. He can't even talk Greek & his outlook & training are entirely English . . . an exiled Greek prince is a sorry sort of job . . . particularly for an outstanding young man like Philip. He is happy in the RN & can easily rise to the top on merit as my father did.'[31] A subsequent letter in May stressed the point, and also made the idea of marriage at least implicit. 'I think your plan of going ahead now with Philip's British nationality & a permanent commission in the Royal Navy excellent from every point of view as it leaves the question of Lilibet open.'[32]

As 1944 progressed, however, the king became increasingly unsure whether a match of this nature was right for his elder daughter. In August, he replied to Mountbatten to counsel both caution and patience – 'I have been thinking the matter over since our talk and I have come to the conclusion that we are going too fast' – although he acknowledged Mountbatten's energetic and practical approach to such matters.† 'I know you like to get things settled at once, once you have an idea in mind.'[33] Mountbatten

---

* See *The Windsors at War*, Chapter Fourteen, for further details of this.
† It was not for nothing that Mountbatten, whose bisexuality was supposedly an open secret among his circle, was nicknamed 'Mountbottom', on the grounds that 'he believed it is better to give than to receive'.

expressed assent to the king, but was more candid writing to his mother. 'Philip entirely understood that the proposal [of his British citizenship] was not connected with any question of marrying Lilibet, though there is no doubt that he would very much like to one of these days.'[34]

When he informed his sister, Princess Alice, of developments at the beginning of 1945, Mountbatten was philosophical but confident, as he suggested that the king and queen no longer needed to be consulted about the potential match. 'The best hopes are to let it happen - if it will - without parents interfering. The young people appear genuinely devoted and I think after the war it is very likely to occur, but any "talk" now would undoubtedly make the situation much more difficult for Philip.'[35] He may have been reassured had he read Channon's diary of 28 October, written after a visit to the Kents' home at Coppins; Channon noted that 'as I signed the guest book, I saw "Philip" written constantly. It is at Coppins that he sees Princess Elizabeth, and I believe she loves and will marry him.' The politician, not always the most accurate of prophets, would eventually be proved right, but it was not an easy path to matrimony.

Philip was both amused and irritated by his uncle's intriguing, which took place everywhere from state rooms in Buckingham Palace to members' clubs in St James. If he had been indifferent to Princess Elizabeth, it might have been considered de trop, but his growing feelings towards her were noticed and aided by Mountbatten, who seemed to relish his self-appointed role of pander. It could, on occasion, go too far. After the end of the war, he wrote to Mountbatten to say, 'Please, I beg of you, not too much advice in an affair of the heart, or I shall be forced to do the wooing by proxy.' Nonetheless, he concluded the letter light-heartedly, saying, 'you can amuse yourself wondering what you are going to do with your Pygmalion next'.[36]

From a procedural perspective, the major obstacle to Philip's being allowed to marry Princess Elizabeth was that he was not a British citizen. There was no desperate hurry on the part of

Buckingham Palace to facilitate such an outcome. Lascelles, who had mixed feelings about the match, wrote in a letter of March 1945 that 'the King asked me recently what steps would have to be taken to enable Prince Philip of Greece . . . to become a British subject . . . [and] how it could be most easily and expeditiously handled'.[37] By August, Lascelles was wearying of the responsibility, and wrote in his diary, 'I suspect that there may be a matrimonial n***** in the woodpile.'[38]

Philip's naturalisation as a British subject in the immediate post-war era was not a simple matter of a couple of documents being signed and a brand-new passport being handed over to a naval hero. Attlee and Bevin had to tell the king that if the prince – who was regarded as being Greek by dint of his father's nationality, even if he had left the country as a baby and barely spoke the language – was to be granted British citizenship, it would be taken as a wider sign of favour towards the entire Greek royal family, and therefore of public support towards the country's royalist movement. Given that, as Sir Alexander Maxwell, Permanent Under-Secretary of State, remarked to Lascelles on 26 October 1945, 'the future prospects of the Greek monarchy are admitted to be dark',[39] it became politically expedient not to consider the matter until early 1946. In any case, Philip was engaged in a lengthy tour of Australia and the Far East, and was spending his time vigorously oat-sowing while he was out there. As his friend and subsequent equerry Mike Parker put it, 'there were always armfuls of girls'.[40]

Nonetheless, Philip maintained his correspondence with Princess Elizabeth throughout this time. At some point, she had obtained a picture of him, which took a suitably prominent place on her mantelpiece. When Crawfie wondered aloud, 'Is that altogether wise? People will begin all sorts of gossip about you', Elizabeth laughed 'rather ruefully' and said, 'Oh dear, I suppose they will.' The next time the governess entered her charge's room, the photograph had changed. It was still of Philip, but this time 'completely ambushed behind the enormous fair beard he had managed to raise while he was at sea during the war'. Elizabeth said proudly, 'I defy anyone to recognise who that is . . . he's completely incognito in that one'. As it happened, she was incorrect – Crawfie observed that 'those oddly piercing, intent blue eyes were much too individual' – and before long, 'one paper came right out into the open and announced it was Prince Philip of Greece whose photograph the Princess kept in her room'.[41] For once, the well-informed media were correct.

Philip may not have been aware of the speculation that his photographic presence in the princess's bedroom had excited in Britain – although it seems inconceivable that Mountbatten did not keep him abreast of such developments – but when he returned from his foreign travels at the beginning of 1946, it was no coincidence that Elizabeth, 'her eyes very bright', informed her governess 'half shyly', 'Crawfie! Someone is coming tonight.'

Between Mountbatten and Crawfie, a degree of matchmaking took place that was almost comical in its intensity. Elizabeth not only took a greater degree of care about her appearance, but constantly played the song 'People Will Say We're in Love' from the Rogers and Hammerstein musical *Oklahoma!* She was seen out in restaurants with Philip, although the two were discreet about their encounters; as Crawfie wrote, almost pruriently, 'one can picture the glances they exchanged as they passed on the dance floor, each with another partner'.[42]

Philip, meanwhile, struggled to find his place in the world. His naval career had given way to tiresome drudgery, overseeing the decommissioning of HMS *Whelp*, and he wrote candidly to Queen Elizabeth that he was 'still not accustomed to the idea of peace, rather fed up with everything and feeling that there was not much to look forward to and rather grudgingly accepting the idea of going on in the peacetime navy'.[43] He may have been 'hatless' and 'always in a hurry to see Lilibet', as Crawfie breathlessly described it, dining as a matter of course *en famille* in the former nursery at Buckingham Palace with Princesses Elizabeth and Margaret. This would be followed by 'high jinks', although Crawfie often took care to remove the younger sister: 'I felt that the constant presence of [Margaret], who was far from undemanding, and liked to have a good bit of attention herself, was not helping on the romance much.'[44] When Margaret's presence became too much, or too 'comically regal and overgracious', as Crawfie put it, Philip 'would give her a good push that settled the question of precedence quite simply'.[45]

Yet when he wasn't shoving teenage girls around, Philip was able to resume his naval career, mundane though it might have been. It was Elizabeth who found herself the subject of open, even insolent, speculation; she returned from one visit to a factory 'rather excited', and said, of the 'horrible' experience, that people shouted at her 'Where's Philip?' Crawfie righteously described this as a 'coarse piece of thoughtlessness',[46] but the reality was that Elizabeth found herself in an unprecedented situation. She was a nineteen-year-old girl who was in love with an older, considerably more experienced man, and whose previous love affairs and flirtations with sophisticated women were a matter of public record. Although it seemed clear to the detached likes of Channon that Philip both valued and welcomed Elizabeth's affections, there were existential difficulties with the continuing relationship. Crawfie compared Philip to Prince Albert – 'another Prince Consort, who had found that role no bed of roses' – and suggested that 'tactful subjugation had been no part of [Philip's] training', going so far as to say, 'there must have been moments when he wondered whether he could possibly face it'.[47]

Regardless of Philip's approach to subjugation, there were other issues as well. Crawfie referred to how 'some of the King's advisers did not think him good enough for [Elizabeth] . . . he was a prince without home or kingdom', just as 'some of the papers played long and loud tunes on the string of Philip's foreign origins'.[48] Although she acknowledged that 'he was a forthright and completely natural young man . . . [with] nothing of the polished courtier about him', his informal, energetic presence riled the likes of Lascelles, who, by Crawfie's account, were given to say things like 'If there is not to be an engagement, the boy ought not to be around so much. There is too much gossip and speculation already.'

Despite the warmth of the relationship, it was generally believed impossible at the beginning of 1946 that Philip and Princess Elizabeth could marry. Tales of his sisters' marriages to leading figures in the Nazi Party did him no credit; as one courtier described it, 'the kind of people who didn't like Prince Philip were the kind of people who didn't like Mountbatten. It was all bound up in a single word: "German".'[49] This impoverished, often scruffy figure, who would write in grand houses' visitors' books that he was of 'no fixed abode' and whose wardrobe was 'scantier than that of many a bank clerk',[50] might even have been accused of being an arriviste, an Arthur Townsend* whose primary designs on the future queen involved securing a financial and social stability he might well otherwise never have enjoyed.

But post-war Britain was a peculiar place. And things could change at remarkable speed, as the royal family were about to discover once again.

---

* The morally compromised antagonist of Henry James's novel *Washington Square*, who is believed to wish to marry the book's protagonist, Catherine Sloper, solely for her money.

Chapter Four

'This Poor Battered World'

Relations between the Duke of Windsor and the rest of the royal family at the beginning of 1946 resembled the experiences of participants in a gruelling war. There were periods of inertia, occasional inconclusive scuffles and long-distance incidents of sniping, and then short, intense rounds of combat, from which both sides would emerge exhausted and demoralised. Victory for either party seemed impossible. Yet dealings between them had not always been so dismal, and one courtier was testament to this. In 1920, when Lascelles was only thirty-three, he was offered the job of assistant private secretary to the then Prince of Wales, on a salary of £600 a year. In this more starry-eyed incarnation, Lascelles wrote that 'I have got a very deep admiration for the Prince', whom he praised as 'the most attractive man I've ever met',[1] and began working for him in December that year.

The relationship between the two lasted until January 1929, when a disillusioned Lascelles resigned, believing that his master's self-absorption, lack of any sense of duty, and general moral vacancy – to say nothing of an absence of Christian faith – made him wholly unsuited to be king. It was a significant turnaround from the beginning of the decade, but when Lascelles had stated that 'I am convinced that the future of England is as much in [Edward's] hands as in those of any individual',[2] he was more accurate than he could have imagined. While, two and a half decades later, the duke was no longer the figure he once was, he still held enormous symbolic importance throughout the world. It might have been easier to have ostracised and ignored him, but such things were not realistic. Even as he and his wife became ever more irksome and demanding, they still had to be afforded the treatment that a former monarch merited.

'I am afraid you are wrong about England', Wallis wrote to her aunt on 3 January 1946. She complained that her husband's home country had been deliberately inhospitable towards him, but also stated that 'the game is how attractive will they make it under those conditions - plus the fact that they really do not want him to have any official recognition anywhere.' Both she and the duke were weary of the situation, and it was an additional frustration that Churchill could not help them ('he has little power now and when he did took the same line as the King and Govt').

Nonetheless, she reported, in her usual stoical fashion, that 'the Duke goes to London tomorrow for another crack at the Court and the powers that be'.[3] It was a sign of the changing times that, after a prolonged (and enforced) six-year absence from his former country, the duke could now visit Britain twice in a matter of few months without the attendant controversy that once greeted him. Yet the tolerance that he now received was also marked by weariness. He could not be forbidden to come to the country that he had once ruled, but he was shown - repeatedly, if needs be - how little interest anyone now had in him. The star attraction had long since been demoted to supporting turn status, and now was in danger of being excised from the show altogether.

There were, in any case, more important issues at hand for his brother to consider. Shortly after President Truman had met him on board the *Renown*, the king was shocked to discover, on 21 August 1945, that the president had signed a document - almost without thinking - that ended the Lend-Lease agreement that Roosevelt had been responsible for in 1941, which had offered Britain a vast amount of food, oil and equipment in order to maintain the war effort. It is possible that Truman's actions were dictated by a newfound disdain for a country that would eject a prime minister

who America knew and liked from office, apparently without any
gratitude for his services during the war, but it is more likely that
it was simple indifference displayed towards their former allies.
After all, the Second World War was over. Wasn't it time for the
United States to look back to their own borders, and to their own
interests?

Although Attlee visited Congress in November 1945, and established a working relationship with both Truman and the Demo-
cratic Party, the king was aware that the situation for Britain was
dismal, and showing no signs of improvement. While he had come
to respect his premier, not least over their shared attitudes towards
the duke, he did not share the prime minister's politics. He believed
that, rather than dealing with the legal restraints on trade unions
or increasing nationalisation of the country's means of production, the crucial actions that had to be taken were to build houses,
to replace both the countless homes that had been destroyed in
the war and those that should have been constructed long before
that.

The new spirit alive in Britain made the king feel marginalised
and without an obvious outlet for his views. While Churchill and
Chamberlain had both allowed him to believe that he had an active
influence in politics, Attlee politely made it clear that the role of
the constitutional monarch - especially with a Labour government
- was to listen and agree, rather than to attempt to impose his own
perspective on matters. Mountbatten's hopes that the king might
be able to exert a more interventionist stance were not met. There
were numerous instances of minor humiliations. It was made clear
by the formerly unquestioning royal servants that they believed
they deserved a pay rise, and that in this new egalitarian age, they
would have no other option than to join a union if their demands
were not met. And although both Churchill and the king had
agreed that Sir Arthur 'Bomber' Harris should receive a peerage,
as well as a promotion to Marshal of the RAF, the peerage was
vetoed by Labour, on the grounds that the destruction Harris's
raids had caused was ultimately disproportionate, not least in the

case of Dresden, which was turned into rubble by the concentrated bombing it received.*

The king may have suggested to Lascelles, in a letter sent from Sandringham over Christmas 1945, that 'I am not downhearted or pessimistic as to the future'.[4] Save the possibility of his eldest daughter's romantic happiness, there was, however, little concrete evidence that things would improve on either a personal or national basis. He and the queen did what they could, once again inviting people to 'dine and sleep' at Windsor Castle - a tradition that had passed into abeyance for decades - but the prospect of the Duke of Windsor dining and sleeping at Windsor, or anywhere else for that matter, was an unhappy and vexing one.

When Edward arrived in Britain on 7 January 1946, having flown from Paris, he found himself received with reluctance by the king and various government ministers. He stayed at his mother's residence of Marlborough House, this time without her present. Lascelles summarised the former monarch's embassy with his usual pithiness. '[Bevin] intended to tell the Duke plainly that he couldn't recommend any form of attachment to the Embassy in Washington.'[5] Although the following day saw the king and duke on sufficiently amicable terms for the former to show the latter into Lascelles' office for a meeting before a state banquet to mark the inauguration of the United Nations organisation, nothing could be achieved. As Lascelles noted, '[the duke] thought that he had made some progress in converting [Bevin] to his Washington plan', but given the Foreign Secretary's comments about the impossibility of such a scheme, the duke's hopes remained, in Lascelles' summation, nothing more than 'wishful thinking'.[6]

The duke's visit was a waste of time and effort. The king noted, pithily, on 8 January, 'David came to see me. He is here for a few

* Harris himself claimed that he was offered a peerage but refused it in solidarity with the crews of Bomber Command being denied a campaign medal for their service. In any case, he received a baronetcy in 1953, when Churchill became prime minister once again.

days. He is still adamant about wanting to be attached to the Embassy and has left an aide memoire both with Attlee & Bevin.'*⁷

Edward was informed by the politicians that he would not be able to accept an invitation from his friend John Marriott, officer in charge of the Guards division in Germany, to visit the army stationed there. Memories of his previous trip to Germany, less than a decade before, and his meeting with Hitler - to say nothing of further embarrassing associations with that country's citizens and sympathisers during the war - meant that there was no way that even a private visit could be made. Attlee and Bevin also knew that the duke would never maintain a low profile. Press conferences, interviews and further scandal would all undoubtedly have followed.

Edward returned to France, dejected, jobless and demoralised, and Wallis summed up the situation in a letter to her aunt on 25 January. 'The English are determined not to give the Duke a big or important job for the reason they think it would take from the King - this in high circles is frankly said. The belief is that 2 Kings can't operate therefore the Duke having made his decision should eliminate himself. In the meantime they search for some camouflage type of position. We have definitely refused any colonial governmentship [sic]. What is the use to bury ourselves away for nothing?' She decided that, if 'camouflage' could not be found, their options were either to lead a private life, 'taking taxes into consideration', or, as the atomic bomb alternative, 'go to England for six months privately naturally and see what the effect would be'.⁸ She did not mention that such a return would almost certainly be vetoed by an appalled government, and their wanderings would recommence immediately.

---

* This 'aide memoire' stated, among other things, 'One of the two questions of burning interest to the American press concerning the Duchess and myself at the present time is: WILL BRITAIN GIVE THE DUKE A JOB AND, IF NOT, WHAT ELSE IS HE GOING TO DO?' Edward suggested that 'The press reaction to a negative answer would be most uncomfortable for all parties concerned.'

Yet as the duke's ambitions of an ambassadorial post appeared frustrated, there seemed to be a sudden shift in his fortunes. The flamboyant and unconventional Archibald Clark Kerr assumed the post of ambassador to the United States from Lord Halifax, and seemed to be a man who would understand the duke's position, given his own eccentricities. Rather than the usual standard-issue Etonian, Clark Kerr was a left-leaning iconoclast. He took delight in boasting that he was tougher than even Ernest Hemingway, and his constant companion was a young Russian named Eugene Yost, who served as his personal masseur and valet; he quipped that Yost was 'a Russian slave given to me by Stalin'. Perhaps surprisingly, given this association, he had once been a suitor of Queen Elizabeth's, and had an equally unlikely wife, a Chilean aristocrat named Doña María Teresa Díaz y Salas. All in all, Clark Kerr - newly created Baron Inverchapel - was the friend the duke needed at this particular juncture.

Emboldened, Edward wrote to Lascelles optimistically on 28 January to say that 'it would be my judgement that Archie would personally place no obstacles in the way', and that although the two had not met in several years, 'I have known him on and off all my life . . . of course, people change, but I would be surprised if he and I could not make a success of the experiment'.[9] He also informed his brother on 2 February that 'in my opinion unless Archie had changed since 1932, he and I could work together very well in America along the lines of my two Aide Memoirs'.[10]

The knowledge that he and Wallis would be giving up their Parisian residence on the Boulevard Suchet at the end of April had galvanised his wish for something to be done, and British attempts to frustrate his hopes of a quasi-ambassadorial post of this nature had not been helped by Bevin's suggestion that the decision lay, to an extent, in the gift of the new ambassador. There seemed, at last, a chance that the duke's schemes might come to fruition.

Lascelles was unconvinced. He wrote to Sir Pierson Dixon, Bevin's private secretary, on 5 February, to say that '[the duke] is delighted to hear of Clark Kerr's appointment . . . he is sure that

C.K. will take a sympathetic view of his proposals for his own future, if he returns to U.S.A. The Duke intends to come to London to see C.K. . . . I don't know to what extent C.K. is in the picture about all this; but it seems to me that it would be a kindness to him to put him there, before his interview with the Duke.'[11]

It swiftly became clear that Clark Kerr, for all his eccentricities, could be an important figure in this regard whichever side he took, and so Bevin acted swiftly. He sent him a telegram on 10 February stating 'the Duke of Windsor has been pressing the Prime Minister and myself to arrange that he should be given some employment in the U.S.A, "comprised within the ambit of His Majesty's Embassy without anything official being designated"', and that 'His Royal Highness has been given no encouragement to think that such an appointment would be possible . . . it obviously raises a most difficult and delicate question of responsibilities between His Royal Highness and His Majesty's Representative at Washington'.[12]

The explicit purpose of Bevin's telegram was to appraise Clark Kerr of the likely approach by the duke; the implicit one to make sure he was on side. And despite his past friendship with Edward, the British ambassador knew what was required of him. He accordingly replied on 12 February, 'Many thanks for letting me know. I fully share your view.'[13] Yet it was difficult simply to put the former monarch back into his box, not least because he was able to telephone the king and argue his case once again. The following week, Lascelles and Pierson Dixon discussed the duke's ongoing conversations with his brother. Their concern was that Edward's charisma - and persistence - might lead to the king offering him a position, in an unguarded moment, that could not then be delivered.

As Pierson Dixon's memorandum to Bevin of 19 February, helpfully marked 'top secret', suggested, 'The King had asked Sir A. Lascelles two questions to which he was not able to give an answer . . . [firstly] how much does Lord Halifax know about the position, [and secondly], how is the Duke to go to America without a job, seeing that he himself had told the American press, on leaving the U.S.A., that he was going to England to discuss the possibilities of getting a job?' Pierson Dixon knew that Lascelles had his own plans in this regard – 'it would be easy to arrange that HM Ambassador at Washington should, if necessary, let it be known to the American press at the time of the Duke's return to the U.S. that, in view of His Royal Highness's position, it was not possible to give him any employment under the Crown' – and that, while Lascelles was keen that the duke and duchess return to America, given the delicacy of matters in France, it could not be with any official imprimatur. Bevin despairingly scrawled on the memo that 'I cannot find him a job . . . it is impossible.'[14]

Nonetheless, the Foreign Secretary was fair-minded, or at least thorough, and so he contacted Halifax – himself a former Foreign Secretary – to solicit his opinion as to the best way of proceeding. Bevin wrote, with careful tact, to the outgoing ambassador to say, 'You may be already aware that the Duke of Windsor has been pressing that he should be given some employment in the United States of America.' He did not call it a sinecure, but he did not need to. Instead, he emphasised that he and Attlee were opposed to the idea, writing, 'it obviously raises the most difficult and delicate questions of responsibilities between His Royal Highness and His Majesty's Representative at Washington', and that he and 'Clam' felt 'it is indeed impossible that His Royal Highness, as former King of England, should exercise any office under the Crown in foreign countries where His Majesty is already represented by the Ambassador'.[15]

Halifax replied contemptuously on 5 March. His dealings with the duke had been coloured by his partial responsibility for him when Edward had been governor general in the Bahamas, and he had become angered at his colleague's arrogance, lack of consideration to his fellow man and inability to do the job to its required standards. It was therefore with righteous irritation that the ambassador wrote, 'the Duke has more than once spoken in the same nebulous terms to me, leaving the general impression on my mind that what he contemplated was some kind of roving public relations work by way of visits, speeches, interviews and appeals'.

Halifax was unconvinced. 'With every desire to assist in [the] solution of the baffling personal and political problems that the Duke's future presents, I cannot but think that anything of this sort would lead to inevitable trouble. It would almost certainly cause embarrassment to the Ambassador and to the Consul, each of whom would be likely in different degrees to find it difficult to keep the Duke on [the] approved line or correct him if he got off it . . . and if he was to do anything in that line, it would presumably be necessary for him (which would no doubt mean the Duchess too) to see important policy telegrams so that he could see what the form was.' Given the duke's commonly known and lamented political sympathies, which had included a level of support for Nazism that was considered inexcusable even before the outbreak of war, it was unsurprising that Halifax could write, 'I should myself feel little confidence in his discretion in all this field.'

There was also a wider issue. Relations between Britain and America were amicable, but Truman was not Roosevelt, and the end of the Lend-Lease agreement had created lingering diplomatic tension between the countries. Halifax therefore anticipated the potential embarrassment that the duke's licensed presence in the United States could cause when he wrote, 'there remains the estimate of the effect that [the duke and duchess] would produce on the American picture. This would no doubt be good and bad. All his personal qualities would win friends; but extent of their press reports of society engagements in Newport, New York and Long Island would, as they have done before, tell heavily the other way.'

Halifax's verdict was straightforward. 'I do not think that any Ambassador would be at all happy to have the Duke serving under him in any recognised capacity officially or non officially; and that most Ambassadors would hope that his sojourns in United States would be neither too frequent nor too protracted.' He ascribed this judgement to 'instinct and experience amassed here of what makes for smooth working and what does not in United States', before concluding, 'I am profoundly conscious that it makes no contribution to the solution of the general question . . . but I am afraid the conclusion in my mind is very clear.'[16]

It was with relief that Pierson Dixon wrote to Bevin to say, 'Both Lord Halifax and Sir A. Clark Kerr share your view that the Duke's proposal is unworkable. On the strength of these opinions by the present and future Ambassadors to the U.S., you may wish to press the King (with the PM's concurrence) to tell the Duke definitively that no prospect of employment in the U.S. can be held out.' Pierson Dixon was pushing at an open door; he subsequently wrote at the bottom of the telegram that 'the King is proposing to do this'.[17]

The king, in truth, was caught between a natural desire to help his brother - and, in so doing, end the chaos that the duke's presence in his life seemed to provoke - and the professional advice that he had received. While he was able to have what Edward described as a 'perfectly amicable telephone conversation' with him on 23 February, during which he suggested that he would be able to offer more concrete news in due course, he realised that he would be hopelessly compromised if he attempted to do anything; he knew that the kind of roving freelance ambassadorial role the duke craved would set an impossible precedent. After all, his younger brother, the Duke of Gloucester, then serving as governor general of Australia, might have desired a similar sinecure, and he would have been unable to deny him.

Therefore, he wrote back to Edward on 20 March to say, 'I have discussed the matter again with both Attlee & Bevin on more than one occasion (hence the delay) & they are both adamant in thinking that at this moment, it would not be a good thing for a near relative of mine to be attached to the British Embassy in Washington in an official position. I have used all my persuasive powers with both of them to make them see our point of view.' Acknowledging that 'I know this will be a blow to you & I am so sorry that I have not been able to arrange it for you', he stated, 'much as I could have wished for you to have had this post, I have the feeling that, with the present state of the world as it is, you could do more with your contacts in America in a private rather than in an official capacity', before concluding, 'I am disappointed that our plan has not come to fruition.'[18]

Before Edward received this reply, he wrote with irritation to the king on 21 March, as he and Wallis prepared to leave Paris, bound for La Croë in the South of France. Chiding him for not giving him any news, the duke wrote, 'Your silence is discouraging and hardly in the spirit of our two talks in London . . . it is difficult for me to believe that the appointment in America really does hinge on the feelings of Halifax's successor, for your command in this personal instance would be obeyed'. Perhaps egged on by Wallis, he seemed to have forgotten his own experiences in this regard. Constitutionally, the king could not take such decisions unilaterally, but instead they had to be approved by his government and ministers.

Although Edward paid lip service to this ('no-one realises better than I do the strain that present world political conditions impose on Heads of State and their Ministers'), it all came down to his own desires. 'I have been waiting for more than five months for a decision on the question of my employment . . . I will continue to bear myself in patience until I hear that Archie Clark Kerr has returned to London from Indonesia. If you then still remain silent on the subject, I can only conclude that you and your advisers have turned down the offer of my services, which places me in a position from which I must retreat without loss of dignity to myself or my qualifications.'[19] Although the letter used George's familiar name of 'Bertie' and was signed 'David', it was just as aggressive as the letters the duke had sent the king in the grim years following his abdication, and just as fruitless. The duke and duchess accordingly left Paris on 1 April: jobless, disappointed and bitter.* They would know this state of affairs well over the coming years.

---

* When the duke eventually received the king's letter, it was of little surprise. He replied on 10 April that 'I have sensed for some time that there was little chance of our plan maturing', and concluded, with the air of a threat, 'As it is now evident that the British Government has no need of my services and as I have no intention of remaining idle, I must look for a job in whatever sphere and country I can find one suitable to my qualifications.'

*

When the royal family were not concerned with the perennially troublesome duke, there were lighter things to consider. Princess Elizabeth attended a lavish dinner party hosted by Channon on 2 February, which the diarist modestly described as 'a shimmering sea of splendour'; he compared his royal guest to 'a gay partridge', whom his friend Peter Coats 'rather got off with'.* The evening concluded at 3.30 with a rendition of 'God Save the King', and Channon walked home reflecting happily on the evening's success; he concluded that 'never has there been so much excitement about a ball', perhaps because he and Coats added Benzedrine to the cocktails. However, 'nobody noticed',[20] and, presumably Elizabeth did not find herself inadvertently pepped up and ready to party after taking a drink with particular vim in it.

Such escapism was rare. As Queen Elizabeth wrote to Eleanor Roosevelt, in anticipation of her visit to Britain, 'So much has happened to this poor battered world since those days when you visited us at Buckingham Palace, & now so many hopes are centred on this great "getting together" which starts next week.'[21] The 'getting together' to which she referred was the United Nations, which had been created the previous October in San Francisco, with the stated aim of bringing about international cooperation, peace and harmony.

It was a noble and high-minded endeavour, and one that would help change the world. The king had delivered a message of support at its foundation, saying, 'I commend this cause to all my peoples. It is their cause and the cause of men and women of goodwill everywhere. If all play their part, the United Nations can be made the guardian of peace, the instrument of progress and a means by which the foundations of a new era in the history of mankind can be established.'[22] Yet its existence did not obscure the fact that things at home were in a desperate state.

---

* Coats was clearly drawn to members of the royal family, and they to him; in the same entry, Channon mused that 'he danced six times with the Duchess of Kent . . . is she in love with him? I have long half-suspected it.'

At the beginning of 1946, as his elder daughter was offered spiked cocktails at parties and flirted with bisexual young men, the king attempted to exert influence over his recalcitrant government. He did this by combining a mastery of detail with a desire to catch out insufficiently briefed ministers. Morrison wrote in his autobiography that 'I was impressed with his up-to-date knowledge; he must have been an assiduous reader of official papers. On occasion he enjoyed trying to trip up his ministers by asking about some detail of which he had good knowledge, but of which they might be ignorant, despite the fact that it affected their office.' Morrison was not to be beaten – 'I got into the habit of checking up details of such people and matters as I surmised might be the subjects of this friendly contest of knowledge'[23] – but the king remained cautious and often unconvinced by the reforming Labour Party. He had told Attlee firmly, on 20 November 1945, that 'he must give the people here some confidence that the Government was not going to stifle all private enterprise . . . everyone wanted to help in rehabilitating the country, but they were not allowed to'.[24]

The relationship between monarch and premier, which had begun inauspiciously, was now closer, but still did not compare to that between the king and Churchill, who was still an informal but trusted counsellor. Lascelles wrote in his diary on 26 February that 'the King's complaint that he can never get anything out of [Attlee] is well-founded. He is agreeable and friendly, but closes each subject with a snap of his jaws, and if you don't try and launch a new one yourself, the rest is silence.'[25] Even by the summer, the king was still uncertain about his premier, writing in his diary on 24 August that 'Attlee still seems to be in a maze.'[26]

It was as a response to this torpor that the king responded enthusiastically to a suggestion by Jan Smuts, prime minister of South Africa, that he should visit his country on a formal royal tour. Although Smuts's initial proposal of a visit in the autumn of 1946 was thought by Lascelles to be impractical, a trip in the spring of 1947 was considered more appealing, not least because it would allow the princesses to undertake their first overseas trip:

an effective means of both demonstrating soft power and also introducing the girls to a far wider audience than they had ever reached before. While the fifteen-year-old Princess Margaret was wilful and mischievous - 'Margaret was a great one for practical jokes',[27] Crawfie sighed, before adding that 'she was now at a girl's most awkward age, neither quite a child nor quite grown up'[28] - Elizabeth was growing into her role as future monarch, and an opportunity such as this would be invaluable for her.

The trip was planned for February the following year. Amid the greyness and devastation of Britain, it would be something to look forward to; it was formally announced on 15 March, and Lascelles was pleased to announce that 'it has had a good press'.[29] Yet the news was overshadowed by a speech that Churchill had made just over a week before. In December 1936, shortly before the abdication of Edward VIII, the then backbench MP had warned of the rise of Hitler and fascism: 'Danger gathers upon our path. We cannot afford - we have no right - to look back. We must look forward.'[30] At a time when appeasement was widely believed to be the best - indeed, the only - option, he was a lone voice. Less than a decade later, it once again became incumbent on him to speak an uncomfortable truth, and to do so with his habitual economy and skill of phrase-making.

In March 1946, the seventy-one-year-old Churchill was weary. He had written to the Duke of Windsor the previous December, apologising for not being able to assist more effectively with the duke's quest for an ambassadorship, and stated, 'The difficulties of leading the opposition are very great, and I increasingly wonder whether the game is worth the candle.' He claimed that he only continued in his present role 'through a sense of duty', and a desire not to '[leave] friends when they are in the lurch'.[31] He might have added that he also wished to continue to serve in the national interest, and to make occasional appropriate interventions on the world stage. On a visit to Westminster College in the small town of Fulton, Missouri, on 6 March, he had his chance.

Although he had dealt with Stalin and Russia in his capacity as

wartime prime minister, he had never warmed to Britain's temporary ally, whom he had called 'a riddle wrapped in a mystery inside
an enigma'. Now, matters had changed irrevocably, and with Hitler
and fascism defeated, the world faced a new adversary. With none
other than the president as a warm-up man – when he had invited
him, Truman had written, 'This is a wonderful school in my home
state. If you come, I will introduce you. Hope you can do it' – the
former premier delivered what he would later call 'the Sinews
of Peace' speech. It became more famous throughout the rest of
the world for his description of how 'from Stettin in the Baltic, to
Trieste in the Adriatic, an iron curtain has descended across the
continent'.

Churchill acknowledged his 'strong admiration and regard for
the valiant Russian people and for my wartime colleague, Marshal
Stalin', and stated explicitly that 'I do not believe Soviet Russia desires war.' Nonetheless, he saw the country's territorial ambitions
as terrifying. Speaking of the way in which Russia had dominated
eastern Germany, he remarked, 'this is certainly not the liberated
Europe we fought to build up . . . nor is it one which contains the
essentials of permanent peace'.

He implicitly compared the present situation to the build-up of
the Second World War, and stated, '[War] might have been prevented in my belief without the firing of a single shot, and Germany might be powerful, prosperous and honoured today; but no
one would listen and one by one we were all sucked into the awful
whirlpool.' His warning was simple. 'We surely must not let that
happen again.'

The speech was criticised in many quarters in America, with
the *Chicago Sun* newspaper saying that Churchill's true object was
'world domination, through arms, by the United States and the British Empire', and calling it 'an address of threat and menace, which
would pose the British and American peoples against Russia to win
"peace" for a "century" through an alliance of the fortunate of the
earth'. The paper decried the speech's 'poisonous doctrines',[32] leading Churchill to respond, robustly, 'as the views expressed here are

the stock Communist output, I feel it might be an embarrassment to you if your publications were in any way connected to me'.[33]

Yet the king found the speech impressive and apt, and during an audience with Churchill at Windsor upon his return told him frankly that he believed it had done much good in the world and that 'Stalin's tirade against W personally* showed he had a guilty conscience.' In his diary that evening, he wrote approvingly that 'the whole world has been waiting for a statesmanlike statement'.[34] The duke concurred, informing Churchill on 5 May that 'I welcomed your bold speech at Fulton, the frankness of which impressed me profoundly. No one but you has the experience to tell the world the true implications of Soviet foreign policy and being out of office, you were free to do so.'[35]

He concluded, 'I can see no hope of avoiding a third global war in our time unless our two countries can think and act in closer harmony than they used to.'[36] For now, an uneasy state of detente existed, between nations and families alike.

---

* On 13 March, Stalin had made what the king called 'a rude onslaught' on Churchill, and had called him a warmonger.

Chapter Five

'Nothing Ventured, Nothing Gained'

'Whither the storm carries me, I go a willing guest.'[1] So Prince Philip wrote in a visitors' book in one of the innumerable houses he stayed at for a few nights in early 1946. Yet asked many years later by his biographer, Basil Boothroyd, whether his movements at this time connoted a definite statement of purpose towards Elizabeth, he was both defensive and bluff. 'During the war, if I was here, I'd call in [to Windsor Castle] and have a meal. I once or twice spent Christmas at Windsor, because I'd nowhere particular to go. I thought not all that much about it, I think.' When it came to his future wife, he was similarly diffident. 'We used to correspond occasionally . . . I suppose if I'd just been a casual acquaintance, it would all have been frightfully significant. But if you're related – I mean I knew half the people here, they were all relations – it isn't so extraordinary to be on kind of family relationship terms. You don't necessarily have to think about marriage.'[2]

The twenty-four-year-old Philip may have been widely ex-pected to propose to Princess Elizabeth during 1946, but he was not someone who went about the country shouting his emotions from the hilltops. As his equerry, Mike Parker, told the royal bi-ographer Gyles Brandreth, '[Philip] was the same, then as now, good at keeping his feelings to himself. He didn't tell me anything and I didn't ask. I might have had my suspicions, but until around 1946, when an engagement was in the air, I didn't know a thing.'[3] Philip himself put it in gruff terms to Brandreth. 'We were cousins; we became friends; we got to know each other better; we became closer; in due course, we became engaged. That's about it, really.'[4]

While Philip and Elizabeth continued to see one another socially throughout the early months of 1946, there was no overwhelming expectation on either of their parts that the friendship could be transformed into anything more permanent. Philip was not yet a British citizen, and his family's German associations were still the subject of rumour and disquiet. In April that year, he travelled across Europe to Salem, where he had briefly been educated, to attend his widowed sister Sophie's second wedding. While such a trip was entirely innocuous for a private citizen, there might have been considerably greater interest in it if his relationship with Princess Elizabeth had been anything other than a casual acquaintanceship.

It did not help that there were many at court who were less than kindly disposed towards Philip, and their opinions could only influence the king and queen. Although Queen Elizabeth felt affection for the dashing blond sailor who had become a regular house guest, her younger brother, David Bowes-Lyon* - memorably denigrated by the aristocrat Gina Kennard to Brandreth as 'a vicious little fellow'[5] - loathed him, and did his best to poison his sister against him, aided by various courtiers who were only too happy to concur with Lascelles' assessment that Philip was 'rough, uneducated and would probably not be faithful'. And the king, despite his own fondness for Philip, felt uneasy at the prospect of his elder daughter marrying and leaving him behind; as Elizabeth's subsequent lady-in-waiting Lady Airlie later commented, she was his 'constant companion in shooting, riding, walking - in fact in everything'.[6]

Princess Elizabeth had also barely seen anything outside of the

---

* Although a married family man, Bowes-Lyon was said to be promiscuously homosexual, enjoying all-male orgies in which the participants were clad only in football shorts. Perhaps in an attempt to avoid scandal, the king and queen attempted to obtain the governorship of New South Wales for him after the war, but they were unsuccessful; the Australians were therefore spared the spectacle of Bowes-Lyon in his glory.

confines of Windsor Castle and Buckingham Palace, bar carefully orchestrated trips to open factories and buildings. As Queen Mary said to Lady Airlie, although Philip and Elizabeth had now been on familiar terms with one another for at least eighteen months, 'the King and Queen feel that she is too young to be engaged yet. [Her parents] want her to see more of the world before committing herself, and to meet more men. After all, she is only nineteen, and one is very impressionable at that age.'[7] Channon's party may have been a raucous, drink-sodden affair, but it at least exposed her to a different set of people than the stiff and often stuffy world of court. The war had taken away the opportunity for her to mix with people of her own age, and so there was the suspicion - barely articulated by anyone, but present nonetheless - that Philip may have been of interest simply because he was the first even semi-eligible man to have crossed her path.

Nonetheless, his continued presence near her, or next to her, did nothing to dispel rumours of their intimacy. He was photographed standing with her on 29 May at the wedding of her lady-in-waiting Jean Gibbs, and even if one newspaper cattily referred to him as 'a figure still largely unknown to the British public',[8] it now seemed quite natural for him to be welcomed into the royal circle. One letter that he sent to the queen in June, while he was serving as a naval instructor in North Wales on board HMS *Glendower*, archly apologised for 'the monumental cheek' of having invited himself to Buckingham Palace, but justified it by saying, 'However contrite I feel, there is always a small voice that keeps saying "Nothing ventured, nothing gained" - well, I did venture and I gained a wonderful time.'[9]

The precisely calibrated tone - polite, but not sycophantic; grateful, but not oleaginous - endeared him to the queen, and soon enough, Philip was granted the ultimate gesture of approval - or was presented with his trickiest task yet. He was invited to Balmoral in August, where he would be on show in front of the entire family. The potential rewards were considerable, but then so were the risks.

*

In the pre-war days, there was a set expectation of the etiquette required when a young would-be suitor visited his aristocratic inamorata's family home for a weekend. He should be polite and formal, but never dull or silent; well versed in current affairs, but prepared never to contradict his hosts, whatever the outrageousness of their opinions or views; well dressed for a variety of occasions, from shooting to formal dinners, but never ostentatious or peacock-like.

He would be surrounded - some might even say confronted - with a host of fellow guests, who might range from the charming to the choleric, and would be expected to overcome the conversational minefields that their disparate presence could also involve. In other words, if he managed to give a good account of himself in the most unpromising and stressful of situations, then it was likely that he would be given the nod to marry the daughter of the house. If he failed, he could expect a letter curtly informing him of his would-be fiancée's betrothal to another, more accomplished man.

The social rules were strict, even harsh, but they existed for a reason. The British aristocracy had not maintained its grip on society by allowing its denizens to marry whomsoever they pleased. Instead, the process was a precisely regulated affair, in which negotiations as to worth began as soon as the women 'came out' - in other words, were launched onto the matrimonial market - and would only conclude once the season's debutantes were safely fixed up with appropriate husbands. Romantic affection was not wholly absent from the exercise, but it was hardly seen as the predominant means of arranging matches between eligible partners.

Yet after two world wars, the rules had been bent, if not broken, not least because there was now a dearth of eligible young men. Had Prince Philip not been a naval hero, it is doubtful that his suit would have been taken at all seriously, given his dubious heritage and uncomfortably close familial associations with the Germans. But when the notice of his invitation to Balmoral was included on the guest list that was distributed to the papers - his name had been absent from the advance list - it was widely believed that he had been invited to the royal family's Scottish home as an audition, and that should he be successful, the notice of engagement would be published before the year was out. If he failed, however, one can only imagine his receiving a regretful letter, written in an elegant hand, beginning, 'My dearest Philip, I am sorry to say that . . .'

The royals headed up to Balmoral on 8 August, and Philip was invited to join them shortly afterwards, for three weeks of grouse shooting, stalking and chit-chat. The length of the invitation connoted purpose; he was not there simply for the pleasure of his company, but for the wider family to see what they made of him. That he might have had opinions about them as well, and that these views might have coloured his later behaviour, did not seem to have occurred to anyone. Nearly a decade earlier, Edward and Wallis had had their own Balmoral holiday, which had ended in chaos, with signs being daubed on Aberdeen streets saying, 'Down with the American harlot!'* It could only be hoped that there would not be a repeat of such a development.

Crawfie subsequently wrote, with the benefit of hindsight, that 'when it was known that Prince Philip was going to Balmoral that autumn, public excitement and speculation brimmed over. The papers carried whole columns of "inside information" and entirely unfounded stories.' She sighed, 'It must have been trying indeed for these two young people, between whom there had as yet been neither proposal nor acceptance.' Yet she knew the truth. 'The generally accepted idea was that this was for Prince Philip a trial trip. The King and Queen were commonly supposed to have invited Philip up to see whether he would be acceptable as a son-in-law.' Crawfie disagreed with this summation - 'the silliness of all this is apparent when it is realised that they had both known him from his boyhood . . . he was asked up because he was a young man they all liked, who would make an amusing addition to the party . . .

---

* The then king had cancelled an appointment to open the new Aberdeen Infirmary in favour of collecting Wallis from the station.

[and] perhaps also to give Lilibet a good long spell of his company, to see how she liked him in large doses'.[10]

However, when Philip arrived at Balmoral, he would no doubt have been dismayed to see the 'vicious little fellow' David Bowes-Lyon dripping poison into his sister's ear about 'the German', along with such courtiers as Lord Eldon and 'Bobbety' Cranborne, neither of whom bore Philip any particular goodwill. Another sort of man might have been cowed into polite silence, or made an especial effort to charm everyone in sight, constantly. Philip did neither.

It has subsequently been put about that the Balmoral sojourn was a wonderful and romantic occasion, during which Philip proposed marriage to Elizabeth and was accepted, and that everything stemmed from the weeks they spent together in Scotland. Certainly, the thank-you letter that Philip wrote to the queen on 14 September seemed to suggest that he had been exceptionally fortunate, and also hinted strongly that he had become at least unofficially engaged. 'I am sure I do not deserve all the good things which have happened to me,' he panted. 'To have been spared in the war and seen victory, to have been given the chance to rest and re-adjust myself, to have fallen in love completely and unreservedly, makes all one's personal and even the world's troubles seem small and petty.' Praising the family's 'generous hospitality' and the 'warm friendliness' of those he encountered, he stated, 'I only realise now what a difference those few weeks, which seemed to flash past, have made to me . . . [the stay] did much to restore my faith in permanent values and brighten up a rather warped view of life', and hinted at the existence of an engagement by writing, 'Naturally there is one circumstance which has done more for me than anything else in my life.'[11]

He may have seemed joyful in his letter of thanks, but it had not been an easy few weeks. As Crawfie described it, 'Lilibet was well aware that . . . some of the King's advisers did not think [Philip] good enough for her . . . there must have been for Lilibet in those autumn days . . . plenty of doubts, plenty of embarrassments, uncertainties, and heart-aches', even if 'her own mind never wavered for an instant . . . it was solidly made up'. The word used about Philip was 'unpolished' - something he himself might have re-garded as a badge of honour. It was seen as decidedly eccentric that he had no plus fours and shot in flannel trousers using a borrowed gun, and that his 'solitary naval valise' contained remarkably few clothes: the only pair of walking shoes he possessed ended up being so worn that they had to be sent to a local cobbler for repairs. The king himself noted in his diary - the sole veiled allusion to his subsequent son-in-law - that 'We have had several young people to stay. Some had never seen a grouse or a stag.'[12]

It is unclear precisely how long Philip was at Balmoral for - Crawfie believed that it was over a month, but this seems unlikely, unless he had arrived immediately after or with the royal family, and had only left on 13 September - but it was a frustrating and unrelaxing time. Not only did Philip have to contend with the sneering and bitching of Bowes-Lyon and others, which he dealt with robustly and uncompromisingly, but he was barely able to see Princess Elizabeth unchaperoned. They went out shooting, and for picnics, but the extent of their time together consisted of the odd drive, and a swift walk around the gardens after tea.

Crawfie was not present at Balmoral, but the impression she had when Elizabeth returned was that 'both Lilibet and Philip had had rather a bad break', and that 'the summer could not have been much fun for them'. Philip was generally well thought of in the wider royal household, as an unpretentious and likeable figure whose naval service stood him in good stead to be accepted into the family. George VI had himself seen combat aboard ships, in-cluding HMS *Jutland* in World War I, and welcomed the idea of a son-in-law having a similar level of dutiful, and distinguished, service. Yet Crawfie also noted that 'the family is a very demanding one, and however sympathetic' - or otherwise - 'the other guests might be, there was little they could do to help. The general feel-ing was that if nothing was to be announced, the boy ought to go south. It was fair to neither of them to keep him hanging around.' She suggested that the royal household were 'all a little bewildered' as to the outcome of the visit – were they engaged, or weren't they? – and wrote, 'I think what it really amounted to was that neither the King nor the Queen could make up their minds what was best for their very dear daughter, and so postponed [a] decision.'

The king's assistant private secretary, Sir Edward Ford, stated pithily of the situation that 'the queen had produced a cricket eleven of possibles, and it's hard to know whom she would have sent in first, but it certainly wouldn't have been Philip'.[13] Although the queen was nothing but charm and gratitude itself when she wrote to her potential son-in-law, it was whispered by her daughter's ladies-in-waiting that she felt he had not set out to charm her, that he was 'cold . . . lacking in our kind of sense of humour', and that his inability to embrace self-deprecation was labelled as that most dreadful of things, 'rather Germanic'.*[14]

It was by no means a done deal that, informal proposal or not, Philip could expect to be accepted into the family. Nonetheless, Lascelles put out a formal statement in September 1946, on behalf of Buckingham Palace, denying the rumour in the *Star* newspaper that the princess was engaged, although it did not completely repudiate the possibility – or likelihood – of such an announcement being made in the future. The statement also announced that both Princess Elizabeth and Princess Margaret would be accompanying their parents on the South African trip early the following year, although there was no mention of Prince Philip travelling with them.

How Elizabeth felt after the Balmoral holiday is hard to assess. Crawfie took the sentimental approach of describing her as a 'quiet and subdued little Princess', and compared her to Prince Albert, referring to his 'touching sweetness of disposition, a shy gentleness that was both moving and appealing'. She suggested that the princess was unhappy about the prospect of heading on the South African trip, saying, 'she would have liked to have matters fixed

---

* In private conversation, the queen went further, labelling Philip 'the Hun' and bemoaning subsequently that his attitude towards the royal estates was 'like a Junker'.

and to be properly engaged before she went away'. After all, 'four months is a long, long time to a girl in love'.[15]

She continued to be in daily contact with Prince Philip, whether by letter or telephone, and they saw each other with a degree of regularity that belied any suggestion of tension or disagreement. Public rumours of a relationship between the two were, in any case, stoked, firstly by the unprompted denial of the engagement – 'Where there's smoke, there's fire', a thousand bar-room pundits dutifully opined – and secondly by newsreel footage of the wedding of Patricia Mountbatten to Lord Brabourne on 26 October 1946. Elizabeth was a bridesmaid, Philip an usher, and a mischievous – or romantic – editor deliberately included a shot of a tender glance between the two of them in the film. When it was shown in cinemas, it was greeted with cheers and applause.

Yet it was not merely Philip's romantic affairs that caused difficulty. He wished to maintain his commission in the Royal Navy, but his foreign-born status and lack of British citizenship made this impossible. He may have walked with kings, and retained the common touch, but it was still problematic for a Greek-born prince to serve in his adopted country's armed forces. Although he had been initially told that he could remain in the navy, the Admiralty now ruled that he would have to become a naturalised British citizen for such a step to be viable.

Philip therefore found himself in an unusual and frustrating situation. His career, potential marriage and perhaps even continued residence in Britain all depended on his being allowed to obtain citizenship, but he lacked an obvious sponsor. While he could count on a degree of warmth and good feeling from the king and queen, they were unable to exert themselves on his behalf, thereby creating a precedent in the process. Even if he had unofficially proposed to, and been accepted by, their daughter over the summer, their hands were tied by issues of protocol. What he truly needed was a maverick, someone who was willing to go against convention and stand *contra mundum*, if needs be. Cometh the hour, cometh the Mountbatten: step forward Uncle Dickie.

*

'Dickie came to lunch and we discussed everything.'[16] So the king wrote in his diary on 14 October. Lascelles had wearied of how what he saw as a family matter was occupying his time, and so had suggested to Mountbatten that he should deal with the question of his nephew's naturalisation himself: the implication was that he was doing so with royal complicity, even if it was made entirely clear that the monarch's name was to be kept away from any she-nanigans of this nature. 'Nothing would suit me better',[17] Dickie cheerfully replied.

The full force of the Mountbatten charisma was therefore un-leashed, and all around him could not resist, even if one enemy of his, Lord Thorneycroft, grumbled that he was 'an elephant trampling down the jungle rather than a snake in the grass'.[18] His intriguing had been more limited in the first half of 1946 because he had been in South East Asia overseeing the transition from war to peace, but the newly created rear admiral had now returned, and his intention was twofold: to see that his nephew was granted the British citizenship he desired, and, by extension, to make sure that there could be no obstacle to a marriage between Philip and Princess Elizabeth.

Mountbatten had been typically active since his arrival in the country. He had cultivated a friendship with the Labour MP Tom Driberg, who he saw as a useful conduit to get anything through Parliament, and attempted to ensure that Driberg was on good terms with Philip. He introduced the two of them over lunch at the House of Commons on 14 August, and later wrote to the pol-itician to say that Philip 'was tremendously thrilled by his day in the House, and very favourably impressed by you', before suavely reminding Driberg of what he had agreed to. 'It is most kind of you to say that you will help to give the right line in the press when the news about his naturalisation is announced.'[19] He did not allude to whether the flamboyant Driberg had taken a liking to the handsome young naval officer, but he was swift to reassure him of Philip's British credentials, saying, 'he really is more English than any other nationality . . . he had nothing whatever to do with the political set-up in Greece'.[20]

Mountbatten was right to be cautious about Philip's Greek roots. Although the country's monarch, King George II, was restored to the throne shortly after Driberg's meeting with the prince, on 28 September, the country was seen as unstable and diplomatically problematic, which meant that the idea of a prince of that nation obtaining British citizenship – and, by necessity, renouncing his Greek nationality – was one that would scandalise.

Yet Dickie was not wasting his time. On 14 November, he was able to convince both Attlee* and Bevin that not only should Philip be a naturalised British citizen, but that he should take the title 'HRH Prince Philip'. Had the Duke and Duchess of Windsor known of the relative ease with which this had been accomplished, given their own – or, to be exact, his – scheming for Wallis to be granted such a distinction, there would have been great anger. In the event, Philip turned down the honour, preferring to retain his naval rank instead.

Eventually, on 5 December, Mountbatten and Philip's wishes were granted, when the Home Secretary, James Chuter Ede, was able to confirm in the House of Commons that 'Prince Philip of Greece' had begun the appropriate bureaucratic rigmarole for a foreign-born citizen who had served in the country's armed forces to be granted naturalisation. Underneath the dry official language, the implication was clear: there was now little, if anything, standing in the way of a potential engagement between Prince Philip and Princess Elizabeth. So inevitable did the match now seem that the *News Chronicle* wrote on 10 December, 'the moment is approaching when the public should be given some explicit information . . . this is not a trivial issue. The British throne has never been held in such good esteem as it is today. It is of the utmost importance that the strong links of mutual confidence should be preserved.'[21]

---

* It helped that Attlee had been assured by the Admiralty earlier that month that Philip was 'in every way above average . . . in short, he is the type of officer we should not like to lose'.

Mountbatten now, disingenuously, put out a press statement to the effect that 'the Prince's desire to be British dated back several years before the rumours about the engagement' - as with the palace's denial, the use of the word 'engagement' simply served to exacerbate the stories - and that, unbelievably, '[I] had no possible connection with such rumours'. Yet there was no pushback from the papers, who seemed happy to accept Mountbatten's half-truths as documented fact.

It was just as well that matters moved fast. A poll in the *Sunday Pictorial* on 12 January 1947, asking whether Philip and Elizabeth should marry, saw the country supporting such a match, albeit by a slim majority: 55 per cent were in favour, 40 per cent against, and the remainder had no opinion either way. But Philip's standing as a foreigner did not endear him to xenophobic elements of the public, and it was also acknowledged that nothing could occur until after the conclusion of the royal family's South African trip, which was scheduled to depart from Portsmouth on 1 February 1947.

It was felt right that Philip should take a new name. His dynastic surname, Schleswig-Holstein-Sonderburg-Glücksburg, was not an easy mouthful, and so it was decided that he should be called Mountbatten: both a nod to his uncle's unstinting efforts on his behalf, and an attempt to place him within the aristocratic lineage of his adopted country. Philip himself later expressed a mild antipathy towards his nomenclature,* saying, 'I wasn't madly in favour [of it] . . . but in the end I was persuaded, and anyway I couldn't think of a better alternative.'[22]

As for the much-rumoured engagement, it seemed that the king had made a deal with Philip. While he had not wished to stand in the way of what was more a love match than any kind of hardheaded dynastic union, there were two conditions to his assent, in addition to Philip's naturalisation as a British citizen. The first was that no formal engagement could take place until Princess Elizabeth came of age, on 21 April 1947 - during which time she would

---

* As did the king.

be coming to the end of her South African trip – and the second was that the trip, which would last for three months, would allow for reflection and a calm consideration of the couple's future. It might not have been romantic, but it was practical. Such considerations temporarily trumped any idea of 'true love'.

In any case, the prime mover behind the machinations was to depart shortly. In December 1946, Mountbatten was offered the position of viceroy of India by Attlee, which, after much careful consideration, he finally accepted in February 1947, pronouncing it an honour to be the man who would be responsible for handing power and responsibility back to the Indian people. He may have felt some reluctance to leave the country behind just as it seemed his greatest opportunity was about to come to fruition, but he could take solace from the knowledge that he had played the hand that he had been dealt exceptionally well. Surely, he mused to himself, there was now an opportunity for something unprecedented to occur: for house Mountbatten to establish itself upon the throne of Great Britain.

Chapter Six

'The Old Values Have Disappeared'

The despairing telegram from Duff Cooper to Ernest Bevin on 5 July 1946 said it all. 'Some Paris papers carry story July 4th that Duke of Windsor sold cigarettes in the streets of San Remo to get Italian money to buy meat.' The denial the duke put forward was unconvincing. 'Although the Duke of Windsor, knowing the shortage of tobacco in Italy did make a few gifts of cigarettes to people who had been of assistance to him, he did not (repeat not) sell any cigarettes.' Cooper's telegram ended with the written equivalent of a sigh. 'You are obviously best judge of whether publication is desirable.'[1]

A decade earlier, Edward had been king-emperor, and one of the most famous, even idolised, men in the world. His every movement had been reported by the press with fascination - even if the details of his relationship with Wallis had been kept out of the British papers, thanks to a gentleman's agreement between Buckingham Palace and the newspaper magnates - and he was believed to have inaugurated a new, more accessible style of monarchy.

This was proved to be half correct, at least: his abdication was unprecedented, just as his marriage to the now Duchess of Windsor had been. But now, jobless, stateless and rootless, the duke was cutting an increasingly pathetic figure, reduced either to selling or giving away cigarettes in the Italian streets. Yet even as his former friends and country seemed content to cut him adrift and forget about his embarrassing presence, a former king with nothing to lose could be a troublesome liability.

One of the few people who remained steadfast was his former counsellor and lawyer, Walter Monckton, though his efforts to help the duke were hidebound by his presence in Hyderabad, where he was serving as the adviser to the nizam in the run-up to Indian independence. Writing to Monckton from La Croë on 31 May, the duke made token efforts to recognise his friend's labours ('I am sure your advice has been the best he could have for his special problem'), but he soon moved on to his favourite subject: himself.

He alluded to a letter that he had written to Churchill earlier that month in an attempt to find work, saying how the king had failed to intercede with Attlee and Bevin on his behalf, and that while 'I am not in the least surprised over the negative outcome of this consideration of this project concerning my future . . . during my two visits to London I could sense definite reluctance to the scheme in Downing Street', he now had to occupy himself in another way. He had said to the former premier that 'as it is now evident that the British Government has no need of my services, and as I have no intention of remaining idle, I must look for a job in whatever sphere and country I can find one suitable to my qualifications . . . I have sufficient confidence in myself to feel that I can still make some contribution towards the solution of some of the complex problems which beset the world today.'

Churchill's reply, as quoted by the duke, was a masterclass in buck-passing - 'I am very sorry about this foolish obstruction by Bevin and Attlee, and I wish I had it in my power to overcome it, but we are all under the harrow'*[2] - and it then turned to Edward to come to his real point. 'It has been suggested to me from not uninteresting quarters that the time has come to write my side of the abdication story.' He justified this by a desire to explode the 'considerable doubt and conjecture' that existed in people's minds about the saga, and sought to elicit Monckton's help should the

---

* The duke sarcastically commented that 'It has amused us a good deal for, after all, he wasn't that cooperative himself during his five-years residence at No. 10 Downing Street.' He neglected to acknowledge that Churchill might have had other things on his mind over the period between 1940 and 1945.

book come to be written: 'It is a subject of such historical and political interest that the lone hand I had to play throughout the negotiations with the politicians, both of church and state, could not be accurately chronicled without the advice and assistance of my liaison officer.' Describing this as an 'interesting idea',[3] he asked Monckton to come and stay in France to discuss it further.

Monckton's presence would have been a useful entertainment. The duke and duchess were bored and frustrated, even if they lived in some splendour. La Croë had a staff of twenty-eight, and Wallis informed her aunt on 24 April that 'I imagine outside of embassies it is the only house run in this fashion in France and probably England today.' Yet even as they hosted guests of the calibre of Noël Coward* and Churchill, it was an uneasy and unsettled time, not least because the post-war situation was a grim one. Churchill may have consoled them by saying, 'I am sure better days will dawn',[4] but they showed no sign of appearing. Wallis summed up pithily the difficulties they faced. 'The cost of food is breaking us . . . wages are ten times pre-war . . . the Duke is very restless for a job . . . Everyone in Europe is searching for the answer to the future and nearly everyone wants to leave France.'[5]

They were both prey for flatterers and false comforters, and one of the most persistent figures in this regard was Kenneth de Courcy: a wealthy businessman, editor of the news digest service *Intelligence Digest* and confidant of the duke. Although he had only been twenty-seven at the time of the abdication crisis, he had felt its effects keenly, writing on 10 December 1936 that 'I am shocked and appalled . . . all our efforts have been in vain . . . They were determined to force him out.' He concluded, 'I expect a disaster will follow. First Germany and then of course Russia. I fear for the British Empire.'[6]

During the war, de Courcy remained a keen correspondent

---

* Who once commented, in relation to the abdication of Edward VIII, that 'a statue should be erected to Mrs Simpson in every town in England for the blessing she had bestowed upon the country'.

of the duke during his governorship of the Bahamas, and shared his antipathy towards anything related to Russia, Bolshevism or communism; he also knew that it could be in his interests to flatter the duke as to his perspicacity around the world situation. His letter of 21 February 1946 praised Edward, saying, 'I never hear from anyone a more statesmanlike or realistic view of the foreign situation as I do from Your Royal Highness . . . It is most deeply impressive.'[7]

De Courcy now proposed an idea that, had it been publicly revealed, would have been seen as treacherous. On 14 March, he made his intentions explicit. Acknowledging that he had always hoped to see the duke and duchess returned to Britain and living there happily once more, he then stated, 'I should be a poor friend and a bad advisor to override the higher interests of the Crown.' He summed up the situation in unambiguous terms. 'I do not think there is very widespread warmth or enthusiasm towards the Crown at present. There is no hostility; there may be a good deal of detached appreciation for the Crown's importance but there is nevertheless coolness and indifference which, if it developed, could be serious.'

His point, however expressed, was not inaccurate. If George VI's standing had never been higher than on VE Day, less than a year earlier, it had undeniably lessened subsequently, as grim, grey normality returned to Britain. The royal family had stood for hope, and the nation had looked to them to provide stability and an exemplar of behaviour in exceptional times, which had mostly been delivered upon. But public gratitude was not an infinite resource, and de Courcy articulated something that had been mentioned more than once privately: a concern that the monarchy was flailing, and that, amid the progressive change that Attlee and Labour had implemented, it was beginning to look anachronistic and irrelevant.

The solution was uncertain, but de Courcy had his own ideas. As he suggested to the duke, 'You are very much loved . . . There is some contact between Your Royal Highness and the minds of the people which . . . is one of those mysterious things which one cannot explain but which is exceedingly powerful.' Hinting that Edward's return to Britain, with this level of public popularity, could lead to the establishment of two separate camps, each with its own loyalties, de Courcy instead suggested that the best idea would be for the duke to maintain a private residence in the country, to be visited 'for very short, sharp and brief periods for business and private purposes only', and that this would bring about a greater sense of normality for his and Wallis's eventual reception in his home country.

De Courcy then combined flattery with realpolitik in a prediction as to what could then ensue. 'Your Royal Highness is young* and extremely able, and . . . possesses talents of the highest kind, and that spirit of service which has been a notable characteristic from the earliest years. There is every reason therefore for wise handling of the problem, for patience, and for watching and waiting so that the best service may be rendered in the most effective way in the right sphere.' This was superficially couched as patriotism - 'Your Royal Highness may later be called upon to perform tasks in the foreign or imperial field which will add immense prestige to the Crown and thus be of the greatest assistance to King George VI and to the whole Royal Family' - but de Courcy's next sentence made matters plain. 'We have to feel our way towards that phase very carefully.'[8]

The duke was delighted with his friend's suggestions, although his response a few days later was appropriately circumspect. 'It certainly is a situation of great delicacy, but, at the same time, one in which it would seem I hold fifty per-cent of the bargaining power in order that the Duchess and I can plan for the future in the most constructive and convenient way . . . For obvious reasons I prefer to say no more in this letter but look forward to another talk with you . . . As you say, it needs very careful thought.'[9]

De Courcy subsequently visited the duke and duchess at La

---

* The duke was nearly fifty-two.

Croë in early May, and then again in June, and the correspondence between him and Edward takes on a more conspiratorial hue
thereafter. On 17 July, de Courcy was sufficiently emboldened to
offer a character sketch of George VI, after 'a long and interesting
talk with an ex-Cabinet minister who is very friendly to Your Royal
Highness'. It was an unflattering portrait, if not inaccurate. 'I am a
simple man, not very clever, awkward in speech, lacking my brother's personality. I never wanted the Throne. I took it reluctantly, it
is a difficult job, I am doing my best without the natural gifts that
make for great success . . . My already difficult position would be
made ghastly if there were the least competition from my brother,
who has a special charm and powerful personality.'

He attempted to dissuade Edward and Wallis from putting out a
press statement suggesting that they would never take up permanent residence in Britain again, on the instructions of the king. De
Courcy described this as something that would do 'immeasurable
harm to yourselves, the Crown and England', and again stressed
his belief that a roving ambassadorial role was the ideal one for
the duke. 'Everyone wants to see you and the Duchess, every door
opens automatically . . . Your letters home could be of the utmost
importance to the King and of value to the Government, and would
live in history as diplomatic documents of the first importance.'
Concluding that this self-created position would make the king
'much, much happier', de Courcy presented himself as the duke's
trusted *consigliere*. 'No one will ever advise with more anxiety to
secure the interests of the Windsors than your Highness's ever-
dutiful [servant].'*[10]

As Wallis suggested to her aunt that her and the duke's interests
lay outside France, whether in the United States or elsewhere,
and that 'I feel the time has come when the Duke should write a
book . . . it is fair that everybody should now know the truth',[11] de
Courcy attempted to recruit her into his schemes as well. A letter

---

* The level of this duty led de Courcy to say, 'I write freely and strongly,
because any friend of royal personages who just says Yes ought to be shot.'

of 26 July, suggesting a meeting the following month, referred opaquely to 'thunderstorms', saying, '[they] do sometimes clear the air, but they very often break up the weather, and sometimes it takes a very long time for it to settle again';[12] he feared that the temptation for the couple to provoke was high, and tactfully counselled against it.

Although the duke and duchess were unable to meet de Courcy in Switzerland in August, as he had proposed, they were sufficiently impressed by his arguments that they might be able to have some kind of life in Britain that they instead arranged a visit for October 1946. They would stay at Ednam Lodge, the home of the duke's friend Eric, Earl of Dudley, which his wife Laura described as their 'suburban villa'. Given that one of her other homes eventually included Blenheim Palace, when she became Duchess of Marlborough in 1972, what would have been grandiose by any other standards was comparatively modest by theirs.

The duchess had not visited Britain since September 1939, and the trip promised to be enjoyable, if low-key. Arranging to meet de Courcy for dinner in Eaton Square on 20 October, the duke wrote – from the Ritz in Paris, naturally – that 'I am certainly anxious for a more private meeting when we could talk confidentially . . . I am very rusty on British politics and have several interesting things to report from France.'[13] The visit was intended to be inconspicuous. There was no press statement made, no potentially score-settling interview arranged with the wider royal family. Instead, it was an attempt to see whether they could once again fit into life in Britain, albeit as private citizens rather than as a former monarch and his notorious wife.

Unfortunately, there were several problems during their stay, which led the duke and duchess to believe that they were *persona non grata* within the country that he had once ruled. They visited their once beloved home of Fort Belvedere outside Windsor, only to find, to their distress, that the long-abandoned house was now in a state of considerable disrepair. There were rumours that official channels were actively frustrating people from being able to visit them. De Courcy wrote angrily to the diplomat Anthony Rumbold on 15 November that two Dutch friends of his had been warned that contact with him was undesirable, 'in view of the fact that I am a friend of the Duke of Windsor, and this is officially disapproved of in London'.*[14] A meeting with the king was amicable but determinedly uneventful: the monarch wrote in his diary, '[Edward] came to tea . . . he looks well . . . Although she is here he never mentioned his wife [and] nothing acrimonious was brought up.'[15]

And worse was to come, in the shape of a crime still unsolved today that would implicate the pair in tales of skulduggery that would linger for many years after it took place.

On 16 October, five days after their arrival in the country,† the duke and duchess headed to Claridge's hotel, leaving Wallis's considerable collection of jewellery virtually unattended in Ednam Lodge. Rather than being placed in the house's strong room, along with the family silver, it was left in a box under a bed. Although the room was being watched by a detective acting on behalf of the duchess, thieves were able to enter the house at around six in the evening, as the detective joined the rest of the household staff for dinner. The burglars were said to have climbed up a long white rope that was attached to a window in the bedroom of Lady Dudley's daughter, gone straight to the duchess's room, ignoring any other items of value there – or elsewhere in the house – gathered the jewel box and left, all undetected by anyone.

---

* Somewhat remarkably, given what he was suggesting Edward should be preparing himself for, de Courcy stated in the same letter that '[the Duke's] constitutional correctness could not be greater, and his loyalty to the Crown could not be more solid than it is'.

† On the same day, their former friend, and German ambassador to Britain, Joachim von Ribbentrop, was executed at Nuremberg for crimes against humanity; the first Nazi to be so disposed of. He remained unrepentant to the end, commenting, 'Even with all I know, if in this cell Hitler should come to me and say "Do this!", I would still do it.' His last words, to the chaplain officiating at his execution, were 'I'll see you again.'

The theft was discovered by chance by Wallis's maid, Joan Martin, who entered the room, saw that the box was absent and triggered the alarm. Within a few hours, Ednam Lodge, which had been intended to be a peaceful and low-key destination for the Windsors' stay, was plunged into chaotic uproar. The local constabulary were called, and immediately began taking statements from the household staff, but the high-profile nature of the victims of the robbery meant that more significant figures from the police force were called. Scotland Yard duly dispatched their assistant commissioner, R. M. Howe, and Chief Inspector John Capstick; they arrived at the same time as the duke and duchess and the Dudleys, who had been staying at Claridge's while their friends had the run of their home.

The robbery was an unlikely development. Either exceptionally strange circumstances had aligned, or nefarious activity was involved. On the one hand, the Duke and Duchess of Windsor were known to carry fabulous amounts of jewellery with them everywhere they travelled, and they would have been an obvious target for opportunistic thieves. On the other, several of the items in their possession, such as a bespoke sapphire brooch in the shape of an exotic bird of paradise, would have been impossible to sell on the open market, given how distinctive they were. This indicated that Ednam Lodge had been robbed by amateurs with no clear idea of what they were doing, instead discovering a haul of jewellery with an estimated value of around £25,000 simply by blind luck. Yet there was also the possibility that the heist was not as coincidental as might have been imagined.

When Edward and Wallis arrived at the house, they behaved with a mixture of panic, anger and something harder to describe. In her memoirs, Lady Dudley later wrote of the duchess that although she was 'in a bad way', she demonstrated 'an unpleasant and to me unexpected side of her character', in that she wanted all the household servants 'put through a kind of a third degree'. The hostess refused, saying that 'all of them except one kitchen maid [were] old and devoted staff of long standing'. Nonetheless,

Wallis saw to it that the maid was treated as if she had committed the crime, despite the complete lack of any evidence against her. While Lady Dudley allowed that the duke was 'both demented with worry and near to tears',[16] the viciousness with which Wallis behaved at what she saw as both an affront to her regal dignity and the loss of her possessions cast her in an unflattering light.

It might have been expected that the thief, or thieves, would simply have fled with their haul, but the first indication that something was awry came the next morning, when eighteen individual earrings were found scattered about the nearby Sunningdale golf course; much to Wallis's continued anger, none of them made for a matching pair. It was equally inexplicable that Fabergé boxes and a string of pearls that had belonged to Queen Alexandra, the duke's grandmother, were discarded as if they were simply worthless trinkets. Rumours spread that an armoured car had been seen nearby, and suspicion fell on virtually any local who had behaved in an eccentric fashion in the past, even though a crime of this nature was unlikely to have been executed by an opportunistic passer-by.

Wallis's distress and fury did not abate. After the party had gone for a walk the next day, with the duchess wearing her only remaining brooch, embroidered with sapphires and rubies and inscribed 'God Bless W. E. Wallis', she asked her husband to put it somewhere especially safe. A few hours later, he was unable to find it, and so was subjected to a tirade from his wife due to his forgetfulness. As Lady Dudley described it, 'We stayed up most of the night; he obviously feared to go to bed empty-handed. I made him endless cups of black coffee while the duke went through his papers.' The search was not in vain, thankfully. 'At about 5 a.m. by some miracle we found it, under a china ornament.' She wrote, with heroic understatement, 'Never have I seen a man so relieved. He was still ashen in the face, but he rushed upstairs.'[17]

The missing jewellery was added up, and a list handed over to the police and the insurance company, Summers, Henderson, which was subsequently printed in the newspapers. It made for an impressive selection, indicating the largesse that the duke had lavished on the duchess before, during and after his time as king. However, the 'et cetera' at the end suggested that some of the items were not to be revealed publicly, which added another layer of mystery to what was rapidly turning into an inexplicable occurrence.

1 x Diamond Bird Clip

One Diamond and Aquamarine brooch

One platinum and diamond bracelet with six large Aquamarines

One Aquamarine Solitaire Ring – 58.2 carats

One gold ring set with One gold sapphire (41.4 ct)

One solitaire Square Cut Emerald Ring (7.81 ct)

One pair of Sapphire and diamond earrings

One pair of diamond ball earrings

One pair of earrings in the shape of a shell, one set with a blue sapphire and the other with a yellow sapphire

One double gold chain necklace with one large blue sapphire and one yellow sapphire

ET CETERA

Once the crime had been made public, it was speculated that the jewellery was worth an unfathomable amount of money, which prompted the duke to say publicly that 'There is absolutely no truth in the published statement that the value of the jewellery was £250,000. Its value was not more than £20,000 and you can say that I said so. I can understand that the quarter of a million figure makes better reading than £20,000 but £20,000 was the value.'[18]

He and his wife were doleful after the robbery. Kathleen Kennedy, daughter of the American ambassador, Jack Kennedy, wrote on 27 October, 'The Duchess* continues to talk of nothing but her robbery and how she has nothing left – so far I haven't seen her with the same jewel. He seems so pathetic but full of charm . . .

---

* The words 'and is really nothing but a bore' were crossed out after 'nothing left' but can still be seen in the manuscript.

Really no one here takes any notice of them and the extraordinary thing is that I actually feel that she is jealous of what I, an American, have got out of England and which has always been denied to her.'[19]

The duke, meanwhile, sighed to his American friend Robert Young that the crime was 'a tough break', both for the 'substantial financial loss' and because 'the sentimental and historical value of some of the objects are [sic] far higher'. He suggested, 'I have not yet given up hope of the recovery of bits and pieces of the haul, but we are both feeling pretty sunk about it right now', and blamed the press for worsening matters, complaining that 'the sensational British newspapers have not spared us in capitalising upon our misfortune'.[20]

It was expected that the police in charge of the investigation would explore every possibility. However, Capstick of the Yard was an unorthodox officer. Deciding immediately that the robbery could not have been an inside job - with or without the complicity of the duke and duchess - he therefore dismissed any idea that the household staff could be responsible. In the initial report that he filed after conducting his interviews, he wrote of Lord and Lady Dudley that 'They, like Bullock the butler, mentioned that there were two safes at Ednam Lodge which could have been used, and they gave the impression that they thought anyone handling valuable jewellery in such a manner deserved to lose it.'

If Capstick shared their lack of sympathy, he did not express it. Instead, he came to the assumption that he was dealing with a gang of master criminals, writing that 'They are seasoned and cunning thieves who have kept very silent about the theft and will undoubtedly be very cautious in disposing of the jewellery.' He sent his findings to the FBI and to the outer reaches of the world. Police forces everywhere from Canada to Uruguay were surprised to find themselves informed about the robbery, and could offer the indefatigable Capstick no practical assistance. Nor was there any obvious suspect nearby. As the increasingly desperate police took to stopping anyone in the street who was imagined to be wearing any of the stolen jewellery – including an incensed Lady Dudley, who was approached by a plain-clothes detective in Mayfair shortly after the robbery and asked to show her diamond clip, which bore a resemblance to the sapphire and diamond Cartier clip that the duchess had worn at her wedding – there was a need to find someone – *anyone* – who could be scapegoated for the crime.

After attempting, and failing, to pin guilt on a local vagrant, Capstick decided that another man, Leslie Holmes, was to blame. At the time of the robbery, the twenty-seven-year-old Holmes, a vain fellow with a self-described resemblance to the actor Clark Gable, had been working on the estate, attempting to fix a statue. In an interview he gave to *The Times* in 2004, he described the almost Javert-like fixation that Capstick developed with him. 'I was going out looting bits and pieces to get money, simple as that. It was small jobs on the ground, anything I could carry. I didn't use ladders or a jemmy. It was train sets, cameras, lamps, household goods – something people did not want.'

Before long, he was arrested, tried for selling stolen goods and given a three-year prison sentence. His proximity to the site of the robbery meant that he became the obvious suspect, and as he later said, 'The police came to see me. They found out I had been looting. They emptied the well and dug up the garden looking for the jewels, but they could not find anything. They could not charge me. They had nothing to go by. They just would not believe me.' Capstick remained certain that he had his man. When Holmes appealed against his sentence, it was increased to five years; as he put it, 'everyone thought I had done the big job'.

Yet the policeman refused to let his quarry go without a full confession. He had him moved from prison in West Yorkshire to Wormwood Scrubs, and regularly visited him, holding copies of Ordnance Survey maps and asking Holmes to place an X on the spot where he had hidden the jewellery, and offering him sums of money in exchange for information. The petty criminal's staunch attempts to maintain his innocence – in this case – were ignored. So certain was Capstick of Holmes's guilt that he informed the FBI in

1951 that 'The identity of the thief is known to police at this office and although - in 1950 - he was released from a sentence of five years for housebreaking offences we have not, as yet, been able to gain sufficient evidence to charge him with stealing the Duke and Duchess of Windsor's jewellery. There is little doubt that he has buried the jewellery and I am convinced he is afraid to dispose of it.'

Capstick's actions now became increasingly bizarre. Fearing that he would be unable to solve the case without a full confession, he attempted to befriend Holmes upon his release. In Holmes's mystified recollection, 'I met him when I got out . . . He gave me a drink. He even gave me a suit . . . There would be a few pleasant-ries and he would get round to the subject. "What about it? Are you going to tell me where it all is?" He became a father figure to me. He called me Mr H. He was a big jovial fellow, always quoting bits of the Bible. He was a very nice chap. I was offered a £4,000 reward to confess and that tempted me. I sometimes thought I should just put a cross on a map.'[21] For years, Capstick sent Holmes Christmas cards, suggesting that the time had come for him to make a clean breast. The malefactor, who now ran a bricklaying business, de-clined to offer him the satisfaction he craved.

It remains unclear as to what really happened. Suspicions of an inside job have persisted, and Leslie Field, the official historian of the royal jewel collection, stated, 'I believe the Duchess of Windsor defrauded the insurers by overstating the numbers and identifica-tions of the jewels which had been disposed of', on the grounds that 'at least thirty' of the items that she claimed had been stolen were sold after her death, by Sotheby's in Geneva in April 1987, and that 'they had from the beginning been in a strongbox in Paris and remained there'.[22] Field's opinion would suggest that either the theft had been planned by the duke and duchess from the be-ginning - which would support Lady Dudley's belief that Wallis's show of outrage and anger was a largely stagey one - or that they capitalised on the crime in order to pocket the insurance money, and exaggerated the losses for their own benefit.

In either case, it overshadowed what remained of their time in England. With the theft remaining unsolved, and the press speculating luridly about Buckingham Palace having sanctioned a break-in in order to retrieve family jewellery that Edward had given to Wallis without consent, the couple prepared to sail to the United States on 6 November, on board the *Queen Elizabeth*. As they left, the duke wrote to his brother, describing his visit as 'an eye-opener'. In addition to decrying the way in which social and economic change over the previous decade had been both rapid and unwelcome, he mentioned his discovery 'the bitter and costly way that Great Britain is no longer the secure and law-abiding country it used to be'.[23] He and Wallis had attempted to see what a homecoming would be like, and had been rejected once again. But in any case, the duke no longer wished to live there. He informed Lord Portal, the former Chief of the Air Staff, that 'the old values have disappeared and been replaced by strange tendencies, and one senses an unfamiliar atmosphere throughout the country'.[24]

What the duke did not mention was that in August that year, he had in fact received permission from his brother not only to return to Britain on a permanent basis, but to reside at Fort Belvedere again. However, the offer came with a sting in the tail. The condition of this repatriation was that it could only take place after his death, and his residence at Fort Belvedere would be within the hallowed confines of a mausoleum.

Chapter Seven

'The Loneliest Man in the World'

'The older I get, the less I like being away from you, and although I am reasonably content, my chief feeling is happiness that one week of the fifteen that I must be away has already gone.'[1] So Lascelles wrote to his wife, Joan, on 7 February 1947 from on board HMS *Vanguard*, as the royal family's tour of South Africa got under way. The king, queen and princesses, as well as courtiers including Lascelles, had embarked at Portsmouth on 1 February, amid much publicity.

The trip was seen as an important one diplomatically, as it would help British ally Jan Smuts secure re-election in the face of the challenge from the right-wing, pro-apartheid Nationalist Party, but it also had two further purposes. The first was to see whether Princess Elizabeth's attachment to Prince Philip would last a four-month separation, and the second was to enable the exhausted king to have a holiday of sorts: he had not left Britain since the end of the war. It was hoped that the two-week voyage would give him a much-needed rest, before the tour began in earnest later in February.

It was not only Lascelles who was uneasy about the trip. Crawfie wrote that Princess Elizabeth dreaded the prospect of being parted from Prince Philip and that she remained 'quiet and subdued'. Although she would not turn twenty-one until 21 April, Crawfie observed that she would have liked to have set off with the security and comfort of a formal engagement in hand. Nonetheless, it was regarded as impossible, even with Prince Philip's soon-to-be-formalised British citizenship, for such a betrothal to become official until at least after the tour.

Crawfie enjoyed supervising the preparations for the trip with her charges – 'the official evening dresses [the princesses] took with them were really beautiful . . . out came the maps of Africa, and we went together over the whole ground they were to cover, and read up on all the places they would visit'[2] – but there was also the question of personnel to accompany the family. As she put it, 'no one quite knew until the last possible moment just who would be chosen to go, and there were many heart-searchings and false hopes'. She was informed that the reason why she herself was not invited was that Princess Margaret – who remained her responsibility – would have no time for lessons. The governess would be able to relax while the royal family were absent, and normal matters would resume upon their return.

Crawfie later wrote that 'I thought Her Majesty did not relish the thought of having to deal alone with what might prove to be a spoiled and disorganized young girl when the party got back . . . I did not entirely relish the prospect myself.' Her greatest fear when it came to a newly emancipated Margaret was that she would not settle down to her previous life with equanimity, especially if her sister's engagement was to become official. She knew that the younger princess was both 'wilful and headstrong', and even as she delicately hinted to the queen that Margaret was unlikely to return to the schoolroom after the trip ('Crawfie, don't suggest such a thing!'[3]), the potential for familial conflict, inflamed by both their enforced proximity and the demands of the tour, was tacitly acknowledged by all involved.

The royal couple were not looking forward to what the king's official biographer, John Wheeler-Bennett, would subsequently describe as 'a great imperial mission'.[4] With the partition of India – which would take place on 15 August that year – now inevitable, South Africa was one of the last remaining territories that remained part of the British Empire, although it had been a self-governing nation state since 1934. And Smuts had been a tireless supporter of Britain, and British interests, during the war. Not only had he been appointed a field marshal of the British army, but he was a member of the Imperial War Cabinet, whose advice had been eagerly sought by both Churchill and the king. If he was now asking a favour as a quid pro quo, then at least the attendant pageantry and profile of the tour would offer its own rewards: the first significant suggestion since the end of the war that Britain remained, in its own estimation at least, a world power, rather than an exhausted and impoverished island still suffering from the after-effects of conflict.

On a personal level, it would also be the last time that the royal family would be together as a quartet. Even if the king and queen continued to have mixed feelings about Philip's suitability as a match for their elder daughter, it seemed all but inevitable that the engagement would be formalised on their return. As Crawfie wrote, 'I have wondered since whether the King and Queen thought that maybe a trip abroad, and the new sights and adventures to be found there, would make Lilibet forget what was, after all, her first love affair . . . Other parents have staked everything on the foreign journey and the long separation, often with some measure of success.'[5]

If this was their intention, it failed. Not only was Philip present at a dinner hosted by Mountbatten* that the royal family attended on 30 January - 'the royal engagement was clearly in the air that night',[6] Mountbatten's butler John Dean subsequently remarked - but when they arrived at Portsmouth on 1 February, a press picture of the royal family showed their respective states of mind. As Crawfie described it, with her customary exaggeration and sentimentality, 'The King and Queen [looked] pleased at the prospect of two weeks' rest at sea . . . Margaret [was] obviously very gay and excited . . . [Lilibet] is standing at the ship's rail looking back sadly

---

* Although Philip was graceful on the evening, writing the queen a letter of thanks for the 'heartening things' she said, which '[would] keep my spirits up' in her and her daughters' absence, he was less sanguine towards Mountbatten. He wrote to him pointedly to say, 'it is apparent that you like the idea of being General Manager of this little show, and I am rather afraid that [Princess Elizabeth] might not take to the idea quite as docilely as I do', before remarking, 'I know what is good for me, but don't forget that she has not had you as uncle loco parentis, counsellor and friend as long as I have.'

towards England.'[7] Yet even before they had departed, and were
taking their formal leave of their staff at Buckingham Palace, Crawfie observed that the king was 'desperately tired' and that Princess
Elizabeth 'was sad and we all thought that she did not want very
much to go'.[8]

Nor were the royal family leaving behind a happy and settled
country. The king saw Attlee on 28 January, and asked him three
times if he was not concerned about the domestic situation in the
country; Attlee did not say, but the monarch wrote in his diary that
day, 'I know I am worried.'[9] As the queen wrote to Queen Mary
shortly before their departure, 'I wish that one could feel happier
about the state of the country, so many homeless is a terrible thing,
and so bad for home life in general.'[10] Prince Philip was conspicuously absent from Portsmouth - a fact reported in the press - and
they embarked on the tour at a time of freezing weather, a national
fuel shortage, enforced daily power cuts and rising unemployment.
Still, it had been long planned, and it might even do some good, on
both international and personal levels alike.

The journey to South Africa was initially uncomfortable and, at
times, tense, negating hopes that it would offer the king his much-
needed rest. He had already suggested to Queen Mary before his
departure that he considered it morally wrong to be away from
his people at the time of national crisis, given that he had 'borne
so many trials with them',[11] but to have pulled out of the trip was
unthinkable. As soon as they left Portsmouth, they encountered a
strong gale - which Lascelles described to his wife as 'a bad dusting'
- which meant that the first days saw the passengers cabin-bound,
save the queen, who made a special effort to keep matters cheerful;
the chief clerk, Ted Grove, who was present on the journey, remarked, 'She was certainly looking better than I felt.'[12]

The passengers amused themselves in various ways in the
'sticky, somnolent atmosphere'. Lascelles described the daily routine as 'deck chairs, deck games after tea, three or four officers
to dinner, a film or dancing afterwards'. There were moments of
greater excitement, usually involving the princesses; they attended

a cocktail party held by the midshipmen - 'like a Turkish bath, but otherwise agreeable'[13] - and on 10 February, they were involved in the 'crossing the line' ceremony, followed by what Lascelles called 'the mummery of "Neptune's Court", with scores of people dressed up, more or less humorously, shavings, duckings in the bath etc. . . . The Princesses went through a token ceremony, and were given elaborate and artistically got-up certificates.' He was able to say that '[they are] enjoying themselves . . . yesterday a treasure hunt was organised for them and the midshipmen, which appeared to be successful'.[14]

During this time, Princess Margaret made the further acquaintance of a young royal equerry, Peter Townsend, who had been in her father's service since 1944. He was married, with two young children, and a decorated RAF officer who had received the Distinguished Service Order and the Distinguished Flying Cross, among other accolades. Matters between him and Margaret would evolve considerably in years to come, but then, Lascelles was able to report, approvingly, that 'Peter T tries hard and is doing well.'[15] Townsend himself reflected, of his life in Britain, that 'it irked me to be restrained, imprisoned, driven in on myself within her shores',[16] and was grateful for the opportunity for escape, even if it could only be temporary.

Princess Elizabeth, meanwhile, managed to forget Philip and instead relaxed into enjoying herself on her first foreign adventure. She wrote happily to Crawfie that 'the officers are charming and we have had great fun with them . . . there are one or two real smashers, and I bet you'd have a WONDERFUL time if you were here'.[17] Yet she was not so frivolous that she could ignore the situation in Britain, which she acknowledged when she wrote to Queen Mary that 'we hear such terrible stories of the weather and fuel situation at home, and I do hope you have not suffered too much. While we were dripping in the tropics, it was hard to imagine the conditions under which you were living, and I for one felt rather guilty that we had got away to the sun while everybody else was freezing!'[18] Matters at home had only worsened; Crawfie dolefully informed

Margaret that 'I had cut my face on an icicle which had formed on my sheet in bed from my own breath.'[19]

The king, meanwhile, had had enough by the time of their arrival in Cape Town on 15 February. He did not feel relaxed or rested, but believed that his absence away from his subjects was irresponsible. Accordingly, he sent Attlee a telegram, shortly before the ship docked, announcing his intention of returning immediately by air and allowing his wife and daughters to carry on the trip without him. The prime minister turned down the offer, on the grounds that the monarch's early return from such a high-profile embassy would not only be diplomatically disastrous, but would also intensify, rather than diminish, the sense of national crisis. The king agreed to continue and serve as an ambassador for his country as best he could. Nonetheless, he was miserable and stressed as he and his family disembarked in what Lascelles called, with typical economy, 'a real Bombay day'. The temperatures in Cape Town had reached 105 degrees Fahrenheit, and despite the warmth of the welcome extended to the royal family, he felt he was in the wrong place at the wrong time.

It did not help that the Nationalist Party was opposed to the visit, both on the grounds of anti-British feeling and because it resented everything the royal family stood for. The British high commissioner, Sir Evelyn Baring, called the pro-Nationalist papers 'unrelenting in [their] hatred of the British connexion',[20] and they, in turn, treated the tour as if it was an affront to their country's dignity. The king addressed the Senate and House of Assembly on 17 February, shortly after arrival, and although Lascelles called this 'most successful, with unexpectedly large and enthusiastic crowds, and vociferous cheering throughout the day', which banished fears that the reception would be a predominantly republican one, the formal dinner that greeted them was an ordeal. Lascelles complained that 'in thirty years of public dinners, I can't recall one that caused me greater misery', although he allowed that 'the King spoke well, and made a deep impression, and to my great surprise, I found when we got home that the Royals had enjoyed it and thought it great fun – especially the young ones'.[21]

Although Lascelles subsequently described Cape Town as a 'roaring success, in outline and in detail', singling out how 'the populace, British, Afrikaans or coloured, could not have behaved better or more enthusiastically',[22] it was not without its problems. The king was mocked by the pro-Nationalist newspaper *Die Burger* for his pronunciation of an Afrikaans sentence at the opening of Parliament on 21 February, and the queen, in an otherwise positive letter to Queen Mary, remarked that the country had 'so many serious racial problems', and that thanks to the hectic schedule of the tour, it threatened to be exhausting; she noted, perspicaciously, 'I do hope it won't be too tiring for Bertie.'[23]

Although the king was able to deliver the set-piece speeches that he was expected to, Lascelles told his wife that he was beset by 'repeated spasms of stage fright, which gave me much trouble'.[24] Even Smuts, the purpose of the trip, was a disappointment: when the royal family dined with him at his home of Groote Schuur on 21 February, Lascelles called him 'a bit tired, and not as amusing as usual'.[25] As Britain teetered on collapse, the king seemed almost bemused by the royal family's presence in South Africa.

After they left Cape Town, they were herded onto a luxurious locomotive, the so-called White Train, which would be their home for thirty-five nights. They were accompanied not just by courtiers and equerries, but by the international press, which included the *Daily Express* journalist James Cameron. Remarking on the monarch's demeanour, he wrote that 'the King kept saying that he should be at home and not lolling about in the summer sun; never was a man so jumpy'. Cameron noticed his 'deadly' boredom, which the monarch attempted to relieve by methods orthodox and unorthodox alike. He offered this vignette of what the now fifty-one-year-old king's life was like, after the train stopped beside a beach near Port Elizabeth: 'Down the path from the Royal Train walked a solitary figure in a blue bathrobe, carrying a towel. The sea was a long way off, but he went. And all alone, on the great empty beach, between the surging banks of the people who might not approach, the King of England stepped into the Indian Ocean and jumped up and down - the loneliest man, at that moment, in the world.'[26]

As the trip continued, the king's mental and physical health declined. The queen's letters frequently referred to his exhaustion and dissatisfaction, most explicitly when she wrote to his mother on 16 April that 'Bertie is rather tired - the pace has been very hot, and the weather at the Victoria Falls boiling. I do hope that the trip home will rest him a little, tho' the journey out was not really peaceful. He has worried so much about affairs at home & this tour has been really exhausting on top of all that.'[27] Even as she professed herself enraptured and impressed by all she saw,* from the traditional tribal dances to the 'profusion & terrific colours' of the local flora and fauna, her husband quickly tired of the 'irrelevant' tour.

His anger and irritation were barely concealed. He hated being under the constant watch of Afrikaner policemen, whom he referred to as 'the Gestapo', and believed that they were attempting to limit his activities. He was also vexed by what he saw as a lack of gratitude towards Smuts, and at one point he lost his temper and said to the queen, of the Nationalists, 'I'd like to shoot them all!' Knowing his moods, his wife replied comfortingly, 'But Bertie, you can't shoot them *all*.'[28]

Nonetheless, Ted Grove's tactful remark that 'we admired the way [the queen] cared and watched over him during the tour when sometimes the continual heat and travel in the confined space of the Royal Train did nothing to improve his occasional bouts of temper'[29] was an understatement. The king resented the way in which his hosts seemed indifferent to the suffering that Britain had faced during the past decade, and frequently made pointed reference to his country's current trials during his public speeches, to

---

* This was, to an extent, an act. The writer Enid Bagnold, who was in South Africa at the time, described the queen's progress on the White Train. 'I waved and she gave one more sickly wave like a dying duck, a sketch of her other waves. She looked as though she would die if she saw just one more woman to wave to.'

some embarrassment. Even Smuts bore the royal temper; at one state banquet in Pretoria, the king was heard angrily telling the prime minister, when asked to deliver a speech, 'I'll speak when I've had my coffee and the waiters have left the room', and then, on being told that people in Britain were waiting to hear him speak, 'Well, let them wait. I have said I will speak when the waiters have left the room.'[30]

As the tour wore on, the king's behaviour grew more erratic and volatile. Although the ever-loyal Lascelles made no allusion to any difficulties in his correspondence to his wife,* the suffocating heat, his exhaustion and the demands being made on a naturally shy and awkward man took their toll. At one point during the trip, he and his family were being driven by Townsend through the Rand area of the country in an open-topped Daimler, engaging in the usual routine of smiling, waving and impersonal interaction. On this occasion, the king snapped, and began to shout incomprehensible instructions at Townsend, to the dismay of his family. Eventually, the equerry, goaded beyond manners, shouted at the monarch, 'For Heaven's sake, shut up, or there's going to be an accident.'[31] Townsend described his own behaviour as being 'with a disrespect of which I was ashamed'.[32]

If this was not enough, worse was soon to come. As the equerry later described it in his memoir, *Time and Chance*, as they arrived in the town of Benoni, he saw 'a blue-uniformed policeman' heading towards the royal vehicle 'with a terrible, determined look in his eyes'. Townsend turned round to see a man, 'black and wiry, sprinting, with terrifying speed and purpose, after the car. In one hand he clutched something, with the other he grabbed hold of the car, so tightly that the knuckles of his black hands showed white.'

Just over a decade earlier, the then Edward VIII had faced an assassination attempt at the hands of the drifter George McMahon, and the following year, George VI had been approached by another madman at the Cenotaph. The fear of being assaulted, or worse, by

* At least not in the published selection to be found in *King's Counsellor*.

a member of the public was an ever-present danger. It was with admiration that Townsend recalled how 'the Queen, with her parasol, landed several deft blows on the assailant before he was knocked senseless by policemen. As they dragged away his limp body, I saw the Queen's parasol, broken in two, disappear over the side of the car.' Even an incident of this nature could not curtail the royal progress, however. Townsend then noted that 'within a second, Her Majesty was waving and smiling, as captivatingly as ever, to the crowds'.[33] The show went on.

Had the man presented a threat, intentionally or otherwise, it would have been an unfortunate but easily resolved distraction, 'one of those things'. Unfortunately, it soon transpired that he had meant no harm at all. Kayser Sitholi, an ex-serviceman, had instead been shouting, 'My king! My king!' He had been holding a ten-shilling note, which he had intended to give Princess Elizabeth as a gift for her imminent birthday.

The king, overcome by remorse and guilt, asked Townsend to seek Sitholi out and make amends on his behalf, adding, 'I hope he was not too badly hurt.' He also acknowledged to his equerry that the strain was getting too much for him, saying, 'I am sorry about today. I was very tired', to which Townsend responded, 'more than ever before, I realised how lovable the man was'. And, he did not need to say, in need of care. A worn-out, drained monarch was prone to make mistakes, and this could be ascribed to human error. But the suspicion - as yet unspoken - that the collapse in his health might soon be terminal came to dominate the thoughts of those around him.

'It was an extremely interesting tour.' So the queen wrote to her sister, May Elphinstone, on 26 April, with great tact, on board HMS *Vanguard* on their return journey. She described South Africa as 'such a complex country, with the white races quarrelling & hating each other, and the black races growing enormously in numbers',*

* The Duke of Windsor, in a letter to the king dated 10 April, remarked, '[your visit] must have been interesting if somewhat tiring and tedious in

but gave May a sanitised version of what their reception had been like. 'They were marvellously kind & welcoming to us - even the old Nationalist Boers, reared to hate England, gave us a very hearty welcome, and I do hope our visit has done good.' Yet she knew that the stated purpose of their trip may have been unsuccessful, even as she suggested, 'it would be a thousand pities if S. Africa became a Republic, because the Crown is really the only link now left, & I do trust this will not happen'; she acknowledged that 'there have been quite strong feelings for one in recent years'.[34]

The fatigue that the trip had caused the family was acknowledged - '[I feel] very, very tired - one feels quite sucked dry sometimes - I am sure that crowds of people take something out of one . . . I can almost feel it going sometimes, and it takes a little time to put it back' - but with typical reserve. 'A little bit of England and Scotland will be heaven',[35] the queen decided. The extreme cold weather had passed, and they were returning to a country that, if hardly restored to prosperity and happiness, had rallied slightly since they had left. The most notable occurrence that had taken place in their absence was the death of King George of Greece on 1 April, which was ignored by the royal family in South Africa - not out of callousness, but because, as Lascelles wryly observed, 'we haven't any becoming mourning with us'.*[36]

The private secretary regarded their visit as having been worthwhile and successful, saying briskly, 'The South Africans are a generous, warm-hearted people and there is no doubt they have thoroughly enjoyed the Royal Family in their midst.' There was an emotional send-off from Cape Town, with the royals being given lavish gifts, the most impressive of which was to Princess Elizabeth: twenty-one diamonds to make a necklace to mark her twenty-first birthday a few days before, which Lascelles estimated

---

parts. I toured South Africa twenty-two years ago, so I know what one is expected to endure at the hands of that curiously mixed population.'

* He also speculated that '[it was said] he died of heart failure but I should not be at all surprised if he was bumped, poor chap'. When the death was announced, many suspected that it was an April Fool's joke.

were worth £200,000. He wrote to his wife, 'I know that [the tour] has been an immense success, and amply achieved its only object (at least from my point of view) – to convince the South African people that the British Monarchy is an investment worth keeping, and that the present Royal Family in particular can mean a good deal to them.'[37]

Lascelles' confidence was misplaced. The next election, on 26 May 1948, saw Smuts ousted from power by D. F. Malan, who promptly implemented the Nationalist policy of apartheid that would eventually turn South Africa into a pariah state until its abolition in 1991. The former prime minister died a disappointed man on 11 September 1950, not long after his eightieth birthday. South Africa's transition into a republic was by then inevitable, and it duly took place on 31 May 1961, following a national referendum.

Judged solely by its eventual results, the royal tour was a disappointment; looked at from the perspective of the king's health, it was little less than a disaster. Crawfie was shocked at how the entire family looked upon their eventual return to Buckingham Palace. 'The King and Queen looked positively worn out. I thought at first the King's hair had gone quite grey in his four months' absence . . . later I saw it was just bleached by the hot sun . . . Margaret looked ill and tired out . . . the worst of them all, and I was secretly very anxious about her.' George VI, never a plump man, lost seventeen pounds in weight on the tour, and began to look drawn and weak, as well as considerably older than his age. This decline in his well-being would only continue, even as he wrote to the Duke of Windsor that the tour had been 'very strenuous but most interesting'.[38]

Yet there had been a broadcast made shortly before its conclusion that not only redeemed it, but would have an existential benefit to the monarchy that was of longer-lasting import than anything that happened in South Africa. Princess Elizabeth had declared, before hundreds of millions, that her whole life, whether long or short, would be devoted to their service. The question of when she would be required to make good her promise as queen lingered, unanswered, even as her father's decline seemed inescapable.

Chapter Eight

'Don't You Recognise an Old Friend?'

When the Duke and Duchess of Windsor arrived in the United States in late 1946, they remained unsure of the warmth of their welcome. Although they had generally been well received during his fleeting visits while he was governor general of the Bahamas and in their post-war sojourn in the country, there was still a lingering enmity towards them both, partly because of their notorious visit to Germany and their meeting with Hitler in 1937, and partly due to the events before and during the abdication crisis.

One correspondent, a G. W. Johnson of New Jersey, had written to the *New York Times* in 1936 to complain that 'the doings of the King, as reported in the American press, have in the course of a few months transformed Great Britain, as envisaged by the average American, from a sober and dignified realm into a dizzy Balkan musical comedy attuned to the rhythm of Jazz', and decried the now duke as 'a hopeless case [and] an irresponsible jazz-mad cocktail shaker', to say nothing of 'a pitiful and bemused lover who is completely enslaved by Mrs Simpson's charms'.[1]

The duke and duchess were, at least, able to live in rather greater comfort in the United States than Mr G. W. Johnson did. They took as their main residence an apartment in Waldorf Towers in New York, which was decorated in suitably regal - if garish - style. Their novelist friend Cecil Roberts* visited them at their new home, and observed that it contained everything from full-length portraits of

---

* And reputed former lover of Edward's late younger brother, the Duke of Kent.

George III and George IV - the latter being the ruler the duke had often explicitly compared himself to - to two liveried footmen, and even napkins embossed with the royal arms. If Edward had wished to portray himself as a king-in-exile, he could not have done so more ostentatiously.* As suited his status, he even called on President Truman, of whom he patronisingly wrote to Queen Mary that 'although no great statesman, the President has a good reputation as a politician for honesty and integrity'.[2]

Yet Edward was unwilling to maintain a low profile, and decided that he would like to return to his former demesne of the Bahamas in early 1947. A despairing telegram from his successor there, Sir William Murphy, to the Secretary of State for the Colonies, Arthur Creech Jones, on 30 December 1946, said that '[his] impending visit is being widely discussed here'. While allowing that 'their visiting Nassau would undoubtedly boost American tourist business', Murphy stated that such an embassy would be 'embarrassing to me personally',[3] and so asked for the Cabinet's opinion as to how desirable the visit was. Bevin replied tactfully. 'Of course there is a distinction between actually settling down in a colony and merely paying it a visit . . . it seems fully clear that if a Governor feels that he is going to be embarrassed by the visit of an ex-Governor we ought to do all we can to prevent this, and this seems to me to be the case here.'

There was, as ever with Edward, a central problem: polite hints simply did not work. Bevin lamented this, saying, 'unfortunately nothing less than a formal message from the PM would be likely to influence the Duke'.[4] As usual, his quixotic actions had to be combated; Bevin asked Attlee to urge Edward not to go to the Bahamas, and to ensure that that would be the end of the matter. Yet much bureaucratic hand-wringing ensued. Murphy observed that any

---

* It seems that in exile the duke also inherited something of his younger brother's flamboyance. Roberts reported how, one evening, 'the duke, in a plum-coloured velvet evening jacket, went to the grand piano and began to sing. He had a large repertoire, a good voice and was excellent in some German, Lancashire, Scottish and Irish songs.'

official objection would lead to an unpleasant amount of publicity, no doubt whipped up by the duke himself, and also that there was no formal rule that former governors of a colony were not allowed to visit, in a quasi-official capacity as honoured guests, once their term had ended.

The situation was defrayed by the suggestion that Bede Clifford, who had been governor of the Bahamas from 1932 to 1934, should visit at roughly the same time, thereby defusing any suggestion that the duke would be setting a precedent; both would be hosted by the antiques dealer and big-game hunter Arthur Vernay. Any implication that the acquisition of the Duke and Duchess of Windsor - even temporarily - would represent another trophy for Vernay went studiously unmentioned.

Therefore, Creech Jones's response to Murphy on 17 January was appropriately diplomatic. 'I think it best that you should offer usual courtesies to HRH as to any other distinguished visitor, and I hope that this will not prove too embarrassing to you.'[5] The duke and duchess visited in February, as proposed, and the visit proved to be thankfully uneventful. Yet with the duke denied the quasi-ambassadorial post that he had wished for - and reminded, during his return to the Bahamas, how irrelevant he now was on the international stage - his thoughts turned to comfort rather than prestige.

Wallis wrote to their solicitor, A. G. Allen, in February to say that 'with the Duke's dislike of cold weather we could spend winters in America from November to April if we had a house . . . if only we could have [Fort Belvedere] for the autumn and spring . . . so we could make our home between England and here . . . Do you see any chance of getting the Fort for this arrangement?' There was a plaintive quality to much of the letter. 'We would not be there long enough to upset the powers that be, and we in our old age could have 2 nice houses where we want them.' She concluded, emotively, 'It is a waste of time being homeless on the face of the earth and most disturbing.'[6]

The duke needed to make money, and quickly, in order to

finance the existence that he and Wallis wished to maintain. Therefore, his attention turned to writing a memoir. During his stay in
America, he met the energetic American publisher Henry Luce.
Luce had founded a series of magazines including *Time*, *Life* and
Sports Illustrated, and was described as 'the most influential private
citizen in the America of his day'. By the mid forties, he was not
only phenomenally wealthy, but he made public interventions into
international policy that a lesser man might have shied away from;
his 1941 editorial in *Life* magazine, 'The American Century', offered
a clear-sighted view of his country's potential foreign policy, not
least a belief that entering World War II was both morally justified
and likely to confirm America's status as the greatest superpower
in the world.

He was proved correct in this, and so, by the beginning of 1947,
he was casting around for other opportunities that would simulta-
neously propagate his reputation and sell magazines. It was inevitable that he would cross paths at some Manhattan cocktail party
or other with the duke, who was disconsolately serving as the
evening's entertainment by offering his fellow guests titbits of his
time as monarch. Luce proposed a deal. Write a series of articles
for *Life* magazine about his childhood and early life, stretching up
to 1914, and he would be exceptionally well paid.

Luce was aware that by limiting the scope of the features to
events that took place long before the duke's short-lived reign and
subsequent abdication, the potential for controversy would be
checked. The duke, meanwhile, viewed the articles as both a means
of making him and Wallis the cash he so desperately craved, and
a stepping-stone to something greater. He had noticed the lucrative deal that Winston Churchill had secured to write what would
become his six-volume history of World War II, and remarked to
the former royal courtier Godfrey Thomas that 'as Mr Churchill
was doing the same thing through his very group, [I] didn't see
why [I] shouldn't, especially as [I am] constantly being asked
by less reputable publishers in the States to write something for
them'.[7] He was rather more reserved when he told Queen Mary the

news, breezily commenting that he had inherited her 'prodigious memory' and justifying the potential betrayal of his family's secrets by saying, 'I am sure that an accurate story of our family life by one of its more prominent members can serve a useful purpose and make a good impression in America and wherever it is read.' He ended by saying, as if his considerable dignity had been implicitly insulted, 'Otherwise I would not have accepted the offer.'[8]

Edward may have airily compared himself to Churchill, but there was a key difference between the two men. The former prime minister was a talented writer with an ear for a killer phrase; the former monarch was an adequate, if verbose, correspondent given to self-pity and unjustified self-regard. Therefore, Luce knew that in order for the articles to be of the literary standard that *Life* expected, the duke would need the services of a ghostwriter. Under normal circumstances, he might have chosen a British author. Instead, given Edward's new-found Americanophilia, Luce suggested one of his editors: Charles J. V. Murphy, a former Chinese correspondent for *Fortune* and an expert on global intelligence matters.

The two had first encountered one another in 1945, when the duke, who had recently completed his stint in the Bahamas, had sounded out Murphy about their working together on some unspecified literary endeavour. Murphy, who was preparing to head off to China, was not especially interested in attaching himself to a man he considered washed up, as well as tainted by his rumoured Nazi associations. However, a combination of pressure from his editors at *Life* magazine, who saw the sales potential of the series of articles, and the duke's continued entreaties eventually persuaded him. He had previously written about Winston Churchill for his magazines, and now turned his attention to another internationally famous Englishman, albeit a less beloved one. It was agreed that Murphy would visit the duke at his home in La Croë in the summer of 1947, and that they would begin work then; the deal was signed in February that year. It would prove to be an epochal collaboration.

The duke and duchess's presence in Britain, at least, was now uncontroversial. After their sojourn in the United States ended in the spring, they returned to England once again, renting a house in Sunningdale, and spent a pleasant, if uneventful, few months there. Wallis later wrote to her Aunt Bessie that 'We saw all the old gang and had week-end guests etc. The Great Family were the same – the Duke made the usual visits – no job from any direction of course and I really feel we have been away from England for so long that it would be difficult to take up the customs and ideas again. So again the question of where to live . . . is really spoiling our days and nights.'[9]

One member of this 'old gang' was Harold Nicolson, who saw them on 29 May at the socialite, and Edward's former mistress, Sybil Colefax's home. He wrote frankly in his diary of his impressions of the duke, who he initially thought of as 'a young man', until Edward called out, '[Don't you] recognise an old friend?' 'He is thin but more healthy looking than when I last saw him. He has lost that fried-egg look around the eyes. He is very affable and chatty. I notice that he has stopped calling his wife "Her Royal Highness" . . . I notice also that people do not bow as they used to and treat him as less of a royalty than they did when he had recently been King. He takes all this quite for granted. I have an impression that he is happier.'[10] Nicolson also talked to the 'improved' duchess, who spoke wistfully about her ambitions for her husband, both in metaphorical terms – 'he likes gardening, but it is no fun gardening in other people's gardens' – and practical ones. 'He was born to be a salesman', she said, '[and] he would be an admirable representative of Rolls Royce. But an ex-King cannot start selling motorcars.'[11]

Permission for the duke and duchess to resume residence at Fort Belvedere was predictably refused. There was no formal rapprochement with the royal family, and the duke was conspicuously not invited to his mother's eightieth birthday celebrations on 27 May; he had to content himself instead with a formal visit to Marlborough House to present his good wishes. If either of them had hoped for more official recognition, it was not forthcoming. Therefore, once their British sojourn came to an end, they returned to their holiday home of La Croë and awaited the arrival of Murphy, to begin work on the *Life* magazine articles.

What neither of them had considered was the possibility that the duke was about to be drawn into a major international scandal that would haunt him for the rest of his life.

The so-called Marburg Files had been discovered in Marburg Castle in Germany in May 1945, shortly after the end of the war. The information contained within them - that the duke had been involved with Nazi agents during his stay in Europe in the summer of 1940, and that his loyalties to his home country were at best ambiguous - was potentially devastating. Attlee and Bevin, newly arrived in office, realised that the files were vastly damaging.* Although the release of the papers was agreed in Cabinet on 9 August 1945, Bevin soon had second thoughts.

He wrote to Attlee on 13 August to ask that the most sensitive details be omitted, namely those relating to the Duke of Windsor's time in Spain and Portugal in June and July 1940. He said of these that 'they describe the efforts of the German government to retain him in Spain, with a view to a compromise peace, and contain second and third hand reports and speculations about the Duke's attitude derived from agents in contact with him'. Suggesting that the documents had no bearing on war crimes or the general history of the war - a dubious statement - Bevin stated that 'they would [nonetheless] possess the highest publicity value on account of the personalities involved and the type of intrigues described'. With commendable understatement, he suggested that 'a disclosure would in my opinion do grave harm to the national interest'.[12]

Lascelles described the revelations as 'at the very least, highly damaging' to the duke and duchess's reputations, and the king was said to be 'much distressed'[13] when he learnt of his brother's

---

* Churchill had commented that 'I earnestly trust it may be possible to destroy all traces of these German intrigues.' Had he been prime minister, he may well have done so, or at least tried to.

activities.* It was agreed that the documents must be suppressed, and it was generally hoped that their contents would never come to light.

Unfortunately, something as incendiary as the suggestion of the former monarch's treachery was hard to keep out of the public gaze. Although General Eisenhower concurred with the British wish to keep a lid on the files, a microfilm copy of them had already been sent from Marburg to the US State Department, and their existence became sufficiently common knowledge for *Newsweek* magazine to run a suggestive story hinting at their contents on 4 November 1946. As a much later memo by the then deputy prime minister Anthony Eden to Churchill tartly stated, 'the position became more difficult as the Anglo-United States project, agreed in June 1946, for the joint publication of a series of volumes of documents selected from the German Foreign Ministry archives developed'.

It did not help that the agreement contained a so-called 'escape clause', by which, in Eden's words, 'either Government could publish separately any documents upon which agreement between them could not be reached'.[14] It became clear that the publication of the Marburg papers was inevitable, and on 30 June 1947, Bevin wrote to Attlee to warn him of such an event, and to discuss what could be done to mitigate the damage. Bevin alluded to a conversation that had taken place between them on 28 February, saying, 'you took the view that it would be dangerous to forewarn the Duke since that would probably lead him to put out precautionary stories by way of defending himself and these in turn might provoke a leakage'. Anticipating that the Americans would wish to push for the full publication of the documents on 3 July, on the grounds that 'they feel that the withdrawal of the file at the instance of one of the Governments in the work of editing constitutes a dangerous precedent', Bevin was uncertain as to whether to acquiesce in their publication or ask the British representative,† John Wheeler Ben-

---

* See *The Windsors at War*, Epilogue, for further details.
† And future authorised biographer of George VI.

nett, to 'adopt stone-walling tactics and seek to postpone the issue'.

Bevin now saw the inevitability of what he called 'the evil day' coming to pass, saying, 'I cannot think of any valid argument with which to confute the [American] arguments.'[15] Nonetheless, he knew that it was obligatory to consult the king or his courtiers and, ultimately, the Duke of Windsor, and warn them that the dam was about to break. It was agreed that he would discuss the matter with Lascelles, who suggested that if the papers were to be selected for publication, the duke, along with Churchill, need only be informed shortly before the actual point when they would enter the public domain: as Bevin wrote, 'I approve this course . . . It assumes that, in the interval, there will be no leakage, but that is a risk that I think we must take.'[16] Attlee scrawled, 'I agree' on the document.

The reason for the acceptance of the document's publication lay in part with something that had occurred earlier that year. On 15 March, the American Secretary of State, George Marshall, together with Bevin, was attending a meeting of foreign ministers in Moscow when he was alerted to the existence of an incendiary document. Accordingly, he sent a top-secret telegram, marked 'For Your Eyes Only', to Under-Secretary of State Dean Acheson that read, 'Bevin informs me that Department or White House has on film a microfilm copy of a paper concerning the Duke of Windsor. Bevin says only other copy was destroyed by Foreign Office, and asks that we destroy ours to avoid possibility of a leak to great embarrassment of Windsor's brother [the King]. Please attend to this for me and reply for my eyes only.'[17]

It remains uncertain as to precisely what this document - which presumably was destroyed at Bevin's request - was. Given the damning nature of the existing material that relates to the Duke of Windsor, the fact that there should be something so damaging that it would have to be destroyed by the Foreign Office can lead to the wildest speculation as to how extensive the duke's Nazi sympathies and contacts were. Whatever happened in March, it was clear by the summer of 1947 that little could be done to prevent the appearance of the remaining files, whatever was contained with them.

Accordingly, the king reluctantly consented in July to the Marburg papers being returned to the archives in Berlin, in the knowledge that their eventual publication would be inevitable. The duke was informed of their existence, but he refused to take the possibility of public humiliation seriously, commenting to Godfrey Thomas that 'the German Ambassador was making up a good story on the lines that he thought would please his chief, Ribbentrop'. That Ribbentrop had once been a friend to both Edward, when he was king, and Wallis was unmentioned; Thomas loyally suggested that this 'had already occurred to us as a possibility'.[18] The story that the art historian Anthony Blunt - later exposed as a Russian agent - and the Windsor librarian and archivist Owen Morshead had been sent on a top-secret mission to Germany to retrieve the documents relating to the duke, and that the contents of these documents enabled Blunt to use his knowledge as a bargaining chip to prevent his imprisonment when his own nefarious activities were exposed, is an amusing piece of Boys' Own intrigue, but, alas, entirely false.

If Edward was concerned about the documents being made public, he was at least distracted in July by the arrival of Murphy at La Croë. It soon became clear to the ghostwriter that the duke intended these initially uncontroversial pieces of journalism to act as a Trojan horse of sorts, and that his truer intention was to begin work on a memoir that would articulate his own story. As Murphy later wrote of their collaboration, 'Edward VIII was becoming as dim and insubstantial as Edward II . . . those handsome features, recently so clear and sharp in the public memory, had begun to blur. To arrest that process, to restore the lustre of his reputation, to assure that his side of the story was presented fairly, and to regain some measure of his self-respect, he decided to write an apologia, although it would be disguised as his autobiography.'[19]

Murphy was struck by the sense of how desolate the lives of the duke and duchess were. They were given over to self-aggrandising theatricality, as if in compensation. He recorded that a couple of his acquaintance remarked how 'a tiny little white table for us four was set on the huge lawn. There were rows of footmen . . . the night was furiously hot, but the Duke was in full Scottish regalia. I thought he was staging a production of some sort.' Murphy was similarly dismissive about the relationship between the duke and his wife. When remarking of their presence at a Monte Carlo gala, he wrote, 'she had on every jewel. He wore a kilt. It was like watching a couple in pantomime - the studied gestures, the automatic smiles.'[20]

The collaboration soon became tense. As Murphy later wrote, 'The Duchess managed to keep the Duke amused at La Croë, but it was at [my] expense.' He became 'increasingly disheartened to see how much time the Duke devoted to idleness and frivolity, and how little he could find for his autobiography'. The duchess wished to become a grande dame of Parisian society, and so would uproot the household to the French capital almost on a whim; Murphy had little option than to go along with the couple. It reduced him to frustration and fury by turns. Had he known that he would continue to work with the duke for several more years, he would have thrown up his hands in despair and left him to it.

Still, they managed to find enough time together to complete the four contracted *Life* articles, even if the duke complained to Thomas that he had never worked as hard or with such concentration. Ominously for his family, he also commented that he had enjoyed the experience and was prepared to write a fuller autobiography. When the *Life* pieces began to run, from 8 December 1947, there was no cause for criticism, given their innocuous nature, but Queen Mary, who considered it deplorable that any member of the royal family should commit their thoughts to public view, wrote to her son to criticise his decision.

His response was both suave and combative. 'I was surprised you thought it a pity I wrote of so many private facts . . . I would submit that the personal memoir of Papa undertaken by John Gore at your and Bertie's request contains far more intimate extracts from Papa's diaries and glimpses into his character and habits than I would have dared to use or thought suitable to include in the story of my early life.'[21] This was something of a shift in his attitude towards his mother, and his wider family. In October 1947, he had been on the defensive, writing in the usual sentimental fashion about his wife. 'I am always hoping that one day you will tell me to bring Wallis to see you as it makes me very sad to think that you and she have never really met. After all ten years is a long time since all the commotion of my abdication and as we are not growing any younger it would indeed be tragic if you, my mother, had never known the girl I married and who has made me so blissfully happy.'[22]

Now, buoyed by the *Sunday Express* editor John Gordon's comments to Allen that the articles, which he had published in Britain in his newspaper, had done the duke's reputation 'immensely more good than anything in years' and that 'in 20 years of editing this newspaper I recall nothing which aroused keener reader interest',[23] he resumed his partnership with Murphy. He was hell-bent on writing his autobiography. The two men came up with *A King's Story* as a working title, and for want of anything pithier, that remained its name. It would first exist as a series of exclusive articles in *Life*, and would then be released in expanded book form.

It should have been a harmonious collaboration, but the relationship between the two men would soon worsen. Yet the duke's difficulties with his ghostwriter would soon be the least of his problems, as his total estrangement from his family was publicly demonstrated once more.

Chapter Nine

'I Felt That I Had Lost Something Very Precious'

As Lascelles returned from the South African trip, and confided his thoughts about the tour to his wife, he could not refrain from a minor indiscretion. 'My impression, by the way, is that we shall all be subscribing to a wedding present before the year is out.'[1] The separation between Princess Elizabeth and Prince Philip had been an attempt to see whether the much-discussed romance could last such distance and, on the part of George VI, to attempt to delay the loss of his elder daughter. Yet although the couple's contact had been sporadic, no estrangement had taken place. Elizabeth returned to England hoping that she would be married before long.

However, not everyone was as excited by the prospect as she was. Queen Mary remained uncertain about Philip, and although Crawfie's account of their conversation paints her in a self-consciously out-of-touch light - 'You think Lilibet will marry him? I know nothing. No one has told me. He seems a good boy, I think . . . we must wait and see, and hope for the best'[2] - she was opposed to the match: at least one account suggests that she was open about her doubts about the engagement. Given the influence and power she wielded within the royal family, it would take an equally determined woman not to be deterred from her wishes.

During Princess Elizabeth's absence, Prince Philip finally secured his British citizenship, on 18 March 1947. His presence at Mountbatten's farewell party that evening, at the Royal Automobile Club on Pall Mall, therefore doubled as a celebration of his own naturalisation. Although he was not present to welcome the royal family back to England upon their return on 11 May* - which led to press speculation that his relationship with Elizabeth was over, not helped by regular formal denials† from the palace that any engagement was planned - he now wrote to the queen on 10 June and said explicitly that while he appreciated the delay, he was still intent on marrying her daughter, and that this was the princess's desire as well. He remained a regular visitor to Buckingham Palace - Crawfie observed that 'his small sports car was again to be seen constantly at the side entrance . . . the old routine began', and she spoke for all in the royal household when she wrote, 'Surely, we all thought, something *must* be arranged now.'[3]

The delay came from the royal parents. While the king's reluctance to let his daughter go was balanced by the respect he felt for Philip, the queen remained ambivalent about the match, perhaps influenced by her mother-in-law. Shortly after she received the 10 June letter from Philip, she wrote to Lascelles‡ to say, 'You can imagine what emotion this engagement has given me . . . It is one of the things that has been in the forefront of all one's hopes & plans for a daughter who has such a burden to carry, and one can only pray that she has made the right decision.' Describing her future son-in-law as 'untried as yet', the greatest endorsement she could offer of the wisdom of her daughter's decision was 'I <u>think</u> she has', indicating lingering doubt about Philip's suitability.

Nonetheless, after several weeks during which Elizabeth and Philip made conscious efforts not to be seen together in public, the

---

* Crawfie expressed her surprise and shock at the princess's appearance - 'I was horrified to see how thin Lilibet had gone . . . she had also lost all her pretty colour and looked pale and drawn' - but noted her 'sort of inner radiance', and how, excited by the opportunity of seeing her paramour once more, 'she had danced a little jig of sheer joy at being home again'.

† A total of five times, including from the South African trip, when it was speculated that a formal notice of engagement would be announced on the princess's twenty-first birthday in April.

‡ The letter only exists as a draft, raising the possibility that it was neither finished nor sent.

queen wrote to her sister on 7 July to confirm that the worst-kept secret in royal circles would no longer remain covert information. 'This is one line to tell you <u>very secretly</u> that Lilibet has made up her mind to get engaged to Philip Mountbatten.' The use of language was interesting – 'has made up her mind' hardly connoted romance, or approval, just as the queen's weary 'As you know, she has known him ever since she was 12, & I think that she is <u>really</u> fond of him, & I do pray that she will be very happy' sounds less like a mother truly happy about her daughter's decision and more like someone resigned to seeing a headstrong young woman about to make a mistake.

Although the news was to be announced imminently, the queen counselled caution: 'we are keeping it a deadly secret, purely because of the Press, if they know beforehand that something is up, they are likely to ruin everything'.[4] Yet the following day, Princess Elizabeth entered Crawfie's room 'looking absolutely radiant', and without the appearance of strain that had defined her since her return from South Africa. She said, 'Crawfie, something is going to happen at last!' and when her counsellor and guide responded, emotionally, 'It's about time', she announced, 'He's coming tonight', kissed her and waltzed away. On 9 July, Elizabeth, of whom Crawfie said that she had 'never [looked] lovelier than she did on that day', walked in and showed off her engagement ring, 'a large square diamond with smaller diamonds either side'[5]: it had been chosen in secret by Elizabeth and Philip, and, although slightly too large, represented the binding commitment between the two.

It was, by then, inevitable that the announcement would be made that evening that 'It is with the greatest pleasure that the King and Queen announce the betrothal of their dearly beloved daughter The Princess Elizabeth to Lieutenant Philip Mountbatten . . . to which union the King has gladly given his consent.' It was a popular match, lifting spirits at a time of national gloom. The *Daily Express* declared that 'today, the British people, turning aside from the anxieties of a time of troubles, find hope as well as joy in the royal romance'.[6]

Every single newspaper - primed by the efforts of Driberg and Mountbatten - was laudatory about the match; as Jock Colville wrote in his diary, 'an effort had obviously been made to build [Philip] up as the nephew of Lord Louis Mountbatten rather than a Greek Prince'.[7] If anything, press reports sought to make Philip more English than the average Englishman; one especially gushing account declared, '[He had] that intense love of England and the British way of life, that deep devotion to the ideals of peace and liberty for which Britain stands, that are characteristic of so many naval men.'[8] Had the famously no-nonsense Philip been shown such a report, he would undoubtedly have rolled his eyes to heaven at the hyperbole.

The international reception to the news was similarly warm. The American diplomat Robert Coe reported to Secretary of State George Marshall that 'the engagement of Princess Elizabeth ... to Lieutenant Philip Mountbatten RN has met with the general approval of the British public'. Coe was not deaf to the gossip - 'the rumours that have been current since last summer were sufficiently strong to have made the British people conscious that this engagement eventually would be announced' - but underneath his professionalism was a touch of sentimentality. 'There was little element of surprise when it took place, as it was widely known that the young couple were in love with each other ... The press has accorded a generous amount of praise of the Princess for her execution of public duties, and to Lieutenant Mountbatten for his meritorious record in the British Navy.'

After (accurately) speculating that Philip would be given a dukedom upon marriage, Coe praised him as 'an agreeable young man, displaying certain characteristics which stamp him as exceptional ... It may be said that the Princess' fiancé has met with general popularity, as he fulfils the requirements of the British public in that he belongs to a Royal House, has been brought up in England, has taken British citizenship, and has a fine record of service in the British Navy.' His fiancée, meanwhile, was described as being 'a firm character ... an intelligent young lady, and a pleasing personality', and was likened to Queen Victoria in her strong-willed disposition.

Evidence of this willpower could be seen by Coe's observation that 'some six months ago it was learned that Princess Elizabeth had determined to marry Lieutenant Mountbatten and declared that if objections were raised she would not hesitate to follow the example of her uncle, Edward VIII, and abdicate'.[9] Although this seems a fanciful assumption for the dutiful Elizabeth, it was nevertheless testament to the strength of her attachment to Philip that such a bold - if no longer unprecedented - action could be considered possible.

Whether or not the queen was wholly delighted about the engagement, she put on a show of contentment about its resolution. She wrote to her friend Sir Osbert Sitwell on 10 July that 'we feel very happy about [the engagement], as he is a very nice person, & they have known each other for years which is a great comfort'. She acknowledged the national joy at the announcement ('Everyone has been so kind') and suggested, in contrast to the international sense of pessimism largely wrought by the Soviet Union, that 'I think that people feel like a moment of rejoicing over a young lady's "Yes!"'[10]

She also knew that she had to assure her future son-in-law of her family's amity towards him. After her brother's continual rudeness and hostility, and whispers that courtiers did not believe that Philip was 'quite the thing', it was necessary to be explicit about his welcome into the royal family, and also hint at expectations now raised of his behaviour in both public and private spheres. Accordingly, while bedridden with laryngitis, she wrote to Philip on 9 July - presumably moments after the official announcement - to say, 'I particularly wanted to see [you] & tell you how happy we feel about the engagement, and to say how glad we are to have you as a son-in-law. It is so <u>lovely</u> to know you so well and I know that we can trust our darling Lilibet to your love and care.'

With the personal encomium thus dispensed with, the queen was clear about what Philip's responsibilities now were. 'There is so much that can be done in this muddled & rather worried world by example & leadership & I am sure that Lilibet & you have a great part to play. It's not always an easy part, for it often means remaining silent when one is <u>bursting</u> to reply, & sometimes a word of advice to restrain instead of to act.' Although she placed 'great confidence in your good judgement', and suggested that '[I] am certain you will be a great help & comfort to our very beloved little daughter', the letter made it plain that Philip was now part of the family, and that he had to defer to the king and queen at all times. Her closing statement that 'you can come & talk to me about anything you feel like talking about, & I shall always be ready to help in any way possible'[11] was more command than suggestion.

A less robust man than Philip might have found the expectations now placed upon him, of both public and private conduct, over-whelming and intrusive. 'The Firm' - a nickname coined by George VI, and one that has lasted to the present day - was a monolithic in-stitution, and his potentially disruptive presence within it needed to be managed carefully: hence the queen's coded warnings and injunctions. Yet he was a sufficiently outgoing character to take the inevitable rigmarole in his stride. It was suggested in the press that he was 'shy' - code for 'he has little interest in making unguarded comments to journalists' - but another expression of his feelings came in Crawfie's observation that the 'tall, rather unconventional young man . . . [who] had made many friends for himself' was seen looking 'very handsome and happy'. When she congratulated him on how everything had resolved itself, he smiled and said, 'I'm so proud of her, Crawfie.' As she wrote - sentimentally - the engage-ment meant that 'the gloomy corridors seemed lighter'.[12]

It was not to be a long engagement. The wedding was fixed for 20 November, and the necessary practical arrangements had to be made swiftly. Overnight, Philip acquired a valet, a bodyguard and a level of public attention that his fiancée had been faced with all her life. He was fortunate in that reception to him, as stage-managed by Mountbatten and Driberg, had been warm and positive, but it was also clear that the royal wedding – the first one* since that of the then Duke of York to Elizabeth Bowes-Lyon on 26 April 1923 – would be an expensive undertaking that ran the risk of seeming extravagant. Britain was a near-bankrupt country, plunged into economic crisis by both the lingering effects of the war and the appalling weather earlier in the year, and it was feared that when the public realised that the much-anticipated event was going to cost a huge amount of money, goodwill would dissipate swiftly.

On 10 July, as Philip and Elizabeth made their first public appearance as an officially engaged couple, at a Buckingham Palace garden party – where, amid the general goodwill,† an unreconciled Queen Mary was heard to mutter, 'Philip is very lucky to have won her love'[13] – and, later, stepped onto the balcony, to be hailed by the excited masses, the *Daily Express*'s headline was 'An Austerity Wedding for Elizabeth'. Although this was not overt criticism of the as yet undecided arrangements for the ceremony, there was a general feeling that at a time of national crisis, it would be both profligate and provocative to spend a vast amount on the event. On the other hand, the wedding offered an opportunity to indicate that Britain was still a world power, capable of spectacular displays of pageantry unmatched by any other nation.

As Mountbatten established himself in India, he remained keenly aware of events, thanks to Driberg's informed commentary. He was pleased at the way in which only the *Daily Worker* offered any negative response to the announcement of the engagement, and stated that 'I am an ardent believer in constitutional monarchy as a means of producing rapid evolution without actual revolution, but only if monarchy is wisely handled . . . I am sure Philip will

---

* The Duke of Windsor's wedding on 3 June 1937 attracted frenzied publicity but was described by one of the (few) attendant guests, Walter Monckton, as 'a strange wedding for one who had been six months before King of England and Emperor of India and Dominions Beyond the Seas'. See *The Windsors at War*, Chapter One, for more details.

† Harold Nicolson wrote in his diary that day that 'everybody is straining to see the bridal pair – irreverently and shamelessly straining'.

not let the side down in this respect.'[14] He, too, was aware of the potential backlash that could be caused by an expensive ceremony. On 3 August, he advised Driberg, 'I am sure that [Philip] is entirely on the side of cutting down the display of the wedding, and his own personal feelings are against receiving any civil list for the very reasons which you give.'

Nonetheless, he felt that Philip had to be granted some public funds commensurate with his new status; he was living on his naval pay of just over £300 a year, and, as his uncle remarked to Driberg, 'as a future Prince Consort . . . I think you will agree that Third-class travel would be regarded as a stunt and a sixpenny tip to a porter as stingy'. Mountbatten concluded that 'you have either got to give up the monarchy or give the wretched people who have to carry out the functions of the Crown enough money to be able to do it with the same dignity at least as the Prime Minister or Lord Mayor of London is afforded . . . I simply cannot advise him to try and do the job on the pay of a Naval officer. He would be letting down his future wife and the whole institution of the monarchy.'[15]

As Attlee and the royal household debated a suitable venue for the ceremony - Westminster Abbey was eventually agreed upon, although St George's Chapel at Windsor and St James's Chapel, which had been used for previous royal weddings, were also considered - Philip headed to Balmoral, now a known and official quantity rather than a speculative prospect. The visit took on an oddly déjà vu quality. In the words of Lord Brabourne, 'They were bloody to him . . . they didn't like him, they didn't trust him, and it showed. Not at all nice.'[16] Tacitly licensed by Queen Mary, and even to an extent Queen Elizabeth, the vicious likes of David Bowes-Lyon and Lord Eldon, unable to be overtly offensive towards the man who was about to marry into the family, took delight in sneering at the bridegroom-to-be's shabbiness and unvarnished manners. It gave particular pleasure to his detractors when Philip, wearing a kilt for the first time and feeling deeply self-conscious so doing, mock-curtseyed to the king; the display of irreverence did not go down well.

Likewise, Philip's manner, a mixture of diffidence and wryness occasionally leavened with irritation, was rather different to the conventional reserve that most of the household displayed. Jock Colville, who was present at Balmoral at this time, commented that Philip appeared 'dutiful' rather than deeply in love, and despite the 'most agreeable atmosphere'[17] to be found in Scotland, he wondered whether the match was a truly equal one. After all, Philip had enjoyed the company of women such as Osla Benning before he had become engaged, and had seen the world; Elizabeth, meanwhile, had only been on one foreign trip, and that in the closely guarded company of her family. In a matter of a few months, she would be a married woman.

When the Balmoral sojourn was over, wedding preparations began in earnest. It was considered unthinkable, in the straitened economic climate, that the people should be expected to fund its cost, and so it was paid for by the king from the Privy Purse; the Chancellor, Hugh Dalton - no friend to the royal family, and vice versa* - took grim delight in declaring in the Commons on 28 October that the taxpayer's sole contribution to the event would be to pay for the decorations outside Buckingham Palace and on Whitehall. Yet even as Churchill, in his capacity both as Leader of the Opposition and chief mischief-maker, agitated for 'a flash of colour on the hard road we have to travel',[18] a balance had to be struck between pageantry and practicality. Princess Elizabeth's dress was designed by the royal couturier, Norman Hartnell, inspired by Botticelli's *Primavera*, but it had to be made with material purchased with three hundred clothing coupons: clothes rationing would continue until 1949. Although the major talking point of the dress would usually be its cost - £1,200, four times Prince Philip's

---

* Dalton also objected to the proposed Civil List annual grant of £50,000 to fund Elizabeth and Philip's joint household. The matter became increasingly heated, until Dalton was - fortuitously enough - forced to resign over an unrelated incident involving the Budget. His successor, Stafford Cripps, was considerably happier to agree to the request, perhaps on the grounds that, as Bevin put it, 'we ought never to lower the standards of the Monarchy'.

annual pay – and the effort that went into its manufacture, on this occasion Hartnell was asked with great agitation about the provenance of the silkworms. Were they Italian or Japanese? With memories of the recent conflict still fresh, Hartnell was able to reassure (or disappoint) journalists hoping for a scoop that the silk was all sourced from China.

Given the relatively short amount of time between engagement and ceremony, its organisation was a logistical triumph. It may have been an austerity wedding, but it was an austerity wedding on the grandest scale imaginable. Fifteen hundred wedding presents were put on public view at St James's Palace,* one of which was a tray cloth from none other than Mahatma Gandhi. Mistaking it for the lawyer's loincloth, Queen Mary loudly complained to her lady-in-waiting, Lady Airlie, that it was 'such an indelicate gift' and 'what a horrible thing'. Philip, clearly no longer caring whether his grandmother-in-law held him in high estimation, upbraided her, saying, 'I don't think it's horrible. Gandhi is a wonderful man; a very great man.'[19] Thus admonished, Queen Mary departed in angry silence.

Such moments were not isolated ones. In the build-up to the wedding, Philip displayed several instances of the forthrightness – some may have called it tactlessness – that became a feature of his life and public standing. On a trip back from Clydebank, where Elizabeth had named a ship, Colville bemoaned Philip's rougher aspects; he wrote in his diary that 'he is a strong believer in the hail-fellow-well-met as opposed to the semi-divine interpretation of Monarchy', and was unimpressed by his 'vulgar' character, as well as his 'quite off-hand'[20] treatment of Elizabeth. Because of his upbringing, Philip was never a demonstrative or tactile man; as one attendee of that summer at Balmoral put it, 'He's not a person who shows love. Given the sort of experience he'd had [when younger],

---

* Channon, attending because he had given an 'ersatz Fabergé' gift of a silver box, described the reception on 18 November as 'crowded', the presents as 'some fine but many horrible' and the bridegroom as 'dazzling'. The royal family were, he noted, 'too surrounded to be approachable'.

you probably would shut yourself away a bit to avoid being hurt. Affection is not his natural currency.'[21]

Amid the excitement, there were also, inevitably, naysayers. Channon sneered on 25 October that despite the popularity of the engagement, 'the wedding (not the marriage) is decried and criticised on all sides; its bogus austerity appeals to nobody; the seating arrangements and unnecessary limited accommodation at the Abbey infuriates all'.[22] A fortnight later, he had not changed his attitude. Writing that even the Duchess of Kent was unhappy about the arrangements, he allowed that 'there are many grumbles especially from the uninvited', but complained, 'little imagination has been shown . . . It is *une occasion manquée*; the whole affair should have been the most splendid ever known in the Empire!'[23] That the Empire was rapidly ceasing to exist was not a matter that concerned him.

When 20 November finally came, there was a sense of barely controlled hysteria, after a build-up that at times seemed wildly disproportionate to the event itself. One American commentator described the jamboree as 'a movie premiere, an election, a World Service and Guy Fawkes Night all rolled into one'.[24] What foreign royals still existed in these post-war days gathered in London, pulling together what they could gather of their finery and jewellery,* and the imminent event dominated every newspaper and newsreel in the country. It was a thrilling and cathartic time for everyone, with one exception: the bridegroom. At a party a few days before the wedding, Philip, 'white-faced', remarked to another of the guests, the musician Larry Adler, 'I suppose I won't be having any fun any more.'[25] On the morning of the wedding itself, his cousin, Patricia Mountbatten, blithely remarked what an exciting day lay ahead. Philip replied, 'I'm either very brave or very stupid.'[26] The previous day, he had received a suitably grand-sounding series of titles:†

---

* Wheeler-Bennett called it 'one of the largest gatherings of royalty, regnant or exiled, of the century'.

† The king wrote to Queen Mary that 'it is a great deal to give a man all at once, but I know Philip understands his new responsibilities on his wedding to Lilibet'.

Baron Greenwich, Earl of Merioneth and Duke of Edinburgh. He was now very much part of the Firm, whether he liked it or not.

Some nerves in his situation were both inevitable and understandable, but this was far removed from Crawfie's blithe comments, about the last night before the wedding, that 'there was a lovely feeling in the Palace . . . we were all of us happy because she was happy'. Even allowing for the sentimental exaggeration inherent in her account, it is still both touching and faintly sad to read of how the princess remarked on her wedding day, 'I can't believe it's really happening . . . I have to keep pinching myself.' After what Crawfie described as 'the usual last-minute crises, the tensions common to any home on a wedding morning', it was time for the great event to take place. Thousands of people had queued on the streets, in a state of excitement that had not been seen since VE Day. The day would be a success; it had to be.

Channon, who was not given a ticket to the main event but instead inveigled his way into the parliamentary enclosure, decried the courtiers as 'slow and narrow-minded', saying they had 'misjudged the temper of the nation and underestimated the enthusiasm of the people'. Sour grapes were responsible for his vitriol, but he was nonetheless pleased to have a prime position for people-watching. The bride-to-be was described as 'shy and attractive', and the bridegroom as 'dazzling and evidently [enjoying] himself'. He was less complimentary about the king and queen; she was written off merely as looking well, and George VI was denigrated as 'wooden and stiff'. He took delight in observing that 'everybody in high society and socialist MPs were angry at being left out',[27] not least the politician Rab Butler, who Channon confidently – and inaccurately – predicted would be prime minister before too long.

One man who was not left outside in the enclosure – and who, whether through carelessness or entitlement, turned up late – was Churchill. The Leader of the Opposition, now seventy-two years old, may have been in the political wilderness, but his favour was still eagerly courted by all parties. He had received a hand-written letter of thanks from Princess Elizabeth for his good wishes when the engagement was announced, and he had remarked to the king that 'the news has certainly given the keenest pleasure to all classes and the marriage will be an occasion of national rejoicing, standing out all the more against the sombre background of our lives'.[28] He had even hosted Prince Philip for lunch shortly before the wedding, giving him an informal pep talk as to what his responsibilities were likely to be. If he expected deference, he would have argued that he had earned it. Channon - no partisan of the former prime minister - wrote that 'the biggest, warmest reception was reserved for Winston; in the Abbey, although he arrived late, everyone stood up - even the Kings and Queens'.[29]

Yet even he could not steal the show. Crawfie, who was present for the ceremony, described it initially as 'nerve-wracking' and felt sick with anxiety, but as soon as Princess Elizabeth appeared on her father's arm and walked down the aisle, she was confident; 'more than once, the King and Queen exchanged a smile and a reassuring glance'.[30] The service was determinedly traditional. Elizabeth promised to 'love, cherish and obey' her husband, hymns such as 'The Lord Is My Shepherd' were sung, and the Archbishop of York, Cyril Garbett, stressed the relatively low-key and austere nature of the event, declaring that the ceremony 'is in all essentials exactly the same as it would have been for any cottager who might be married this afternoon in some small country church in a remote village in the Dales'.[31] Only the presence of two thousand guests at Westminster Abbey - and as many as two hundred million people watching or listening to the event worldwide - undermined his well-meant sentiments.

The wedding breakfast at Buckingham Palace afterwards was similarly low-key by royal standards - a mere three courses, as opposed to the ten-course banquets of previous days, and a comparatively trifling 150 guests lunched on partridge and ice cream, albeit laid out on gold plate and served by scarlet-coated footmen - while the speeches were terse at best. As Crawfie described it, 'The King hates them and has always dreaded having to make one . . . he was brevity itself . . . The bridegroom, another sailor, had just as little to say.'[32] There was a toast, and then the newly wed couple headed off on their honeymoon, the first part of which would be spent at Mountbatten's home of Broadlands in the New Forest. Their departure was a predictably emotional moment; the king and queen joined other well-wishers in racing to the gates at Buckingham Palace, hand in hand, to throw rose petals at the couple's car, and Crawfie noted, not without surprise, 'the Queen picked up her silk skirts and came right up to the railings with us'.[33]

The day had been a triumph. Despite the cavilling of Channon and the excluded politicians and other public figures - Sir John Reith, former director general of the BBC, wrote in his diary of the 'miserable royal wedding day', on which he felt 'completely out of phase with everything and everybody through not being asked to the Abbey'[34] - it was not just the longed-for union of a glamorous young couple, but also a reminder, after the many disappointments of the previous two and a half years, that the royal family could still manage to pull off a grand set-piece occasion of this nature, albeit with austerity garb cloaking the pageantry. Crawfie confided emotionally to the king, 'I feel as if I, too, have lost a daughter.' He was superficially calm, replying, 'they grow up and leave us, and we must make the best of it', but he was concealing his own feelings of turmoil.

His relationship with his elder daughter was vitally important for him, both emotionally and practically. It is not overstating the case to argue that from VE Day onwards, she was the single most important figure in his life: steadier and more dutiful than her younger sister, and less capricious and partisan than her mother. The pictures that show the two of them together demonstrate an unusually close and warm relationship, devoid of the formality that members of the royal family usually demonstrated to one another in photographs or in public.

A hint at the depth of his emotion at her departure came when he remarked to the Archbishop of Canterbury, during the signing of the register at the service, that 'it is a far more moving thing to give away your daughter than be married yourself',[35] and when

Elizabeth and Philip had left, and the excitement of the day began to dissipate, he quietly headed back to the royal apartments and wrote a letter to the newly married princess.

It is probably the most affecting thing he ever wrote. It was the speech he was unwilling, or simply unable, to make publicly, and is hard to read without being moved by his mingled feelings of pride and loss. It was sent to Broadlands shortly after the honeymoon began, and it is not hard to imagine his daughter's response at receiving the poignant and heartfelt letter. It bears reproduction in full.

> I was so proud of you and thrilled at having you so close to me on our long walk in Westminster Abbey, but when I handed your hand to the Archbishop I felt that I had lost something very precious. You were very calm and composed during the Service and said your words with such conviction that I knew everything was all right.
>
> I am so glad you wrote and told Mummy that you think the long wait before your engagement and the long time before the wedding was for the best. I was rather afraid that you had thought I was being rather hard-hearted about it. I was so anxious for you to come to South Africa, as you knew. Our family, us four, the Royal Family must remain together, with additions of course at suitable moments!
>
> I have watched you grow up all these years, with pride under the skilful direction of Mummy, who as you know is the most marvellous person in the world in my eyes, and I can, I know, always count on you, and now Philip, to help in our work.
>
> You leaving us has left a great blank in our lives, but do remember that your old home is still yours and do come back to it as much and as often as possible. I can see that you are sublimely happy with Philip which is right, but don't forget us is the wish of your ever loving and devoted,
> Papa[36]

Chapter Ten

'The Future Is a Gloomy One'

'I think the answer to the question "were you invited to the wedding" should be the plain truth "no" and then refuse to comment, don't you?'[1] So the Duchess of Windsor complained to her aunt on 11 September 1947. The royal family's refusal to invite the duke and duchess to Princess Elizabeth's wedding was not an unpredictable snub, given the events of the previous years, but it was still a salutary reminder that the couple were seen as *infra dig* and that their presence at such high-profile - and supposedly joyful - public events was neither required nor welcome. The duke had offered the king his congratulations on the 'interesting announcement' on 8 July, and suggested to his mother that 'I certainly hope they will be very happy',[2] but it did not translate into him and his wife being welcomed back into the fold.

Wallis was not happy. Informing her aunt that the duke was being asked for comment as to his presence at, or absence from, the forthcoming wedding, she said, 'Naturally the English do not want this so definite and the Duke has been told he should avoid answering! Why should we go on protecting their rude attitude after ten and a half years? I can't see how any sane person should think I would be asked after all this time and I don't think it hurts to answer the truth, do you?'[3]

The lack of an invitation to the wedding was the first substantial proof they had that despite their indifferently received return visits to Britain, they would never be accepted back into the royal family, or treated with anything other than contempt. They were in New York for the ceremony, in their rented home at Waldorf Towers, and watched it disconsolately on television. Irrelevance bit hard. Edward wrote angrily to the Earl of Dudley on 16 October to say, 'I shall be very interested to know if you are able to get the low-down on the marked indifference of the Press in general to my presence in Great Britain', and was sure that he knew the reasons why. 'It is difficult to believe that it was not acting on a directive from Buckingham Palace.'[4]

There were those who agreed that the couple's treatment had been shoddy. The duke's younger sister, Princess Mary of York, who had remained close to him since the abdication, did not attend the wedding, citing ill health as a factor, as well as her continued mourning of the recent death of her husband, Henry Lascelles, Earl of Harewood. That she was seen out in public two days later at another event indicated either that she had a more robust constitution than many of her family, or that she had deliberately boycotted the event in tacit protest as to how her elder brother continued to be treated.*

And the duke found some unexpected support, perhaps unbeknown to him, from 'three American women'. They wrote to the king on 4 October angered at the lack of an invitation for both Edward and Wallis. The anonymous correspondents stated that 'For ten years the treatment accorded Her Highness, the Duchess of Windsor, by the English Government and the Queen Mother, particularly, has been an insult to every American. Surely, no really great person stoops to be discourteous to anyone regardless of their station in life.' The letter struck an egalitarian note: 'The Duchess is not of Royal Blood, but is there such a thing as Royal Blood? Isn't it fast becoming just a Fairy Tale? Are we, today, not striving for a United World devoid of trivial snobbery and such?'

The women were undoubtedly angry - 'How can the Queen

---

* In a letter of 12 November to her friend Dame Mary Tyrwhitt, Mary suggested that the wedding festivities 'might prove too great a strain', and that while she was 'very disappointed' to miss the event, 'November 17 or 18 the Press must announce I have a chill or something of the sort'.

Mother do justice to her people when she has so little concern for her own son's happiness, and for ten years has hurt him so deeply?' – and concluded by asking, 'Don't you think it about time to do something about all this? It has no place in our distressed world of today.'[5] The king's reaction to the declaration of solidarity with his brother and sister-in-law was unrecorded.

Others remained partisan too. Edward's great supporter Kenneth de Courcy was quick to reassure him of his undying loyalty. He wrote on 17 November from London that 'the nuptial celebrations have started here but I must confess to a feeling of coldness on my part as I deplore the absence of the Duke and Duchess of Windsor ... I also think it perfectly preposterous that the three sisters of the bridegroom have been invited just because they are married to Germans.'

Nonetheless, de Courcy remained optimistic about the duke's future, even if few others were. 'We are on the verge of very great political changes here, not only affecting the parties but large philosophical changes, and I think it may well be that presently other views may prevail.' He also suggested that a return to prominence was not just likely, but inevitable. 'I need hardly tell you, sir, that so soon as it is possible some of us who feel strongly will I hope be in a position to insist that those who advise the Crown advise that you should govern one of the great dominions, if indeed Your Royal Highness felt so inclined ... One day an arrangement of that kind must be offered and if I have anything whatsoever to do with it, as one day I may have, such an offer will be made.'[6]

De Courcy was amusingly certain about the extent of his own influence, but no doubt his continuing confidence in the duke acted as a pick-me-up in otherwise difficult times. As Edward and Wallis continued to drift between America and Europe, the former king might have been mordantly amused to know that even if he was not wanted by his family, there were still those who were keen to be associated with him. One enterprising individual, D. M. McCausland, formed the 'Duke of Windsor pipe band' and asked for formal permission for the duke to be associated with the organisation. Although Edward's great love of the bagpipes was a consistent, if sometimes regrettable, feature of his life,* his secretary, F. J. Dadd, replied, straight-faced, that 'I am to say that the Secretary of State regrets that this is not a case in which, in accordance with established practice, he can make a favourable recommendation to the King, whose consent is required to the use of Royal names and titles.'[7]

Bagpiping aside, America proved to be a mixed experience for the duke and duchess. Many of their belongings had been sent there at the outbreak of war in a panic, and were still in storage in New York, reinforcing the sense that their existence was a transitory, uncertain one. A permanent life there seemed undesirable because of the taxes they would be expected to pay as residents, and the duchess felt personally aggrieved at the attention – usually unflattering – the American papers paid her.

Edward expressed his discontent with the country's 'leftist thinking', and was particularly upset that Truman won re-election in the autumn of 1948. He complained to Beaverbrook that 'the departments in Washington and even the White House will escape the thorough house-cleaning of liberals and fellow-travellers, if not Communists, which is long overdue'.[8] Yet he felt no more fondly towards Britain, which he decried to Queen Mary as ruined by 'decades of Liberal and Socialist legislation'; he commented wistfully that 'so much of the traditional elegance we used to know has already vanished or is vanishing . . . until one hardly has the heart to revisit the haunts of one's youth'.[9] As he aged, he became increasingly conservative and reactionary in his views. The previous year, he had written sorrowfully to the king to say, 'I can well imagine how you must be considerably harassed by the turn economic and political events are taking in Great Britain, which are so deplorable and discouraging as to be beyond comment from this distance.'[10]

---

* Diana Cooper remarked to her friend Conrad Russell, after being treated to a performance by Edward while king at Fort Belvedere, 'It's clever to have chosen the pipes as one's "shew off" for which one of us can detect mistakes, or know good from bad artistry?'

It was not long until the Windsors left the United States - on board the *Queen Mary*, in the company of none other than their long-standing friend Lord Beaverbrook - and after a brief sojourn in Britain, they returned to France and La Croë in August 1948. Wallis wrote miserably to her aunt shortly after their arrival about their current circumstances. 'We have had a disturbed time - you remember I was not looking forward to this journey to Europe . . . the Duke has had colitis and when he is sick as you know he be- comes the real invalid. Also the Russians have him down and he wants to get everything out of this country at once . . . The Duke is in a strange mood - upset over the world and plans which are hard to adjust for us around taxes.'[11]

Edward's strange mood was not helped by his correspondence and association with de Courcy, who skilfully - or foolishly - fanned the flames of his paranoia. Even as he wrote on 22 July that 'I do not for the moment think that there is going to be a war this summer as some sensational people have forecast', de Courcy repeated his usual belief in Britain's decline. 'I cannot help but feel that we shall be reduced to a mere Military Mission, despite all our protests and strong speeches . . . What is the good of saying that we are going to make a strong stand at any cost and then Cabinet Ministers going around saying that we are going to avoid war at any costs?' His attitude, as expressed to the duke, was reassuringly, even naïvely, straightforward. 'By the use of a few atom bombs on the [Soviets'] main concentration points, the thing could be fin- ished within a month and the world could settle down to at least a century of peace, if not more.'

He was warmer about the king and queen than he had been before - 'they make a very good impression . . . she is absolutely magnificent'[12] - but the duke's response of 28 August made no ref- erence to his family. Edward did, however, return to his favourite theme: how dreadful the world had become, and how little could be done about it. After referring to his recent illness ('I was quite sick . . . firstly from an overdose of penicillin given me as an anti- dote to a bite sustained in separating the two Cairns in one of their monthly scraps, and secondly from an attack of colitis'), he concurred with de Courcy's worldview. He suggested that although the experts he had consulted agreed that it would be better to stand up to Stalin now, 'it is a big chance to take for time is on the side of the Western Powers and Russia knows it and another World War will anyway destroy the last remnants of what is left of free enterprise in Great Britain and the economic structure of America'.

He blamed the late President Roosevelt for this situation; he considered that Roosevelt had been excessively servile towards Stalin and Russia. 'There is no escape from the fact that the future is a gloomy one and that inevitably the East and West must eventually shoot it out. I would not be surprised if you bypassed Grosvenor Square nowadays to spare yourself the disgust of having to look at the statue of the man most responsible for the jam in which the Western Powers now find themselves.' He concluded with inadvertent bleakness. 'If there's no shooting before October, I expect to go to Great Britain the latter part of that month.'[13]

There were other distractions. By the time he and the duchess had established themselves in France once again, *Life* magazine wished to resume business with him. The magazine's editor, Dan Longwell, wrote to him on 10 September to agree to the duke's two provisos: no time limit in finishing, and the understanding that, in collaboration once again with Murphy, the duke would be primarily writing a book, and that *Life* would excerpt appropriate sections upon its completion in order to have another successful run of articles. Longwell struck a breezy note - 'I do believe that both of you will do your best while enthusiasm is running high' - but despite his assurances that there was no hurry to finish writing, he hinted that they might yet be scooped, or as he put it, 'someone else might jumble much of the story in some popular way and create a legend that would be hard to catch up with in reality'.[14]

If this was intended to galvanise the duke into action, it did not work. He and Wallis had recently hosted Monckton and his wife at La Croë, and the time had been spent drinking cocktails

- 'I must confess to finding [it] very hard to take [them] at our advanced age', the duke good-naturedly complained in a letter to Monckton - and having what Edward called 'the opportunity of undisturbed reminiscing'. They had discussed the abdication at length, which the duke had enjoyed: 'it was fascinating to recall the stirring events of 1936 and to test our memories in connection with those momentous days'.[15] Churchill was presently a guest of the couple,* enjoying the opportunity to be away from politics and to paint, and Beaverbrook was expected imminently; a reminder that the duke continued to have connections in high places, even if he railed against his home country and its dwindling relevance.

Monckton, however, was less delighted at the prospect of the book being massaged into existence.† After his reappointment to the position of attorney general to the Duchy of Cornwall by the king, he wished to look to the future, rather than obsessively dwell on the past. Not only was he uncomfortable at the idea of his own recollections of the abdication crisis ever making it into public view - he described his memoir to Lascelles, who hoped to be able to have a copy for the Royal Archives, as 'too full and too intimate for publication, even after the lapse of years‡[16] - but he was also fearful as to what the duke's memoir would contain. He complained to Edward's former equerry, Major Gray Phillips, that '[I] fear that he really is getting down to writing the long threatened book . . . I always hoped a) that it would be postponed to the Greek

---

* Although a disappointing one; a subsequent letter complained that 'Although I was able to get Winston to talk a little about 1936, I found him more reticent and cagey than I had expected.' Beaverbrook, on the other hand, '[had] been more than cooperative', and Monckton was prevailed upon to extract 'valuable dope' from various sources - the American slang perhaps reflecting the length of time the duke had spent in the United States.

† The duke's solicitor, George Allen, was another naysayer, believing that the publication could only cause harm.

‡ Fortunately, Monckton's memoir can today be found in the Balliol College archives, and was invaluable for the creation of *The Crown in Crisis*.

kalends* and b) that I should be able to operate an effective blue pencil.'

As the book was inevitable, Monckton's best hope was to prevent its worst excesses. He commented to Phillips, caustically, 'one cannot help seeing how much more interesting it is for him to occupy himself in recapturing those exciting days than in any other pursuit now open to him'. He was not blind to 'the final attractions' of the book – 'presumably largely in hard currency' – but he also attempted to enlist Phillips' help in curbing the duke's worst excesses. 'You and I and all his friends must try to dissuade them from publishing matter . . . where we feel that the very fact of their publishing it will injure them in the eyes of the public.' He noted that the 'pleasant and understanding' Murphy was 'mainly interested in the sales of the book, and this will, of course, drive him to want to publish just those things I want to stop'.[17]

Murphy, however, was finding the task of collaborating with the duke increasingly irksome and unpleasant. As time went on, numerous difficulties arose. Edward was concerned that his co-writer wanted the book to be sensationalist, gossipy and liable to cause more offence than he wished it to; Murphy, meanwhile, found the duke insufferable. He blamed the duchess in large part for this, later writing that 'a dozen times a day she would telephone to the Duke in his workroom . . . the Duke's reluctance – or inability – to concentrate being abetted by his fear of crossing the Duchess, [made me] helpless, with no ally and no appeal'.

As he caustically suggested, 'the flow of the Duke's narrative could never, even at best, invite comparison with a cataract; his span of attention . . . was two and a half minutes maximum, and when the story of the preceding night was plainly written in his trembling hands and bloodshot eyes,† [I] knew that another workday would have to be scrubbed'. Murphy cited an adage of

---

* Or 'a time that will never come'.

† The now fifty-four-year-old duke was spending most of his nocturnal hours in various nightclubs by this stage, often remaining out until dawn. One can only be impressed by his stamina.

Rubens to explain how difficult his working life had become: 'Long experience has taught me how slowly princes act when someone else's interest is involved.' Anyone with any previous experience of the duke could only have confirmed the veracity, as well as the timelessness, of the statement.

There was a point in the middle of 1948 when Edward considered abandoning the memoir altogether. It was Beaverbrook who counselled him against so doing, and indeed stressed the importance of celerity. The magnate wrote to the duke in July, 'It is clearly of high importance that such a work [as yours] should be prepared without delay. If there is any postponement, the facts will inevitably become blurred and distorted. Such a book must be a historical document of the first importance. It must shape the work of all the historians of that era for all time. It is imperative that you should write the record yourself. No-one else can do it with such authority . . . the British people have never really understood the story of the Abdication. If your account is given to them, you may be sure you will get an overwhelming response.'[18]

Beaverbrook had informally advised Edward many times when he was king, often with some success. The duke's biographer Philip Ziegler commented to me that Beaverbrook was the only man he would ever listen to, and so it proved. The duke professed himself 'both interested and gratified' and replied that 'The telling of the events of 1936 will be difficult and will require all the tact and skill at my command . . . The unsettled state of the world and the war clouds which hang so heavily over us hardly create an atmosphere conducive to quiet thought and reminiscing.'[19] Although the unkind, or battle-weary, might have questioned whether the duke possessed either tact or skill, he now agreed a formal deal with *Life*: in addition to the continued services of Murphy, he would receive a $25,000 advance, any research or secretarial assistance he needed and carte blanche to deliver the finished series of articles when he wanted. It was a deal that any other author would have sold their grandmother for, but Edward, after all, had been king. This unprecedented degree of *noblesse oblige* seemed only justified when it came to telling this particular monarch's story.

Murphy, meanwhile, was less impressed. Fearing that the duchess would destroy the project - 'her disruptiveness grew by the week'[20] - he begged Luce to be allowed to escape the madhouse and return to the relative sanity of Truman-era America.* He was denied his wish. Murphy would be stuck with the increasingly demanding couple for a further two years; a Sartrean vision of damnation, complete with better tailoring. He began to suspect that the duchess did not want the book to be finished, partly because of the further opportunities it would create for malicious gossip to be directed towards her, and also, as he put it, because 'she wanted to deny the Duke the satisfaction of finally carrying something - anything - through to completion'.[21]

At this stage, the ghostwriter hid the worst of his irritation. He headed to London to interview Monckton, and the duke wrote happily to the lawyer on 8 December that '[Murphy] enjoys your company and the stimulation of your conversation.' As well, no doubt, as much-needed variety from the company of the duke and duchess. Edward now announced his planned deadline for finishing the book - Labour Day, the first Monday of September 1949 - and alluded to Longwell's restlessness at its slow progress. Nonetheless, the duke seemed impressed by Murphy - 'he is a good egg and quite a brilliant journalist' - who, presumably, did not reciprocate such feelings.

When Edward was not bothering someone - whether it was his literary collaborator, an old acquaintance such as Monckton or Churchill, or the royal family - or forcing himself to write, he played golf, gardened and complained about the state of the world. Those who encountered him were struck by an attitude that lay

---

* Truman's re-election, on 2 November 1948, surprised many who had expected the Republican candidate, Thomas E. Dewey, to win. One of those surprised had been Henry Luce, who had printed a picture of Dewey and his staff travelling across San Francisco's harbour on *Life*'s cover, with the caption 'Our Next President Rides by Ferryboat over San Francisco Bay'.

somewhere between naïvety and a complete lack of interest in any aspect of modern life that did not concern him. He once sat next to an American journalist, Marietta Fitzgerald, at dinner, and she asked him how George I's ascent to the throne had come about through his relationship to the Electress Sophia. The duke looked at her blankly and said, 'I think my mother would know that. I could send her a telegram, if you wish.' Fitzgerald tried a simpler question: was the Irish Republic a member of the British Commonwealth? The same near-panicked expression, and then a moment of clarity. 'I think my mother would know that, too.'[22]

It was left to Wallis to attempt to keep matters buoyant. The letters she wrote to her aunt during the second half of 1948 were by turns pessimistic ('people here are quite resigned to war in a year or two'), snippy ('there is a lot to be said against as well as for royalty - there is no doubt their upbringing makes them hard with no understanding')[23] and, when it came to describing the terminal illness of her friend Katherine Rogers,* profoundly sad. 'It is all heartbreaking and their courage you could not believe . . . nobody really knows about this dread disease . . . I feel so upset over the poor things.'[24]

The duke was often away in London, visiting Queen Mary or cajoling memories from his friends and acquaintances for his memoir, and Wallis alternated between stoicism ('I seem to have plenty of friends to prevent me from being lonely')[25] and misery. She complained on 1 December that 'there is nothing to do here and no-one to see . . . I don't see how my friends live in the *grande luxe* and pay those taxes.' As ever, matters financial dominated her thoughts. 'Americans are certainly rich and have the opportunity of making money - whereas the Duke has none and [investment] incomes nowadays are not much good.'[26] They were caught in the difficult position that their capital was tied up in Britain, and it

---

* Katherine and her husband Herman gave Wallis shelter at their villa in Cannes when she needed it during the abdication crisis: see *The Crown in Crisis*, Chapter Ten, for more details.

could not be taken out of the country due to post-war restrictions on currency importation, and so the need to make money, always looming large in both their minds, was now doubly pressing. It was with some bitterness that the duchess wrote on 18 December that 'I think I should go down in history as Wallis the home maker. I am fed up with my movie star and his house decisions.'[27]

As the decade approached its end, both the duke and duchess were in a state of flux. The memoir offered him, at least, some interest and distraction, but the endless frustrations of their lives meant that neither of them was able to look to the future with anything resembling optimism. Still, if they were in a rut, it had the virtue of being lined with diamonds and other baubles. And as events in England changed dramatically, perhaps there was something to be said for dull consistency after all.

Chapter Eleven

'An Unkind Stroke of Fate'

British monarchs have often suffered from less than robust health. One thinks of Henry VIII, grotesquely overweight and riddled with leg ulcers, diabetes and hypertension, or Charles II, who apologised for being 'an unconscionable time dying' after what was believed to be a fatal apoplectic fit. Edward VII, the so-called 'Edward the Caresser', was afflicted with severe bronchitis in between bouts of (surprisingly athletic) lechery with actresses, and George III's mental illness has led everyone from doctors to playwrights to attempt to diagnose what was truly the matter with him.

Yet these ailments have passed into popular consciousness because of their dramatic nature. The decline in George VI's general well-being was nowhere near as attention-grabbing as any of his predecessors as king, but in its own way, it was an even sadder fate, not least because it would eventually result in the untimely death of a comparatively young man, and thereby plunge the monarchy into its second succession drama in less than two decades.

Compared to his elder brother, whose gilded youth seemed a carefree one, the then Duke of York struggled with a crippling stammer, and was beset by everything from severe seasickness to debilitating gastric problems. In 1916, he was diagnosed as suffering from a duodenal ulcer, which was eventually successfully operated on in November 1917, and the following decades saw him undergoing everything from a poisoned hand to rumoured fainting fits and epilepsy.* Yet it was the Second World War that led to the greatest strain on his health, as he began smoking heavily to cope with the stress and exhaustion he felt. Had he been able to rest in 1945, as Churchill eventually did when he was defeated in the election, he might have been able to recover at least some of his constitution. But kings do not have the luxury of being able to take holidays when they choose, and as his official biographer, John Wheeler-Bennett, put it, 'his temperament was not one which facilitated a rapid replenishing of nervous and physical reserves'.[1]

Although the success of his daughter's wedding in November 1947 brought personal comfort to the king, his already fragile health had been strained during the South African tour earlier that year, and by the beginning of 1948, he began to complain of severe cramp and numbness. Queen Mary sighed to the Duke of Windsor on 12 February that 'Politics as usual are very depressing and I am so sorry for poor Bertie, & it is all such a worry.'[2] The monarch was suffering from Buerger's disease, which had been brought on by his heavy smoking; the blood vessels in his lower feet and legs expanded, making it difficult for him to walk. By August, he was said to be 'in discomfort most of the time',[3] something that he tried to relieve by violently kicking his foot and leg against his desk, in a vain attempt to restore the circulation. The only place where he found even fleeting peace was Balmoral, which he visited late that summer; the steep hill walks made him feel more energised and gave him hope that he was recovering. Yet even so, while walking with Peter Townsend towards Arthur's Seat in Edinburgh, he kept muttering, 'What's wrong with my blasted legs? They won't work properly!'[4]

Unfortunately, upon his return to London in October 1948, the pain had become even more agonising. He found himself unable to sleep, thanks to his left foot feeling perpetually numb and the right one going in a similar direction. He was examined by the splendidly

---

* His youngest brother, Prince John, suffered from severe epilepsy and died of a seizure at the age of thirteen.

named Manipulative Surgeon to the King, Commander Sir Morton Stuart, who pronounced himself 'gravely alarmed' at the monarch's condition. Yet something - protocol; concern at making too hasty a diagnosis; ignorance, even - meant that although Sir Thomas Dunhill, Serjeant Surgeon to the King, and Professor James Learmouth, Regius Professor in Clinical Surgery, were also consulted, Learmouth did not examine the king until 12 November.

Between his arrival in London and Learmouth's examination, the king had undertaken the state opening of Parliament on 26 October, and was preparing to head to New Zealand and Australia on a visit that would mirror the previous year's trip to South Africa. There had also been a Remembrance Day service at the Cenotaph to attend, the Territorial Army to review, and the usual round of receptions, investitures and the general business of monarchy to attend to.

His diminished state was obvious. Channon, who had seen him on 20 October, wrote in his diary that 'I shall remember the King looking sunburnt but snarling and I thought far from well - his figure remains young but I thought that all youth had left his drawn face.' The diarist pronounced the monarch 'utterly charmless', which may have been sour grapes: 'I thought that he glared at me and so did not approach him.'[5] The idea that someone might not have wanted to talk to the ever-waspish politician seemed beyond him. Others were more concerned. The queen, who had been worried about her husband for some time, suggested to Lascelles that 'I am not at all happy' about the way in which his health was not being attended to, and impressed the necessity of 'making a real break'[6] for him.

Learmouth's diagnosis a few weeks later was both alarming and depressing. He confirmed that the king had arteriosclerosis, brought on by years of heavy smoking, and suggested that it was possible his right leg would need to be amputated. The news was horrifying; as the queen wrote to Queen Mary, telling her that the trip to New Zealand and Australia would now need to be cancelled, 'I have been terribly worried over his legs, and am sure that the only thing is to put everything off, and try & get better. I am sure that Australia & NZ will be desperately disappointed – but what else could one do – I do hope they will understand that it is serious.'[7]

A statement had to be issued to explain both the king's temporary withdrawal from public life and the possibility of his health declining further, and so, on 23 November, a bulletin was released to the press. It stated that the king was suffering 'from an obstruction to the circulation through the arteries of the legs', and that this had 'only recently become acute'. Although the general tone of the message was as upbeat as could be expected in the circumstances, it concluded that 'the strain of the last twelve years has appreciably affected his resistance to fatigue'.[8] It was now public knowledge, amid the various other tribulations that the country faced, that its monarch was unwell. Channon remarked witheringly in his diary that '[the King's illness] is the result of his restlessness and inability to sit still . . . he never sleeps in the afternoon, never rests – now he is an invalid'.[9] The statement may have been inevitable, but it was no less humiliating for the national prestige. Or what remained of it, anyway.

There had been happier news recently, as well. Princess Elizabeth and Prince Philip had settled into married life with great pleasure, despite their first home being in Buckingham Palace: the necessity of their having an independent household had to be weighed up against the inevitable expense that such a move would require.* Elizabeth was sufficiently enraptured with her new husband to write to the queen that 'Philip is an angel – he is so kind and thoughtful, and living with him and having him around all the time is just perfect', and even went so far as to say that it seemed 'as though we had belonged to each other for years'.[10] Her mother professed her delight, saying not only that she and her husband already adored Philip as if he was their own son, but 'that you and

---

* Channon wrote on 17 December that 'I have been asked if I would lend or let my house to them for some months; and I refused.'

Philip should be blissfully happy & love each other through good days and bad or depressing days is my one wish', as she praised her 'unselfish & thoughtful angel'[11] of a daughter.

Philip, meanwhile, regarded his marriage with a mixture of genuine happiness and concern for the future. Jock Colville described him as 'a shade querulous',[12] even as he acknowledged that this was an intrinsic trait of his character. When the queen's new son-in-law wrote to her a few weeks after the wedding, it was with a mixture of genuine love and determination. 'Lilibet is the only "thing" in the world which is absolutely real to me, and my ambition is to weld the two of us into a new combined existence that will not only be able to withstand the shocks directed at us but will also have a positive existence for the good.' In response to the queen's desire that he should 'cherish' her daughter, the prince took issue with the term, albeit light-heartedly. 'Cherish Lilibet? I wonder if that word is enough to express what is in me. Does one cherish one's sense of humour or one's musical ear or one's eyes? I am not sure, but I know that I thank God for them, and so, very humbly, I thank God for Lilibet and us.'[13]

Nonetheless, although he was very much consort rather than master in public, in private it was another matter. His wife acknowledged that Philip needed to be 'boss in his own home',[14] and this was made difficult by the constraints of married life in Buckingham Palace. The two had separate bedrooms - faintly ridiculously for a young, newly married couple - that were linked by a sitting room, and although the Duke of Edinburgh had been given a role at the Admiralty, where he now worked as an operations officer responsible for, in his words, 'shuffling ships around', he felt frustrated and compromised. Lord Brabourne later said of Philip's difficult relationships with the palace staff that 'it was very stuffy. Lascelles was impossible . . . They patronised him. They treated him as an outsider. It wasn't much fun. He laughed it off, of course, but it must have hurt.'[15]

The prince's response to such condescension and rudeness was much the same as it had been on his summer visits to Balmoral:

grit his teeth, refuse to rise to the bait and ignore his persecutors as far as he could. He also knew that as soon as his wife became pregnant, his place within the royal family would be doubly reinforced, and so it was with relief that, early in 1948, he and the princess discovered that she was expecting. It had been a matter of intense national speculation since the wedding – although not before, for propriety's sake – and the princess had commented drily to Crawfie that 'Probably we shall read about it in the papers before we really know ourselves.' When the 'frightfully pleased' Elizabeth was able to confide the news to her former nursemaid, the information did indeed make it into the papers. As Crawfie observed, 'no one knows just how it is these things leak out . . . there must be some form of jungle or bush telegraph that operates in the Palace and has not yet been discovered'.[16]

The news was formally announced on 4 June, when the pregnant princess appeared at Epsom Downs racecourse on Derby Day, and as soon as it became public knowledge, she and Philip were inundated with letters offering everything from unsolicited but well-meant advice to almost surreal invocations from the half mad, the desperate and the lonely. One woman wrote, 'My son is in prison. He has been there three years. You who are now so happy in expecting a baby could have him released for me.'[17] While it would have been infra dig for the princess to respond to this and countless other begging letters, she might have responded that her responsibilities, while admittedly numerous, did not include meddling in the criminal justice system.

There was a strange custom relating to royal births that had begun in 1894 and had last been observed in 1926, when Elizabeth was herself born. It was considered obligatory that the Home Secretary of the day – in her case, the thoroughly authoritarian William Joynson-Hicks – should be present to observe the birth of any royal child, something that Lascelles subsequently described as 'out-of-date and ridiculous'. The private secretary considered that in the post-war world, such an invasion of a young mother's privacy was an unnecessary and anachronistic imposition. As he later wrote, 'the Home Office made exhaustive researches and assured me that it had no constitutional significance whatsoever, and was merely a survival of the practice of ministers and courtiers, who would flock to the sick-bed, whenever any member of the Royal Family was ill'.[18] The current Home Secretary, James Chuter Ede, a Unitarian and former local government official, was similarly unimpressed by the tradition, writing in June that 'the custom is only a custom . . . it has no statutory authority behind it and there is no legal requirement for its continuance'.[19]

It is unlikely that Ede relished the prospect of being present at the birth of a strange young woman's first child, nor that he would have enjoyed Prince Philip's attitude towards his presence there. Yet both the king and queen were initially in favour of this particular practice being maintained, partly out of a sense of duty, and partly because the queen feared that the abeyance of the tradition was nothing less than a threat to the dignity of the throne. After all, little connoted regality more clearly than an uncomfortable-looking middle-aged politician watching as the heir to the throne gave birth. Therefore, Lascelles was directed to inform Ede on 21 August that 'It is His Majesty's wish that you, as Home Secretary, should be in attendance when Princess Elizabeth's baby is born.' He may have wished to wash his hands, Pilate-like, at the ridiculousness of it all, but ultimately he knew that it was not his responsibility to attempt to affect change. What he needed instead was a higher authority to intervene.

This duly came, in the unlikely form of Norman Robertson, the Canadian high commissioner. On the course of a routine visit to the palace in early November, Robertson asked after the princess, who was due to give birth later that month. Lascelles alluded - probably without warmth - to the necessity of Ede witnessing the event, and the high commissioner pointed out that should the Home Secretary be present, there was a requirement that the equivalent politicians from the Dominions should also attend. It was an inadvertently hilarious image: a septet of grey-suited, grey-haired men, Disney's Seven Dwarfs raised to bureaucratic respectability, all solemnly observing a young woman's labour pains. Lascelles was therefore able to say to the king, not without wryness, that 'as [you have] no doubt realised, if the old ritual was observed, there would be no less than seven Ministers sitting in the passage'.[20] It was one of the more admirable qualities of George VI that he was a husband and father first, monarch second, and the idea of his daughter being subjected to this indignity was enough to ensure that on 5 November, a statement announced that the 'archaic custom' would no longer be observed.

Yet such moments of protocol came almost as light relief as the king's health continued to decline. Even as he was passed from doctor to doctor for examination, he was required to attend to constitutional matters, issuing letters patent to ensure that the future child would be a prince or princess from birth, rather than the Earl of Merioneth or Lady Mountbatten. Details of her father's condition were kept from the princess as far as possible, so as to avoid any undue anxiety as her confinement approached.

Elizabeth pronounced herself stoic about what was coming, saying to Crawfie that she had complete faith in the doctors and regarded childbirth with a mixture of equanimity and anticipation. 'After all, it is what we are made for', she observed. Finally, just after nine p.m. on 14 November 1948, a baby boy was born, weighing 7 lb 6 oz. Philip, who had been playing squash with his equerry, Mike Parker, to distract himself from his wife's protracted labour - it had begun the previous day - was told the news by Lascelles, and bounded in to see his wife and son with jubilation. He ordered that bottles of champagne be opened to toast the new arrival, and summoned bouquets of carnations and roses for the princess. For a man who often struck those around him as moody or even grumpy, the uncomplicated happiness and bonhomie that he now displayed was a welcome development.

It was a rare moment of unalloyed good tidings, for both the royal family and the nation. When the birth was publicly announced, there was spontaneous cheering from the crowds of thousands of well-wishers gathered outside Buckingham Palace, and renditions of 'For He's a Jolly Good Fellow'. Across the country, bonfires were lit, and congratulatory telegrams and letters arrived in their thousands. Within a couple of days, the boy's name was announced - Charles Philip Arthur George - and Cecil Beaton was summoned to the palace to take official photographs of the proud, if exhausted, mother with her baby. He wrote in his diary that 'Prince Charles, as he is to be named, is an obedient sitter . . . he interrupted a long contented sleep to do my bidding and open his blue eyes to stare long and wonderingly into the camera lens', something that Beaton described, all too accurately, as 'the beginning of a lifetime in the glare of publicity'.[21]

Crawfie, who saw the infant Charles within the first few days, noted his strong resemblance to George V - or perhaps a reflection of the late king's affinity with newborn babies - and spoke approvingly of his 'absurdly mature look . . . he was very healthy and strong, and beautifully made, with a flawless, silky skin'.[22] The queen, relieved and joyous at the safe arrival, mused to Queen Mary that 'one has lived through such a series of crises & shocks & blows these last years, that something as happy & simple & hopeful for the future as a little son is indeed a joy'.[23] As for the princess herself, she was able to write to her aunt, May Elphinstone, of her pleasure in her 'too sweet' boy, and that 'I can still hardly believe that I really have a son of my own - it seems quite incredible - and wonderful!'[24]

Yet for all the excitement and happiness at the birth, there was no concomitant relief for the king. The damage to his leg was sufficiently severe for him to be confined to bed, clamped in a fiendish-looking device known as an occlude that was designed to improve his circulation. Crawfie economically conveyed the shock that those in the royal household felt when they discovered the extent of his indisposition, as well as remarking, indiscreetly, that the queen was 'quite distraught with anxiety'. She continued, '[we] had thought the King looked tired and ill, but had put it down to the excitement of the wedding, and the birth of his first grandchild. So the news of how ill he really was came as an immense shock to all of us. He must have known for some time how ill he was, and as usual he had refused to face it, had carried on till the baby was safely born, and then, probably, had hoped he would somehow manage to get through the Australian tour. But the time came when he had to listen to his doctors, and give in.' As his younger daughter, Margaret, was said to have remarked, 'When Papa decided he could no longer struggle to keep going, he went to sleep for two days.'[25]

Friends offered what support they could. Churchill wrote to the king on 22 November to support the cancellation of the trip, saying, 'I had been concerned to think of the instances of prolonged exertion the tour would have demanded from both Your Majesty and the Queen. They would have "killed you by kindness"! The distances are enormous and everywhere there will have been delighted & loyal crowds. One must not understate the strain of such enjoyable contacts with enthusiastic friends.' He reflected on the national situation, and expressed a hope that they would soon be in partnership once more: 'I trust that the rest & relief will restore your health, and enable you to add long years to your reign. It has been a time of intense stress & trial. It may well be that history will regard it as "our finest hour"! I am proud to have been your First Minister in all these great adventures. I can hope in spite of my age to stand at your Majesty's side once again.'*[26]

Even Edward was shocked out of his usual self-absorption to offer his brother some sympathy. He wrote on 6 December to say, 'What bad luck that your leg has gone back on you and laid you up for a while. I could not be more sorry for you or think of anything more boring for an active man like yourself. However, you are very wise to take your tiresome ailment in hand in good time and give yourself all the requisite rest and treatment.' He expressed his regrets for not having written before - 'I [have been] laid low with

---

* Churchill also wrote a terser and less poetic letter on 2 December, saying, 'I trust & pray Your Majesty's progress is good. I think so much of you sir in these days & of all you have done & have still to do for our country in these dangerous & depressing times.'

a severe gastric attack' - and inadvertently acknowledged his own detachment from events by saying, 'The newspapers report an improvement, so I hope you are not in too much pain and that you will get well much quicker than you expect and be able to spend Christmas at Sandringham.' The man who had once been monarch was now reduced to reading the newspapers for information about his brother's condition.

The letter was typical of the duke. It contained brisk 'David-knows-best' advice ('I was very relieved when you abandoned the Australasian tour . . . it's too far for the King to absent himself with the world in its present explosive condition'), recommended some quack chicanery that bore the imprint of Wallis ('a French professor, Leriche . . . internationally known as the inventor of a special new operation for the relief of circulatory ailments') and, sympathy extended, made a despairing comment on the horrors of the world they inhabited. 'News from all fronts gets worse and worse wherever one looks. Truman's victory was very discouraging, although the leftist trend of the world in mind I personally thought that the Republicans were over optimistic.'[27] What it lacked, as ever, was an iota of real empathy.

The king did not recover his health sufficiently to be able to head to Sandringham for several weeks, and his Christmas broadcast to the nation struck an appropriately rueful tone. Calling the past year 'a memorable one', he played down his illness, describing it merely as one of several 'vivid personal experiences', and saying that 'I have been obliged to submit, for reasons of health, to a spell of temporary inactivity.' Yet he put an optimistic spin on it. 'Even this, like every other cloud, can have a silver lining . . . [and this] is the grateful recollection of the volume of good will and affection that they brought from all over the world to me and mine.'

He acknowledged the inevitable disappointment that the cancellation of the Australian and New Zealand tour had brought - 'by an unkind stroke of fate, it fell to me a month ago to make a decision that caused me much distress' - but he tried to be positive, saying, 'against my own disappointment, and my regret at the disappointment that I knew I was causing others, I can see the wave of sympathy and concern which flowed back to me not only from the Australians and New Zealanders themselves but from friends known and unknown in this old country and in every one of the great brotherhood of nations to which we all belong'.

The broadcast concluded with the king advancing a Christian belief that the adversity he had faced had given him a new lease of life. '[My experiences] have left me with a fuller understanding of the work which I have been called upon to do. They have shown me that kingship is no isolated, impersonal function, no abstract symbol of constitutional theory; they have shown me that it is, rather, one pole of a very real human relationship, depending on ties that are invisible, and unaffected by changes in internal form. These ties may be difficult to explain, but are none the less powerful for good. Our Commonwealth - the British Commonwealth - has been subject to the laws of evolution; we would not have it otherwise. But it is stronger, not weaker, as it fulfils its ancient mission of widening the bounds of freedom wherever our people live, and for myself I am proud to fulfil my own appointed share in that mission.'

The sentiments, presumably written by Lascelles, were heartfelt, but also, in the year that the king's first grandson was born, indicated fresh engagement with the future of the monarchy. A year earlier, on 17 December 1947, Channon had written in his diary that 'I don't think that the royal family is popular; certainly not the King and Queen who are tolerated. Nobody hates them; nobody loves them.' This may have been the usual sniping of a man who was increasingly disappointed with both his country and himself, but Britain was changing. When Hugh Dalton learnt of the arrival of the future king, he wrote in his diary that 'if this boy ever comes to the throne . . . it will be a very different country and Commonwealth he'll rule over'.[28]

With the birth of his grandson, his daughter's pre-eminence as a public figure and his own declining health, George VI was faced with looming obsolescence in his lifetime. He did not deal with it with the calm equanimity that his public appearances might have suggested. He was given to outbreaks of temper - his 'gnashes', as they were known - at anything from the failings of politicians to insufficient deference; he once lost his composure because a man walking past him at Sandringham did not remove his hat in his presence. At his worst, he could be as irritable, petty and demanding as his elder brother, displaying a lack of curiosity in others and the wider world that indicated his family's limited intellectual horizons all too clearly. Channon's sneering opinion that he was 'a dull little man, admired, liked by nobody . . . there is hardly anything to hate'[29] was not uniquely held.

Set against this, his virtues as a husband and father were not simply ephemeral niceties, but tribute to the way in which he had absorbed his parents' teachings of duty and principle and managed to pass them on to his own children with a human face, rather than the unchanging facade of monarchy. And it was the next generation that he now looked to. There had been two spectacular successes for the royal family as an institution in the post-war years - the wedding, and now the birth of Charles - and neither had involved him directly. The duke's biographer, Philip Ziegler, even suggested that around this time, 'in a curious way, he was written off . . . Elizabeth was the future.'[30] As the king confronted his mortality, and the creeping knowledge that he was unlikely to see his grandson grow up, there was one consolation. He had hoped to revitalise the monarchy, but would run out of time before he could do so. It now seemed clear that his successor would have to continue the job for him.

Chapter Twelve

'Untold Injury in Every Quarter'

If 1948 was a year of turbulence and upheaval for the royal family - something the queen described to Churchill as 'almost too vampire . . . [the experiences] have drained away something of the joy of living'[1] - 1949 was one of betrayals. The first was relatively small in scale, if still quietly devastating. Crawfie left the family's service after fifteen unblemished years of faithful and diligent endeavour, during which she had behaved almost like a second parent to both Elizabeth and Margaret, who were deeply fond of her.

When the queen wrote to her on 1 January, acknowledging her imminent departure, she called her a 'true and trustworthy friend'. It was with genuine affection that she acknowledged everything that Crawfie had done for the family. 'I can never tell you how grateful I am for all your devotion & love for Lilibet & Margaret. It was such a <u>great</u> relief to me during the war, to know that you were by their side, through sirens, guns, bombs & pantomimes - keeping everything cool and balanced & good humoured. Thank you with all my heart.'[2]

The queen hoped that Crawfie would find happiness with 'the hub of your universe', Major George Buthlay, whom she had married in September 1947. By Crawfie's subsequent account, she had wished to leave the royal family's service shortly after her marriage, but was prevailed upon to stay, if only by the queen's injunction that 'I do hope you won't think of leaving us just yet . . . it is going to be such a busy time.'[3] She remained in service for a further fifteen months, during which time she was granted Nottingham

Cottage, a grace-and-favour Christopher Wren-designed residence at Kensington Palace,* as well as promised a full-salary pension for life upon retirement and a suitably well-recompensed job for Major Buthlay. At the start of 1949, it would have seemed to any observer that Crawfie was the very model of a former royal employee.

By the end of the year, she was disgraced and cast out of the circle of trust that the royal family had bundled her in, at times suffocatingly so. Her crime was to attempt to capitalise on her experiences and memories in an inoffensive, if ill-considered, fashion, and her punishment was a warning to any other courtier as to what they might expect if they transgressed in a similar fashion. Yet it was as nothing compared to another, potentially greater betrayal, which started as a result of the king's illness. It took its form in shadowy intrigues and half-suggested machinations that would, if they had come to pass, have been nothing less than treacherous. And naturally, it was the man who had caused most harm to his family over the previous decades who was behind it.

Kenneth de Courcy did not hold back when he wrote to the Duchess of Windsor on 13 May, after a period of travelling in Europe. 'There are some things which I want to talk over with you and which I think to be of great importance.' Nor was she kept in suspense for long. 'The issues involved are, to my mind, of first importance in view of the King's illness.' De Courcy stressed that he had previously advised against the duke returning to Britain, due to the 'overwhelming natural advantages' that Edward presented, showing up his brother as the poor royal timber that he was. ('The consequences might have been very embarrassing to both of them.') However, 'an entirely different situation has arisen now'.

With a brutal lack of sentiment, de Courcy outlined the situation as he saw it. 'The King is gravely ill and out of circulation and

---

* It was later occupied by the Duke and Duchess of Sussex, and Prince Harry claimed it was the venue for an angry altercation between him and his brother, Prince William, that ended with him lying on the floor, his necklace ripped, a cracked dog bowl cutting into in his back.

he will not be in circulation again. The Royal Family is grievously reduced in numbers and . . . I am of the opinion that the Dynasty - I prefer to say that rather than the Crown - is facing a time of great crisis, the outcome of which is unforeseeable, but it might be extremely serious.' He suggested that he knew more about the king's health than the monarch himself did, stating that the 'grievous malady' he suffered from was incurable, and that 'barring accidents in other parts of the body the King faces the fearful tragedy of losing first one leg and then the other within two or three years'. Listing the various indignities and illnesses he could expect to face, he concluded that 'in these circumstances therefore it is perfectly clear that the King will be able to do extremely little and moreover that those around him will gain greater and greater power'. Then he produced his most damning provocation. 'I may tell you most confidentially that a Regency has already been discussed and it seems likely enough that presently one will be appointed.'

Although Princess Elizabeth, as de facto next in line to the throne, was already beginning to assume greater responsibilities in preparation for her eventual accession, de Courcy positioned himself as the man in the know. 'I have no doubt from my information that the Mountbattens, thoroughly well informed of the situation, will do everything in their power to increase their influence, first with the public regency, secondly with the future monarch.' He hinted that Prince Philip was likely to be in line for preferment thanks to his Mountbatten connections, but that 'the King has already had occasion to be extremely angry with this young man and unfortunately there is an ever widening public beginning to hear about the consequences for this'. This, in de Courcy's estimation, could lead to little less than the destruction of the monarchy as it stood. 'If this particular person should in consequence of what is happening incline more and more to seek help and succour from Mountbatten, it is perfectly easy to imagine how things will work out.'

The apocalyptic situation thus outlined, de Courcy could make only one suggestion: send for the Duke of Windsor, albeit in an 'unofficial and most discreet' capacity, and allow him to function as regent. 'If the Duke were prepared to be advised and to devote his great abilities and his utmost energies to the task, his influence could be decisive at a most critical time in English history, thus making that of the Mountbattens of relatively little importance . . . I am not suggesting that the Duke's influence should be with the Royal Family but with the people.' This was not so very far from the suggestion, made around the time of the abdication crisis, that the then king should be head of an unelected, unaccountable political organisation known as 'the King's Party', with Churchill as prime minister and Lord Beaverbrook as the shadowy *éminence grise* behind the monarch.

In both cases, a failing of Edward's - a willingness to ignore all norms of acceptable behaviour - could now be regarded as a virtue. As de Courcy, channelling Machiavelli, put it, 'in the times of great kingship Princes who were determined to bend the wills of men and nations to their policies and leadership did not care in the slightest degree for little things like rank and protocol; what they cared for was the winning of power and the service of the nation, and all the ceremonial things followed naturally'. He suggested that rather than attempting to regain the throne by conventional means, the duke might devote himself to something even more important, namely 'in laying entirely fresh foundation stones in the place of those which are now endangered, upon which the Monarchy of the latter part of the 20th and the whole of the 21st century might be built'. Maintaining that Edward should concentrate on avoiding publicity - 'a rigid refusal to be seen anywhere which might in the faintest degree give enemies the chance of putting out a play-boy propaganda' - de Courcy concluded his heartfelt, if treacherous, counsel by suggesting, 'I venture to say that if this advice were followed the results would be remarkable.'[4]

No reply exists from either the duchess or the duke to de Courcy's extraordinary letter. Under normal circumstances, discretion or simple common sense would have entailed a rebuttal of the measures suggested, but if a response was written, it has

Above The landslide election of Labour leader Clement Attlee after the rigours of World War II led to the formation of the welfare state, but the relationship between the new prime minister and George VI and his courtiers was not always harmonious.

Left Princess Elizabeth and Lieutenant Philip Mountbatten, 1947. The relationship between Elizabeth and Philip was one of the worst-guarded secrets in the royal family, despite regular denials put out about their engagement, until its formal announcement on 9 July 1947.

Left Kenneth de Courcy, 1947. The Duke and Duchess of Windsor's friend believed that Edward should return to Britain and perform a regency, and stated this near-treacherous aim in candid letters to the Duke.

Below Fuel crisis, 1947. At the beginning of 1947, Britain was plunged into the dual crisis of war-torn austerity and a freezing winter, which necessitated everything from 'no power' periods in the mornings and afternoons to a virtual state of national emergency.

Above The royal tour to South Africa, 1947. A diplomatically important tour by the royal family to South Africa in early 1947 led to the beginning of the final decline of George VI's health, although his daughter's famous broadcast on her twenty-first birthday established her unparalleled popularity.

Right George VI and Alan Lascelles, 1947. The king's indefatigable private secretary, Sir Alan 'Tommy' Lascelles, was a stickler for propriety and decorum at all times, but his letters and diaries reveal his frustrations with those he had to deal with - most notably, the Duke of Windsor.

Left Princess Elizabeth and Prince Philip's wedding, 1947. The wedding of Elizabeth and Philip on 20 November 1947 was one of the few pieces of unalloyed good news that Britain had had since VE Day in 1945.

Below left A crowd waiting for the wedding day, 1947. The youth and glamour that both Elizabeth and Philip offered ensured that their union was hugely popular with virtually all the country, and 200 million people worldwide listened to its broadcast on BBC Radio.

Below King George VI and Queen Elizabeth, 1948. This picture, taken on the royal couple's twenty-fifth wedding anniversary, demonstrates the great affection that the two held each other in, which sustained the ailing monarch until the end of his life.

Winston Churchill and Alan Lascelles, 1949. When the former prime minister was swept from office in 1945, he believed his political career to be over, only to return to power in 1951.

Princess Elizabeth and Churchill, 1950. The relationship between Elizabeth and Churchill, who became her first prime minister, was a warm and affectionate one, even if Churchill's first response after her father died was to say 'She is only a child.'

Left Duke and Duchess of Windsor, 1951. Edward and Wallis's bond was a close one, epitomised by their joint nickname of 'W.E'. Yet the post-war years saw them shuttling between Britain, France and the United States in a stateless and rootless existence.

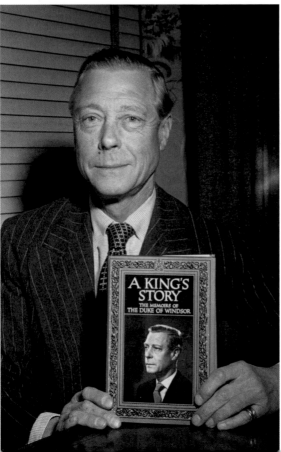

Below left The Duke of Windsor, 1951. The former Edward VIII, incensed by what he saw as poor treatment of him and his wife Wallis, eventually took revenge by writing a bestselling memoir of his early life, *A King's Story*.

Opposite page, left Marion 'Crawfie' Crawford and George Buthlay, 1952. Marion Crawford was a much-loved governess to Princess Elizabeth and Princess Margaret, until, egged on by her husband George Buthlay, she wrote a revealing book about her time with the royals and was subsequently ostracised.

Opposite page, right Louis Mountbatten and Prince Philip, 1952. Philip's charismatic uncle, Louis 'Dickie' Mountbatten, was as responsible as anyone for matchmaking the union between his nephew and Elizabeth – to Philip's occasional chagrin.

Opposite page, below George VI, Queen Elizabeth and Princess Margaret, 1952. Princess Elizabeth headed off on a royal tour of the Commonwealth on 31 January 1952 by air, but her trip was curtailed by her father's death a few days later.

Left George VI's farewell, 1952. The king's death was sudden but not wholly unexpected, and it allowed Churchill, in a moving eulogy, to say that 'During these last months the King walked with death as if death were a companion, an acquaintance whom he recognized and did not fear.'

Below George VI's funeral, 1952. The king's death on 6 February 1952 from a coronary thrombosis, at the age of fifty-six, threw the country into shock and mourning, and led to the return of the Duke of Windsor in an attempt to see what he could salvage from the situation.

Right Queen Elizabeth, 1953. When Elizabeth had her coronation, at the age of twenty-seven, on 2 June 1953, the appallingly unseasonal weather could not dampen the spirits of the millions who lined the streets of London to see her be crowned queen.

vanished. Certainly, the relationship between de Courcy and the couple was in no sense tarnished by his suggestion that Edward should effectively all but seize the throne and capitalise on his brother's indisposition by taking on the office of regent. Not only was de Courcy writing to the duke on 2 June to criticise Churchill ('his interventions in home politics are uniformly disastrous . . . if he would only stop making speeches we might possibly win the next election'), but the continuing friendship between them was shown by his subsequent letter cheerily suggesting potential dates to meet for dinner at the Ritz in Paris later in the year. If the duke wished to back away from such a scheme, he did not try very hard.

Nor, in fairness, did he attempt to return to Britain permanently. The beginning of 1949 saw him sequestered in France, with the reluctant company of Murphy, in the ongoing attempt to write his memoir. Unsurprisingly, the relationship between subject and ghostwriter had deteriorated sufficiently by this point for a miserable Murphy to write candidly to Monckton on 23 April that 'my own spirits stand sorely in need of replenishment'. Pithily, he explained the current difficulties he faced. He had been summoned back to New York and to *Life* magazine, who were worried at the absence of progress; as he put it, 'Operation Belvedere is at a point of special crisis.' There had been some talk about abandoning the project, but he now wrote to the lawyer that 'We have decided to make one more try . . . if this last try is to succeed, I shall greatly need your help . . . It is now all too clear, painfully clear, that our famous friend must continue to count upon you.'[5]

Murphy's central problem was that in the absence of the duke being able to remember certain salient details, he was having to piece together the events of his past with help from former courtiers, politicians and the *haut ton*. Some of these people were less than thrilled by the prospect. Godfrey Thomas wrote to Monckton on 19 June to say, plaintively, that 'Of course I'll do what I can to help about the earlier part of HRH's life . . . as it happens, I'm going over to Paris to see him this next week-end . . . He rang me up this morning & sounded full of life and good spirits.' With an Eeyorish touch of pessimism, he grumbled, '[he is] likely, I should say, to see "us both" out'.*[6]

Before long, it was clear that there were intrinsic difficulties in the creation of the book. Although at this point the royal family were cooperating tacitly - Lascelles received Murphy on a visit to Britain in the early summer of 1949 - it was also clear that there was the potential for great embarrassment in the duke's treatment of the abdication crisis. Monckton wrote to Lascelles on 8 July, fearing the worst. 'I am particularly anxious to do all I can in the general interest but could do with some wise and helpful advice . . . I shall not have an easy time for what I have written to the proposed author will undoubtedly cause offence.'[7] A letter to Murphy written on the same day suggested the various difficulties the account could lead to: 'errors of fact which other people with Notes and Memoirs will rush to correct if they feel hostile in any case . . . breaking the rules of constitutional propriety . . . libel, particularly if the facts are not correct'.[8] He concluded to Lascelles, with the put-upon attitude that he had displayed ever since the abdication crisis, 'If I go too far, I shall lose what chance I have of exercising the pruning fork, which becomes more and more necessary at every stage.'[9]

Unsurprisingly, the effort and anguish involved with these efforts caused Monckton to become ill, and he had to have an eye operation in August. The Duke of Windsor expressed rote commiserations in a letter of 13 August, in which he asked for Monckton's continued fact-checking assistance, on the grounds that 'I know from my own experience how stale one's memory gets after a lapse of thirteen years, but where I may have forgotten you will remember, and vice versa.' The kinds of questions he had in mind would have baffled even the most sage counsellor - 'When did I actually decide to abdicate?'[10] - and Monckton replied with his usual patience, while convalescing at the stately home of Madresfield.

---

* He was to be proved correct. Thomas died in 1968, Monckton in 1965, and the duke continued until 1972.

'You were always determined to abdicate if that was the only way in which you could marry the Duchess . . . I was always desperate lest you should fall between two stools, i.e. abdicate and then find that the Duchess was not free.'[11]

He knew that the book's very creation was riddled with difficulty. A despairing letter from Murphy of 4 August had noted that 'the written record is scanty in the extreme, and our friend's memory, much as he prides himself on it, is weak and scattered'. He even hinted that the memoir might not come to pass. 'You will be interested to hear that for the moment the book has been completely put aside. We are now concentrating on the articles and toward that end I have now begun to cut the abdication chapters . . . With the narrowed focus the margin of error will tend to diminish.'[12] The implication was clear: if everyone cooperates in the appropriate fashion, the chances of a scandalous and embarrassing memoir ever making it into the public domain were drastically reduced. Murphy no longer hid his irritation with his collaborator, observing on 1 September that 'I have delayed writing until the Duke of Windsor's plans become clearer – a not always successful process', and bemoaning the 'agonising slow rate' at which work was being done, as well as sneering of the duke, 'it is his habit not to commit himself'.[13]

At last, in October 1949, some chapters were ready, and were sent to Monckton for his professional opinion. After he passed them over to Allen, the solicitor did not hide his horror at both their content and their style. Revealing his unfamiliarity with the ghostwriting process, he gasped, 'I do not think that HRH himself could possibly be the author of these chapters . . . I feel that they are so bad that I am impelled to suggest to you that it may be our duty to advise against publication, because if they appear in their present form, they will be condemned and must do him untold injury in every quarter.' Allen's approach to journalistic and publishing matters was commendably right-minded, if somewhat naïve in its view of the duke's inclinations. 'I should have thought the wiser course would be to rewrite the articles on a basis of truth

and generous fairness to everybody, in a manner which would stir
world sentiment in his favour, and place him on a new pedestal
for all time.' He concluded, 'I believe that the task would be by no
means impossible in the right hands.'*[14]

Allen, ever the punctilious lawyer, sent Monckton a series of
notes about the chapters. He was especially exercised about what
he felt amounted to an ad hominem attack on the former prime
minister, Stanley Baldwin† ('legally, the criticism of S. B. might
be said to go beyond fair comment and to constitute . . . an attack
upon him personally, imputing to him base and sinister motives'),
and stated that 'the propriety of a member of the Royal Family, and
former King, entering upon political controversy and speculation
might be criticised'.[15]

Monckton, when he read the material the duke and Murphy
had produced, was no more impressed. In his own comments, he
wrote, 'there is much to eliminate that is not worthy of him . . .
all this will seem very negative criticism but I am so sure that the
pruning fork will be needed and will leave a better result in what is
left . . . that I must make these suggestions'. He wondered out loud
whether Murphy might be replaced by 'a sympathetic, experienced
and brilliant friend and writer'[16] such as Duff Cooper, and wrote
despairingly about some of the basic errors of comprehension,
which included describing Attlee, then the Labour prime minister,
as a member of the Liberal Party. On 4 October, he washed his
hands of involvement with the project. 'I can take no responsibility
for the book, for its presentation of the Duke's case, or for the accuracy of its statements of fact . . . It is of vital importance that this
should be made plain, because others who played principal parts
at the time are likely to rush into print and also to write to me for
confirmation of their memory, and I want to be able to decline to
enter into any controversy at all.'[17]

---

* One of the reasons for Allen's disenchantment was, as he sighed in the
postscript, 'I see my name is wrongly spelt throughout, which shows a new
hand.'

† Helpfully, for the purposes of libel, Baldwin had died in 1947.

Monckton had done what he could. In a subsidiary note, he listed what he had achieved in his edits. 'I have succeeded in securing the deletion of the attack on Hardinge* and practically all criticism of the Archbishop.† There is and could be nothing critical of the Royal Family or any member of it. Any minor observations in relation to any of them to which objection might be taken I have already been able to delete or hope to do so.' Yet for all his skill, tact and diplomacy, he was unable to stand against the duke's increasingly obstinate desire to see the project come to fruition. Edward may not have decided to take de Courcy's advice, and prepare himself for a potential regency, not least because another matter of a deeply personal nature continued to occupy him. But if he wanted to take his revenge on those who had wronged him, the best thing he could do would be to publish and be damned.

This was, separately, the same conclusion that Marion Crawford also came to. Yet her rationale was rather different to the duke's. Crawfie had no desire for revenge on a family who had been good to her and had treated her as a trusted intimate for many years. She had observed the happy marriage of the king and queen, their devotion to their daughters, and the impressive development of Princess Elizabeth into a young woman who dealt with unlooked-for responsibility with grace and charm. (The more wilful and wayward Princess Margaret was another matter.) With her own union with Major Buthlay, she might have hoped for a similar degree of personal contentment, and the ability to enjoy a long, comfortable and fruitful period of retirement, with no financial imperative to work and the chance to dedicate herself to good causes, if she so wished. She would have joined the ranks of many of the ladies-in-waiting and other trusted household servants who performed their duties cheerfully, discreetly and without ever seeking to betray the

---

* Sir Alec Hardinge, the king's private secretary at the time of the abdication crisis.

† The Archbishop of Canterbury, Cosmo Lang; a noted opponent of Edward VIII.

omertà they had embraced by being a member of the royal family.

Unfortunately, Major Buthlay was not one of life's gentlemen. He was instead a semi-disgraced military man who would have probably been played by Terry-Thomas had a film been made of his life. A divorcé fifteen years Crawfie's senior, he had been involved during the war with a company known as UNNRA (United Nations Relief and Rehabilitation Administration), which might have had noble intentions but was stymied by some of its senior members involving themselves in an Albanian smuggling ring. When Buthlay's attachment there came to an end, he secured himself a minor position with the Bank of Scotland, courtesy of Ulick Alexander, the Keeper of the Privy Purse and, far from co-incidentally, a director of the Scottish Union Insurance Company. This gave him a facade of respectability, but none of the financial security he desired. Therefore, his intentions went the same way as many weak men through the ages: exploiting his wife's good nature to further himself.

Buthlay saw Crawfie's attachment to 'the Firm' as a means of parlaying himself into positions of power and influence. Once she had left their employment, he proceeded to nitpick at the honours and gifts she had received, criticising everything from the size of their grace-and-favour home to the CVO (Commander of the Royal Victorian Order) she was given upon retirement for 'personal services'; he persuaded her that she should have been given a damehood instead, and that she had been cheated out of her rightful reward. Like a serpent dripping poison into her ear, he gradually convinced her that she had been hard done by, and that her long years of service had been barely noticed, let alone rewarded. Therefore, he argued, it was almost her responsibility to herself to write down her story about her involvement with the royal family. It wouldn't hurt anyone; it would just be a fair way of putting her story across, and would have the happy by-product of providing for them financially as well.

Crawfie moved swiftly. By April 1949, she had obtained a literary agent, and had asked Queen Elizabeth for permission to write a magazine story about her time with the princesses. The queen, however, was unhappy about the idea, and wrote to her on 4 April to politely dissuade her from continuing with the project. She stated, 'I do feel, most definitely, that you should not write and sign articles about the children, as people in positions of confidence with us must be utterly oyster, and if you, the moment you finished teaching Margaret, started writing about her and Lilibet, well, we should never feel confidence in anyone again.' The letter combined the usual regal flattery ('you have been so wonderfully discreet all the years you were with us') with straightforward threat: 'You would lose all your friends, because such a thing has never been done or even contemplated among the people who serve us so loyally.'

She ended with an observation about the temptations Crawfie would be faced with, and how to deal with them. 'Having been with us in our family life for so long, you must be prepared to be attacked by journalists to give away private and confidential things, and I know that your good sense and loyal affection will guide you well. I do feel most strongly that you must resist the allure of American money & persistent editors and say No No No to offers of dollars for articles about something as private and precious as our family.'[18] It was reasonably meant and sensible counsel and Crawfie would have been well advised to take it. After all, whatever she earned from her indiscretion would have to be set against the shame of becoming a pariah.

It was unfortunate, then, that Bruce and Beatrice Blackmar Gould, the co-editors of *Ladies' Home Journal*, were so fixated on Crawfie's revelations. They visited London in May and assiduously pursued her, eventually coercing her into signing a contract on 25 May that agreed she would produce a manuscript of around forty thousand words. Royal permission to publish letters from the queen, the princesses and others was desirable but not essential, and she was promised the aid of a ghostwriter, Dorothy Black, who the Goulds suggested would be 'immensely helpful in making your story a story that will enlist the sympathy of the Queen as well as our readers' - which, they noted, was 'not an easy thing to accomplish'. A more cautious woman might have read over her letter from the queen, with its injunction that she should be 'utterly oyster', but Crawfie, leant on by the Goulds and her husband - who dismissed her literary agent, on the grounds that he could do the job better - got to work.

She was pleased with what she and Black produced, believing that it trod a fine line between discretion and retaining the interest of the reader, desperate for titbits of royal gossip. She wrote* to Bruce Gould on 19 September that 'my story will bring America & Britain closer together in real friendship & understanding. I feel that our Foreign Office will welcome the chance. Like you, we pray all will go well & that the Queen will not only agree but also write a preface in her own handwriting.'[19]

Her hopes were, inevitably, dashed. The queen read the manuscript in October and wrote to her friend Lady Astor to say, 'we have worried greatly over this matter, and can only think that our late & completely trusted governess has gone off her head, because she promised in writing that she would not publish any story about our daughters, and this development has made us very sad'. Repeating the royal family's commitment to secrecy - 'we have to trust our people completely, and such a thing has never happened before & is a bad example to others' - she expressed a hope that the Goulds might remove 'some of the inaccurate or dangerous bits, which would indeed be a *great* relief'.[20]

The tactical error the royal family then made was to ask for thirteen points of fact to be addressed in the text: these were mainly the removal of trivial details, such as Queen Mary being asked to assist with the education of the princesses, and the king, queen and Princess Elizabeth watching an air raid from the Brunswick Tower in Windsor Castle and having to be asked to stop doing so. Unfortunately, both the Goulds and Crawfie took the removal of

---

* There is some suggestion that several of her letters from this period were either dictated or written by Buthlay.

these anecdotes to mean that the queen and others were offering consent to publication, which they certainly were not. As Dermot Murrah wrote to Bruce Gould, 'the Queen has dug her toes in firmly and is not going to budge on the principle that all former royal servants are forbidden to write under their own names about the royal family', which, inevitably, meant that, as Murrah put it, 'Mrs Buthlay has blotted her copybook for good and all.'[21]

Up to this point, Crawfie had believed, apparently sincerely, that she was acting with at least tacit approval from the queen. When she realised that she was likely to be ostracised by her former friends, and that her grace-and-favour house and pension might be withdrawn, her previously amicable disposition shaded over into anger. She, or rather Buthlay, announced her intention to Gould on 25 November of monetising her treachery, saying, 'I would be wise to make as much as I can while the going is good as a) I shall certainly require every penny I can earn if the Queen's displeasure is brought to bear against me, and b) if events cause Her Majesty to smile upon me, whatever I do to make *The Little Princesses* more popular, will only add to my favour in the Queen's eyes.'[22] In the latter point, at least, she was either naïve or delusional. Her husband's fear that publication was going to lead to a cessation of expected income led him to write – and Crawfie to sign – a letter on 26 December stating, 'I have no fear of what might be called "consequences" because I have adhered to the terms of my understanding with the Queen, and if she decides to be unfriendly, or worse, she will be the loser. If any action on Her Majesty's part is brought to bear on me to my detriment, I shall not hesitate to expose it in the Press if necessary, and if an attempt should be made to eject me from this house and/or deprive me of my pension, I shall fight in Court and have the facts made public if I am driven to do so.'

The aggression and bravado could only barely conceal the fear both Buthlay and Crawfie now felt, and their concession that 'the Queen will merely feel she should show a certain amount of disapproval'[23] indicated their hope that the publication of *The Little Princesses* would be greeted with temporary *froideur* and then business as usual would resume. They were well recompensed for the book, to the tune of $80,000, and unsurprisingly, it was a bestseller in both Britain and the United States, with millions of copies of the *Ladies' Home Journal,* which had excerpted *The Little Princesses,* sold; the book itself was the highest-selling title in the United States in 1950.

Not all the public were delighted by its existence. On 30 December, a Vera M. Brunt wrote to Lascelles to say, 'Can nothing be done to suppress Miss Marion Crawford, the *Evening Standard* and *The Ladies Home Journal of Philadelphia?* That anyone who has been trusted as a Royal Governess for 17 years can so demean herself, and cheapen all that she should protect, has been a great shock to one of His Majesty's most loyal servants.'[24] Lascelles, who was privately as horrified and disgusted as his employers by what became known as 'doing a Crawfie',* responded with a sigh. 'The Private secretary regrets that it is not possible to take any steps such as Miss Brunt proposes, and can only suggest that Miss Brunt, if she wishes to pursue the matter, should address herself to the authoress of the book in question.'[25]

Crawfie's exclusion from the royal family's wider circle was not immediate. She received a Christmas card from Princess Elizabeth at the end of 1949, was provided with central heating for her home by the royal household, and was invited to the royal garden party in the summer of 1950. Although she never heard from Queen Elizabeth directly again, it was not until the autumn of the following year that she appreciated the extent to which she and her husband 'were shunned by colleagues from top to bottom'.[26] Realising that she was never going to be welcomed back into the fold, she devoted herself to more of the same bland and often factually inaccurate writing, which led to a libel suit from the Duke of Windsor, offended by the description of his wife in the serialised version

---

* He wrote to Monckton on 10 May 1950 to say, of the articles, 'I have always felt that any outward interference would be a grave error of policy, though I believe it would be legally possible to restrain the publication of certain letters. But anything that could be represented - as it ultimately would be in certain newspapers - as "Palace persecution" would be unwise.'

of *The Little Princesses*; he especially disliked Crawfie's description of how Wallis 'appeared to be entirely at her ease, but rather too much so . . . she had a distinctly proprietary way of speaking to the new King'.* The offending passages were subsequently withdrawn, but it was yet another black mark against her previously sinless name.

The end of her public career came swiftly and embarrassingly. She had become a regular journalist for *Woman's Own* and was commissioned to write a piece on Trooping the Colour and Royal Ascot for the magazine in June 1955. She produced the usual anodyne gush - 'the flashing of the swords in the sunlight' and suchlike - but was undone by the fact that she wrote her copy long in advance, which was then exposed by the events being cancelled because of a rail strike. There had been widespread suspicion that much of *The Little Princesses* was exaggerated or fictionalised - an accurate assumption, given that the Goulds had rewritten it to make it more interesting, accuracy be damned - and this seemed to confirm it.

Crawfie was finished as a writer, and faced public mockery, a state of affairs the royal family did nothing to ameliorate. When the queen had remarked that the inevitable consequence of her publishing her book would be that 'You would lose all your friends', she was not exaggerating. Facing life as an unpopular outcast, Crawfie removed herself from London society, and she and Buthlay retired to Aberdeen, leaving their grace-and-favour home behind.

They remained an unlikely couple, unable to shake off the taint of notoriety; her doctor described the pair as 'very, very presbyterian, [she] sitting with a blank face as her husband cracked barrack-room jokes'.[27] Buthlay died in 1977, and Crawfie had a miserable widowhood, apparently beset by guilt over her actions. Before her eventual death in 1988, she had made at least one unsuccessful suicide attempt; the emergency services who saved her life found a note that said, 'The world has passed me by and I cannot bear

* The final book merely says 'she was a smart, attractive woman, with that immediate friendliness American women have.'

those I love to pass me by on the road.' Although Balmoral was less than fifty miles away, she would never be visited by any of its residents again.

Both Crawfie and the duke had betrayed the royal family. The difference between the two of them was that as an employee – even, whisper it, a servant – she was ultimately dispensable, for all the queen's talk of affection and loyalty. The duke, despite his far greater provocations, could not be cast out into outer darkness, much as his family might have wished for it. But as his brother's health continued to hang in abeyance, he decided to return to a long-fought battle, and hoped that this time his wishes would finally prevail.

Chapter Thirteen

'In My Faith and Loyalty I Never More Will Falter'

When Queen Elizabeth wrote to D'Arcy Osborne on 5 March 1949, it was with apologies for tardiness. She, at least, had good reason for it. 'The last year has been rather like the war in a minor degree! Daughters getting engaged, and daughters marrying, and daughters having babies, & the King getting ill, & preparing for a tour of Australia & New Zealand, & then having to put it off - all these things are very filling to one's life.' She indicated her great love for the infant Charles - 'very delicious, and [he] makes for a very nice soft innocent topic of conversation in a rather horrid, unkind world!' - and suggested that her husband was, at last, on the mend. 'The King is really getting on very well, though it will be fairly slow progress, and one good thing is that he is having the first rest since 1936.' Signing herself 'your sincere but totteringly aged friend',[1] the queen tacitly acknowledged that it was not just George who was feeling less than regal, as the most eventful of decades drew unceremoniously to its close.

Her allusion to the monarch's health was not entirely candid. He had rallied very slightly at the beginning of 1949, and had been able to visit Sandringham to shoot, but he was now, reluctantly, coming to terms with the knowledge that he would be an invalid for the rest of his life. Lascelles commented to Lord Hardinge that 'the [King] continues to please his doctors, but he won't be out of the medical woods for many weeks yet'.[2] Even if Harold Nicolson, who was engaged in writing a life of George V, heard his son

described as being 'as sweet and patient as can be'³ - a far cry from
the often impatient and splenetic man he had been over the previous years* - it was still both a personal and a national humiliation
for the king to be bedbound and immobile.

His mood was not helped by his being told by Professor Learmouth that he would require a right lumbar sympathectomy operation: a complex procedure that was intended to restore blood
supply to his leg by cutting a nerve at the base of the spine, and
therefore give him a degree of movement again. Get it wrong, and
the risks could be paralysis, or death. The king was irritated by
this, believing that it suggested the previous treatment had been a
waste of time, but Learmouth assured him that the months of tedious bed rest had been necessary for him to gather his strength for
the operation. He was more candid with a courtier who earnestly
asked him how the monarch could become robust enough for such
an operation. 'With iron pills from Boots'⁴ was Learmouth's prag-
matic response.

On 12 March, after a bespoke operating theatre was constructed
in the Buhl Room of Buckingham Palace, the procedure took place.
The king had been forbidden cigarettes to keep him as healthy as
possible, but even as he blithely announced his lack of concern as
the anaesthetic took hold, it was yet another reminder that he was
all too mortal. The monarch's optimism was rewarded: the operation was a success, and his leg was saved, dispelling fears - or, in
some treacherous quarters, hopes - that he would be perpetually
disabled.

Nonetheless, he was instructed to take the next months as
quietly as he could, avoiding both mental and physical stress and
instead concentrating on domestic matters. Unfortunately for his
equilibrium, he had a telephone call with the Duke of Windsor,
who wrote to their mother to say, 'it was a good conversation and

---

* In his biography of the queen mother, Hugo Vickers writes sorrowfully
of George VI that 'he had been known to kick a Corgi across the room at
Windsor'. Those of us who have had the misfortune to come into contact with
the yapping terrors might feel some sympathy with him.

he made light of having to submit to Professor Learmouth's knife on Saturday', but pronounced the situation 'very disappointing', and 'tough luck on Bertie'.[5] The queen, meanwhile, wrote to Princess Margaret on 8 May to say, 'Papa is down at Royal Lodge this week, & I think that he is <u>really</u> better. He is taking an interest in his rhododendrons, & making plans for more planting, & altogether beginning to perk up.' It was with determined optimism that she confided in her daughter that 'if he can go on as he is doing, & not get exhausted in London, he will soon be back to his old form'.[6]

On 21 March, Nicolson had an interview with Queen Mary, ostensibly to discuss the life of George V for his biography, but he soon found that she was more interested in talking about her ailing son. She hinted that his decline was the result of his elder brother's behaviour: 'he was devoted to his brother, and the whole abdication crisis made him miserable. He sobbed on my shoulder for a whole hour . . . but he has made good. Even his stammer has been corrected.' Maternal feelings overcame regal reserve, as, 'in such a sad voice', Queen Mary said, 'and now he is so ill, poor boy, so ill'.[7]

At first, the indications were that Learmouth had performed a kind of miracle. By 17 June, the king was sufficiently recovered to be able to dance at a ball at Ascot, albeit with discreet breaks during which his leg was placed in a foot rest,* and in July, he performed investiture ceremonies, wearing black suede shoes; a necessary contrast to the formality of the evening dress he wore for the events. His recovery seemed a blessing, and an enduring one. On 21 July, the queen could write, with genuine rather than forced confidence, to Eleanor Roosevelt, responding to her enquiries about her husband's health, that 'I am glad to be able to tell you that [the king] is <u>really</u> better, and with care should be quite well in a year or so. It is always a slow business with a leg, and the great

---

* Channon described the monarch as 'bronzed' and the queen as 'unfortunately so fat', but was pleased that both were 'very gracious and both called me "Chips"'. He later called the king 'rather red in the face' and possessed of 'prominent teeth', indicating that his characteristically waspish nature had not been tamed by these pleasantries.

thing is not to get overtired during convalescence.' Acknowledging the problems with this forced inertia - 'you can imagine how difficult this is to achieve with the world in its present state, & worries & troubles piling up' - she nevertheless stated, 'he is making such good progress, & for that I am profoundly grateful'.[8]

While the king rested and rallied, his elder daughter and her husband, unencumbered by the responsibilities of looking after their infant son, began to establish themselves as society figures. They associated with the leading actors and comedians of the day, including Danny Kaye, Laurence Olivier and his wife Vivien Leigh, and generally provided a youth and glamour that the princess's parents were no longer able to offer. Channon, who remained besotted by Philip, wrote on 17 June in his diary, with an atypical touch of sentiment, that 'the two Edinburghs made a somewhat late appearance [at a ball] and they looked superb. They were like characters in a fairy tale.'[9] A fortnight before, he had been wildly - perhaps characteristically - inaccurate. 'Princess Elizabeth's pregnancy is becoming more obvious but nobody yet knows officially* . . . I am told . . . that the Windsors are getting on very badly; but I don't believe it.'[10]

In early July 1949, the family moved into Clarence House in St James's. The building had been designed by John Nash in the mid 1820s for the former Duke of Clarence - and subsequent William IV - and was once regarded as one of London's finest private houses. However, years of neglect and the bed-blocking antics of the Duke of Connaught, the last surviving son of Queen Victoria, had turned it into an unsanitary wreck; it had been bombed in the war and was in desperate need of refurbishment to make it habitable, let alone luxurious.

Philip, who had not had a permanent home of his own in decades, undertook the renovation with typical vigour. He was helped by a grant of £50,000 - around £2.2 million in today's money - that the family had been given by Parliament to make the accommodation

---

* She was not pregnant and would not become so until much later that year.

acceptable for the future queen, which did not include allowances for some of the extravagant gadgetry and luxuries that the Duke of Edinburgh desired. These included everything from a basement private cinema to an automated closet that would spit out a suit of its wearer's choice at the touch of an electronic button; sophistication that was only rivalled by that most modernistic of inventions, the electric trouser press. The total cost, unsurprisingly, came in at £28,000 over budget, despite countless gifts provided from well-wishers. It became almost a badge of honour for Commonwealth countries to provide samples of everything from timber to indigenous art, leading to the logistical nightmare of where to place often incompatible or unwanted products so as not to cause offence to their eager donors.

Philip and Elizabeth had what most would recognise as a thoroughly modern marriage.* Although each retained their own bedroom, kept apart by a dressing room, valets and other members of staff were somewhat abashed to see the two of them together in bed on more than one occasion, and James MacDonald, Philip's valet, reported that the Duke of Edinburgh was blithely naked in his wife's presence. They had separate bathrooms - Philip's, naturally enough, was painted blue and decorated with pictures of the ships he had served on - and at a time when virtually no home in the country had a television, Clarence House could boast several, including one installed in the servants' hall: a wedding gift from Uncle Dickie.

By now, those who were living in close quarters with the couple could observe their characters. The nursery footman, John Gibson, who was responsible for the gleaming maintenance of Prince Charles's pram, described them as 'just ordinary people . . . a lot less formal than some people I came across'.[11] Philip's often brusque and straightforward manner did not obscure a genuine

---

* Though I would hesitate to go as far as Lord Longford, who informed Elizabeth and Philip's biographer, Gyles Brandreth, that 'The Queen enjoys sex, as I do. People who ride tend to. It's very healthy.'

interest in and, when needed, compassion for those who were paid to look after him. He continued his work at the Admiralty, which bored him, and threw himself into other activities to compensate. As Mike Parker said to Brandreth, 'He crackled with energy. He made things happen. He made things jump . . . He wanted to make a difference and, if necessary, he was ready to make a noise.'[12]

His wife, meanwhile, was not one of life's natural noisemakers, being given to a public reserve that some could take for shyness, or simply a desire not to overshadow her husband. When it was announced in October 1949 that the duke was to be posted to Malta as first lieutenant and second in command of HMS *Chequers*, there was no hesitation on either Elizabeth or Philip's part that she should accompany him. As Parker informed her biographer, Ben Pimlott, 'this was a fabulous period when it was thought a good idea for her to become a naval officer's wife'.[13] Perhaps surprisingly, the ultimate approval came from the king himself. Two years earlier, he had been overcome by emotion at seeing his daughter marry, but now he was sanguine about the prospect of her leaving the country with her family. After all, he had other things on his mind.

Philip left for Malta on 16 October, delighted to return to naval life proper, and Elizabeth was due to follow on 20 November. Their son would, as was customary, be left behind in Britain, to be cared for by nannies. In the intervening month, however, she became embroiled in controversy for the first time in her life. On 18 October, she addressed a Mothers' Union rally at Central Hall in London. Her theme was a deeply conservative one - the evils of divorce - and it was to tumultuous applause that she denounced 'the current age of growing self-indulgence, of hardening materialism [and] of falling moral standards', and declared that 'we can have no doubt that divorce and separation are responsible for some of the darkest evils in our society today'.[14]

She was applauded warmly, with the assembled audience delighted at the strong moral line she took - in a speech presumably written by her private secretary, Jock Colville - but others were less enamoured by an attitude that might have struck the more progressive as Victorian. The 1923 Matrimonial Causes Act had given women more rights in divorce than before, but it was still a complicated and humiliatingly public business to obtain a legal separation from one's spouse. The Marriage Law Reform Committee's comment that 'the harm to children can be greater in a home where both parents are at loggerheads than if divorce ensues' might strike contemporary readers as nothing more than common sense, but it was the royal imprimatur that had been given to the subject that seemed both unnecessary and almost insulting.

It may have been the case that, as one courtier put it, 'King George and Queen Elizabeth were completely satisfied that their daughter had been right, for their views on marriage and family life were the same',[15] but it is unlikely that her husband would have shared her scripted opinions. Not only had his own parents separated, but his liberal political outlook and generally progressive, even libertarian, stances were decidedly different to the rule-bound ones held by the family - and institution - he had married into. Should his personal views collide with shibboleths that were held virtually sacred, the results could only be dramatic.

The most recent member of the royal family to fall foul of divorce laws, meanwhile, paid a brief visit to the country in April 1949, shortly after his brother's operation. Although the Duke of Windsor's return did not attract any particular attention on this occasion - Channon remarked that 'apart from a hideous photograph in a newspaper he has caused not a stir'[16] - his increasingly frequent trips to Britain carried with them a purpose that bore the inevitability of death and taxes: the desire for his wife to be recognised with the title Her Royal Highness.

It had been an *idée fixe* of the Duke of Windsor's since his abdication that Wallis should be recognised on the same terms, and on the same level, as he was. This was expressed in ways both petty - on their wedding day, he insisted that his wife's prayer book be inscribed with the words 'Her Royal Highness' by the presiding clergyman - and profound. Letters patent published on 28 May

1937 declared that 'the Duke of Windsor shall, notwithstanding his act of Abdication, be entitled to hold and enjoy for himself only the title, style or attribute of His Royal Highness, so however that his wife and descendants, if any, shall not hold the said title or attribute'.[17] This had rankled at the time, and had been a continuing cause of anger and division between the duke and the king ever since.

Yet after the end of the war, Edward's conditional acceptance within his family depended in large part on his being quiescent on this matter and not creating an embarrassing fuss. Towards the end of 1948, he decided that his silence was no longer appropriate. He may have been influenced by an incident that took place earlier that year at a dinner in Palm Beach, when Wallis was insulted by the Duchess of Sutherland, who claimed that she herself was a 'proper' aristocrat and worthy of higher standing than the arriviste Duchess of Windsor. Wallis mused to Allen on 23 February that 'do I as the wife of a royal duke sit ahead of the wife of a non-royal duke? I am sure you can get an opinion or ruling from the Lord Chamberlain's Office or whoever knows the correct precedence . . . What a pity it was not all settled in 1936.' She, unlike her husband, had a wryly accurate idea of her standing, both in Britain and overseas. 'I am convinced that the Lord Chamberlain's Office would prefer not to have me at the table at all!'[18]

Nonetheless, the duke considered such treatment of his wife both insulting and morally wrong. He waited for his moment to make a fuss, and eventually its pretext arose from an unexpected quarter. Monckton had been served with a divorce petition by his wife, Polly, in 1946, on the grounds of adultery, and it was successful, leading to his forced resignation as attorney general to the Duchy of Cornwall; it was considered inappropriate for any member of the royal household, however honorary their role, to remain in post under such circumstances. However, Monckton was indispensable, and after he quietly married his former mistress, Bridget Hore-Ruthven, on 13 August 1947, he resumed his position in late 1948.

A decade previously, this would have been inconceivable, and even now, it was more a mark of Monckton's high standing than the arrival of a more liberal perspective. However, it did not escape the duke's notice that this return could be weaponised, and his letter to the king of 7 December concealed its intent beneath heavy-handed civility: 'One of my main objections to the official attitude towards divorce in Great Britain has always been the regrettable loss of the services of able and experienced men, which are not infrequently incurred thereby.'

He had already made his feelings known to his brother, and Lascelles had drafted a suitably trenchant letter in response; he suggested to the king that 'Perhaps I should make quite certain that Attlee would take the line I have said he would. I can easily do this privately if you wish.'[19] The letter itself was a firm one. It stated that 'I have been thinking over what you said about giving the title "HRH" to your wife. I do not see how this could be done. As you will remember, the present arrangement came into force through Letters Patent under the Great Seal, approved by me on May 27 1937, on a submission by the Prime Minister.'

Lascelles, in the name of the king, continued in similar vein. 'More Letters Patent could not be revoked, and fresh ones issued, without another submission; I have been told that there is no chance of the present PM, nor any of his colleagues, ever agreeing to make such a submission and that in all probability the PMs of the Dominions might have to be brought into it also. I am told, too, that there would be very strong feeling in this country, and in most parts of the Empire, against one cast making controversial issues out of all that happened in 1936, as any attempt to alter the Letters Patent would be bound to do.' He concluded with an admonishment. 'I don't believe that you would want to have such things thrashed out again any more than I do, and it would certainly not be a good thing from the public point of view at this particular moment.'[20]

Yet Edward was not a man who would simply admit defeat. He asked for, and was given, permission to have an audience with

William Jowitt, the Lord Chancellor. If anyone might have been able to offer legal opinion that the letters patent were ineffective or invalid, it was him, and the duke had the advantage that Jowitt had already informally advised him, while a private lawyer, that he stood a good chance of having them overturned if he wished to mount a formal challenge.

The Lord Chancellor's subsequent account of his interview with Edward, which took place on 14 April 1949, was freighted with embarrassment. He sent it to Lascelles with the note 'Herewith my official report - but what a difficult position for me! I hope I did right.'[21] Jowitt had acquired a reputation for playing all sides in his political career, having served at various points as a Liberal, National Labour and now Labour politician, in order to secure the high office that he now currently enjoyed. He came to resemble a latter-day Vicar of Bray, a fictionalised clergyman who was notable for his versatility in adapting his clerical and political principles to whichever monarch happened to be on the throne. He had also tried to curry favour with the Duke of Windsor, to keep the patronage and support of a man who might conceivably have been of use to him; he may have been forgiven for sighing under his breath that 'whatsoever king may reign, still I'll be the Vicar of Bray, sir'.

In any case, he was now faced with a situation where 'in my faith and loyalty I never more will falter'. He reported that when he saw the duke, 'I did not know on what subject he wished to see me',* but 'I thought it probable it would be on the question as to whether the Duchess should be accorded the title of "Her Royal Highness"'. He alluded to the previous, now discredited, advice he had offered - 'any embarrassment I might have felt in view of my present position in discussing this matter with the Duke was allayed when he told me that he had mentioned to the King that he was going to ask me to come and see him to discuss this topic and

---

* On the letter from Jowitt to Lascelles in the Royal Archives, someone - presumably the private secretary - has drawn a large and implicitly sceptical question mark in the margin at this point.

when he added that the King had raised no objection' - and then the majority of his statement consisted of backpedalling in legalese.

He informed a no doubt sceptical Lascelles that 'my previous Opinion given in 1937 . . . had been that the Letters Patent of 1937 really proceeded upon a misapprehension of the law. In the view expressed in my Opinion it was erroneous to suggest that the fact of his Abdication and the fact that he had ceased to be in succession to the Throne involved the proposition that he had thereby ceased to be "His Royal Highness". The Opinion was based upon the view that he became "His Royal Highness" not by virtue of any Letters Patent, but for the simple reason that he was the son of his father who was the Sovereign of this country.'

As regards Wallis, Jowitt stated that 'it was of course clear that the Duchess could not found any claim on the Letters Patent of 1937; but supposing that she had a perfectly good claim apart from any Letters Patent, did the Letters Patent of 1937 take that claim away?' His attitude had, he declared, changed over the past decade. 'I expressed the view in that Opinion that the Duke was entitled to the style "His Royal Highness" because he was the son of the Sovereign; that he had never for one moment of time ceased to be "His Royal Highness" by his Abdication or in any other way; that it was a misapprehension to suppose that there was any need for new Letters Patent if it were desired to create him a Royal Highness; and that the Duchess was entitled to an equivalent rank because she was his wife.' However, he now declared that 'at our interview yesterday, I pointed out to the Duke of Windsor that whatever subtle arguments lawyers might adduce, the fact was that the Letters Patent of 1937 issued by the King on the advice of his responsible Ministers, plainly contemplated that the Duchess should not enjoy this honour'. This was highlighted by Lascelles with suitable gravity.

Jowitt now attempted to suggest that the matter of the duchess's title was not a legal one, but simply one of etiquette. 'The marks of respect which the subject pays to Royal personages are, I said, in no sense a legal obligation. They are rather a matter of good manners. The question for instance whether ladies should curtsey to the Duchess would depend in practice, not upon the view they formed upon a legal question, but upon their desire to uphold and carry out the intention of His Majesty the King as the fountain of honour.' He then washed his hands of the affair. 'I said therefore, that if this situation were to be reversed, it could only be effectively reversed by the issue of fresh Letters Patent; that such Letters Patent would not be issued by the King save on the advice of his Ministers, either in this country alone, or possibly throughout the Commonwealth.'

According to Jowitt, this was greeted with irritation by the duke. 'The Duke of Windsor expressed his anxiety to end the present situation, which he thought had gone on all too long. It certainly needed tidying up. Its continuance amounted to nothing less than an insult to his wife, to whom he had been most happily married for many years past. He said that the position which had arisen was exactly what would have happened had there been a morganatic marriage; and this was exactly the position which Mr Baldwin had said was impossible in this country, and was a position to which the Duke of Windsor, when King, would never have assented.'

He concluded that Edward wished to speak to Attlee about the situation, in an appeal to higher authority, and had requested that the Lord Chancellor should put his case forward to the king, to which Jowitt had replied that 'of course I am available if His Majesty cared to send for me'.[22]

Lascelles retained a certain scepticism about the lawyer's turncoat ways. As he described it, candidly, to the king, who was still recuperating, 'it is the best example I have ever seen of a clever lawyer trying to eat his own words without giving himself indigestion'. Although he allowed that 'on the whole . . . Jowitt seems to have taken quite a sensible line', he also noted that 'the statement "I did not know on what subject he wished to see me", is not, I am afraid, 100% true. Walter Monckton assured me that Jowitt knew perfectly well what the Duke wanted to see him about.' Still, the prime minister could be relied upon; as Lascelles wrote, 'It is quite certain that Attlee will not hold out any hopes at all of changing the present state of things.'[23]

The duke, however, felt that the meeting had gone as well as could be expected. He made a note of the interview, in which he wrote, 'Letters Patent: although in existence and beside the point must be rescinded by the King on advice of his Ministers. No legislation required of Parliament. Ld Chancellor would like to explain it all to Bertie. Advises me to talk to Attlee. Dominion PMs here next week. Winston? He is writing Lascelles to report our meeting. Everything above board.'[24] Jowitt might have suggested that he had given the duke a clear indication that his suit would not - *could not* - succeed, but Edward's lifelong determination only to hear what he wanted meant that he believed it was only a matter of time until his wish was granted, and he visited Attlee for an interview in this spirit of optimism.

The prime minister disliked confrontation, but he knew that something had to be said to check the duke's hopes. Accordingly, he wrote to him on 26 April to say, after '[my] most careful consideration', that the 'personal matter' that concerned the duke had been discussed at length with Jowitt, and that while Attlee understood and was 'very sensible' of Edward's desire to remedy the situation, 'I feel bound to say that I do not think it advisable or opportune to take any action at the present time'.[25]

The duke, unsurprisingly, was furious. He initially blamed the Lord Chancellor, and on 3 June wrote him a coruscating tirade in which he declared that 'I cannot attempt to disguise my intense disappointment at Mr Attlee's letter, all the more so as the opinion you gave me in 1937 and your understanding attitude the other day gave me high hopes to believe that your influence in my favour would be considerable.' After all, if you cannot trust a Lord Chancellor - even one who has changed political allegiance more times than most people have enjoyed hot dinners - who can you trust? Edward went on to complain that he had not heard from the king and 'therefore I am uninformed as to whether he ever sent for you so that you might explain the invalidity of the Letters Patent of 27

May 1937', before concluding angrily that 'embarrassing situations created by the denial to the Duchess of my royal status are not infrequent and always undignified . . . after twelve years of loyal self-effacement, we should now be spared the social rudeness involved, a source of unnecessary pain to both of us'.[26]

Jowitt, at least, felt he had done all he could. He refused to see Edward again, sending him an understandably brief letter on 13 June, in which he expressed his sorrow that it was 'not, of course, a matter in which I can in any way help Your Royal Highness'.[27]

The duke was incensed, and as usual, his attention turned to his brother, who he had always blamed for his misfortunes. Yet this time, George VI was not prepared to offer the usual mixture of indulgence and blame-shifting that he had previously deployed to keep the peace as far as he was able. He had become aware in the autumn of 1949, when he was still recuperating from his illness and operation, that his brother's intention to write his memoirs, rather than merely a series of articles for *Life* magazine, was not mere gossip. Harold Nicolson described him as being 'very distressed at the news of the Duke of Windsor's autobiography'[28] on 20 October, but this was, if anything, an understatement. Over the past dozen years, the king had witnessed his brother's betrayal and mendacity over and over again, from his Nazi sympathies to his aggression towards his family, and he felt a sense of righteous aggravation towards the duke.

At last, in December 1949, the two men met to discuss the increasingly vexed situation. It did not go well. In a letter to Princess Elizabeth, the queen described it with commendable understatement. Remarking that 'Papa seems well but gets a bit tired with all the worries', she went on to relate, rather as if she was writing to a child, what had occurred when the royal brothers had been together. 'Uncle David came & had one of his violent yelling conversations, stamping up and down the room, & very unfairly saying that because Papa wouldn't (& couldn't) do a certain thing, that Papa must hate him. So unfair, because Papa is so scrupulously fair & honest about all that has happened.'

The queen was increasingly irritated with her brother-in-law's antics, and reflected, 'It's so much easier to yell & pull down & criticise than to restrain & build & think right – isn't it.' She might also have suggested that a degree of personal animosity played its part: she had been an implacable opponent of the duke since his abdication, believing that his selfish actions had affected her husband's health irreparably, and was entirely disinclined to use her own influence – which was considerable – to sway wider judgement and allow the duchess the use of the title that Edward so desperately coveted for her.

Lascelles did what he could in the circumstances. He wrote to Attlee on 9 December to thank him for his 'helpful advice' and to impress upon him the continued importance of his support. 'This is a case where the decision rests largely with the Sovereign . . . It cannot, however, be regarded as entirely a personal and family matter.' Briskly outlining the constitutional difficulties that would ensue were the letters patent to be overturned, not least the sense that the abdication was still not a settled matter, he concluded, with a not-so-veiled hint of command, 'the King trusts, therefore, that in any further discussion on the subject between himself and yourself . . . these considerations will not be forgotten'.[29] Attlee's reply was suitably conciliatory. 'I entirely agree that, while the decision in the matter . . . rests largely with the Sovereign, the consequences of any action have public significance . . . Should the Duke approach me again on this matter, I will ensure that he is fully impressed with this and the other considerations which you have brought to my notice.'[30]

The king was nonetheless placed in a near-impossible position. Given the decline in his health, he was even less inclined to be conciliatory than before, and so, after his contretemps with his brother, he began to write a broadside against the troublesome duke, who had apparently announced his suicidal thoughts. In the draft that exists, dated 11 December, he set out what he called 'his case' with clarity. 'In our talk the other evening you told me that your life was not worth living; that you resented the fact that I would not revoke the Letters Patent depriving your wife of the title HRH & that in not doing so I must hate you.' He refused to spare Edward's feelings, on the grounds that 'all this, although you may not realise it, has hurt me very much'.

Describing the abdication as 'that ghastly moment', he channelled years of frustration at his brother's selfishness into the letter. 'What you did do, you have never given this fact any further thought even if you knew [it] was to leave a most ghastly void in everybody's life both here, in the Empire & in the World. I had to try and fill this void in the first few months with nothing but sympathy for what had happened. 1937 was Coronation Year (yours, don't forget). I don't suppose you have ever given a thought to the effect on the people of this country & the resentment they felt towards you at the time.'

Likewise, the king saw his brother's lack of commitment clearly. 'You find this difference of status a hindrance in your private life. This I am afraid is one of the consequences of your position. I gave you, for yourself, what I thought would be the proper & brotherly status to one who has held the highest position in the land.' In text crossed out from the draft, the monarch added, 'I can see now that you must have everything to make life worth living . . . [you] will not rest content with what you have.'

His contempt for Wallis was unabated – 'Your wife was not a fit & proper person to be your Queen Consort & neither your family nor the public would & could receive her . . . therefore she cannot become an HRH now that you have abdicated' – and the king, atypically for him, ended with a sneer. 'The only way to rectify this position is for you to give up & renounce your HRH which would mean of course your giving up your right to honours of knighthood & your rank in the Services . . . and this I know you will not countenance doing.'[31]

This was too strong – Lascelles suggested that 'I think p.4 would be best omitted'[32] – and the private secretary produced a toned-down version, in which the monarch now suggested that 'When you abdicated, you accepted the view of the great majority of your subjects, that your intended wife was not the right person to be the Queen Consort. For that reason you renounced the Throne for yourself & your descendants. What you now ask me to do would be to reverse that decision which was your <u>own</u>. If your wife now became a member of our family there is no reason why she should not have become your Queen in 1937.' He concluded that 'It wouldn't make sense of the past, and it would be just as unacceptable to a great many people now as it was then.'[33] Wallis would never, it seemed, be welcomed into the royal family, any more than she would ever be accepted into public life in Britain.

The duke did not reply for nearly six months, after which time the second round of *Life* articles, entitled 'The Education of a Prince', had been published. When he did finally deign to answer his brother's letter, on 6 June 1950, it was with a combination of icy politeness and anger. Describing how he wished to 'naturally reserve this highly personal and confidential subject for verbal as opposed to written discussion between us', he reiterated how happy thirteen years of marriage to Wallis had made him, and then stated his case. 'No more did I get into "that state of emotion" as you infer ... Considering the manner in which you have been temporising with me since I raised this subject almost two years ago, I have remained commendably calm and patient.' He acknow-ledged his 'greater frankness', but put this down to the fact that 'having found a normal approach ineffective and unproductive of any response from you, I merely stated my case and registered my feelings over what I consider an injustice to an innocent person, my wife'.

He was not disposed to look back towards the past, remarking that 'the 1936 and 1937 "skeletons" you have now pulled out of the closet are hardly in line with some of the questions you asked me at our last meeting ... I refer, for example, to your wanting to know whether the granting of my rightful request on behalf of Wallis would alter my attitude towards living in Great Britain.' He then attempted to assert his ancestral rights as an elder brother with a suitably dismissive valediction. 'From the things you and various people have told me since I raised this subject I cannot accept what you call "the facts of the case" as a reason for withholding my request - a tortuous and unconvincing thesis to which you have never so much as hinted in our conversations and which, quite frankly, I can neither follow nor understand.'*[34]

The duke may well have hoped to press his case in person again, and eventually wear the king down by a process of attrition. If so, he would be disappointed. Not only did the monarch have less than two years to live by the time Edward sent his scornful and dismissive reply, but that bad-tempered and vituperative encounter between the two in December 1949 would be one of the final times they ever saw one another.

---

* He ended by asking his brother if he had received the *Life* articles from New York - either an intentional insult or a typical example of determined obstinacy.

Chapter Fourteen

'The Incessant Worries and Crises'

On 26 February 1950, the results of the general election were announced. Given the distractions that Attlee had faced over the past few years in his transformative attempts to build a new Jerusalem - from the lingering mistrust with which he was treated by the royals and courtiers alike to the ongoing, unresolvable saga of the duchess's HRH title - it was unsurprising that he was unable to repeat the landslide victory he had won in 1945, despite obtaining the largest popular vote ever achieved in an election.* Then he had enjoyed a majority of 146; less than half a decade later, amid widespread grumbling about continued austerity and the country's apparent inability to return to a pre-war state of normality, this was slashed to a mere 5 seats. It may have been a Labour majority still, but it was very much in hung parliament territory.

The prime minister had other reasons to feel on edge, too. His perceived lack of charisma had almost been a selling point in 1945; compared to Churchill's showmanship and swashbuckling, the idea of an unfussy managerial type who would get on with the task of putting the country back into business was both persuasive and necessary. Yet he had not grown more flamboyant during his years in Downing Street, and his once-lauded qualities were now stale and boring. A line from Angus Wilson's 1949 short story 'The

---

* A total of 13,226,176 votes. To put it into perspective, the population of Britain in 1950 was 50 million, which meant that virtually one in three adults able to vote did so for Labour; by way of contrast, the Conservatives managed 12,494,404 votes.

Wrong Set', 'An empty taxi drove up to No. 10 and Mr Attlee got out', seemed to epitomise his absence of presence. Little wonder that one commentator, Colm Brogan, speculated in the *Daily Express* that many of the prime minister's colleagues hoped for a different version of the story: 'An empty taxi drew up at 10 Downing Street – and Attlee got in.'[1]

It did not help that he was facing a revitalised Churchill, who travelled around the country by limousine and was received with enormous warmth by those who had apparently forgotten that they voted his party out of office five years earlier. He was able to make hay with the apparent failings of the Labour government, and suggested that the Conservatives would make Britain great once more. In a party political broadcast of 17 February, he declared that through 'one heave of her shoulders, Britain can shake herself free'. The previous day, he had also suavely addressed the persistent (and far from inaccurate) rumours of ill health that had dogged him for years. 'I am informed from many quarters that I died this morning. This is quite untrue. It is however a good sample of the whispering campaign which has been set on foot. It would have been more artistic to keep this one for Polling Day.'[2]

Although his party lost, sparking whispers as to the now seventy-five-year-old Churchill's suitability to lead the Conservatives to victory in the future, not least because he had suffered a stroke the previous year, it increased its standing in the Commons from a meagre 213 seats to a more respectable 298, turning it into a far more formidable opposition. It was therefore without undue arrogance that Churchill was able to write to Lascelles on 27 February 1950 and suggest, 'Whatever happens, I think that another General Election in the next few months is inevitable.'[3] If he had seen the events that had unfolded at Downing Street the previous evening, he may have been more forthright in his beliefs. According to the reporter-turned-novelist Frederic Raphael, who was reporting Attlee's return to office – 'power' seems too strong – the prime minister, clad in 'signature funereal rig', was insulted by an American reporter, who shouted, 'Make up your mind, Mr

Attlee, you going or staying?' The prime minister's intendedly statesmanlike response – 'We shall carry on' – was delivered 'in a modest voice' that led Raphael to comment, '[he] was never going to inspire anyone to fight on the beaches'.[4]

The royal family's reaction was measured. Although Churchill remained their preferred politician, the queen took a studious, only faintly partisan line when she wrote to Philip in the aftermath of the election on 3 March. 'We are just beginning to recover ... the excitement was terrific, and though unfortunately the result is a stalemate, it was very well fought, polite and reasonable & people took it seriously thank God. For the problems are so tremendous, & one really needs all men of good will to combine their brains & talents to bring us through the difficult days.'[5] She was probably unaware that Attlee had so little faith in his government's ability to pass legislation that on 9 March, he suggested to his colleagues that should they be defeated in the Commons, 'he was inclined to think that his proper course would be to advise the King to send for Mr Churchill'.[6]

Labour's wafer-thin majority threatened to cause a constitutional furore of sorts, as it was now believed that in the event of the government being voted down in the Commons and therefore unable to function, the king would be forced to step in and take decisive action. After several weeks of speculation, Lascelles decided to put an end to the imaginings of overeager, or bored, journalists, and wrote a letter to *The Times* under the pseudonym 'Senex', in which he firmly stated the rules of engagement when it came to the relationship between monarch and premier in this situation. In doing so, he established the 'Lascelles principles', a term still used today. The letter bears reprinting:

> Sir, It is surely indisputable (and common sense) that a Prime Minister may ask – not demand – that his Sovereign will grant him a dissolution of Parliament; and that the Sovereign, if he so chooses, may refuse to grant this request. The problem of such a choice is entirely personal to the

Sovereign, though he is, of course, free to seek informal advice from anybody whom he thinks fit to consult.

In so far as this matter can be publicly discussed, it can be properly assumed that no wise Sovereign – that is, one who has at heart the true interest of the country, the constitution, and the Monarchy – would deny a dissolution to his Prime Minister unless he were satisfied that: (1) the existing Parliament was still vital, viable, and capable of doing its job; (2) a General Election would be detrimental to the national economy; (3) he could rely on finding another Prime Minister who could carry on his Government, for a reasonable period, with a working majority in the House of Commons. When Sir Patrick Duncan refused a dissolution to his Prime Minister in South Africa in 1939, all these conditions were satisfied: when Lord Byng did the same in Canada in 1926, they appeared to be, but in the event the third proved illusory.

I am, &c.,

SENEX[7]

Stability in government was of paramount importance. On 25 June, the North Korean People's Army invaded South Korea, backed by communist China; this duly led to an American declaration of war against the People's Army, and a condemnation of the attack by the United Nations Security Council, to which Britain belonged. Another world war, which had been a subject of dread speculation since 1945, seemed to be all but inevitable, pitting the West against the combined forces of North Korea, China and, eventually, the Soviet Union. Attlee was nobody's idea of an inspirational leader at a time of war, which he knew and indeed played up to. While Churchill might have seen this as an opportunity to grandstand and sabre-rattle, the prime minister prized caution and discretion. It was no wonder that the *Manchester Guardian* wrote dismissively of his broadcasts, '[one is] soothed and lulled by the stupefying illusion that nothing was seriously wrong'.[8]

Even *in extremis*, the adversarial relationship between Attlee and

Churchill - albeit one rooted in a mutual respect that had been established during their working partnership in the war - continued,
and the king had to be kept informed of matters. On 18 August, the
prime minister wrote to the monarch to appraise him of the results
of a meeting the previous day between him, Churchill, Bevin, Eden
and the Liberal leader, Clement Davies, to discuss the situation in
Korea. It had not gone well. As Attlee put it, 'Mr Churchill talked at
considerable length on the dangers of the present situation mostly
on the lines of his last speech in the Defence debate in the House.
I was unable to find any suitable reason for an earlier recall as it
did not seem to me that another debate ... would be useful. Mr
Churchill showed considerable annoyance and suggested that in
not accepting his date the Government was acting dictatorially. I
was unable to accept this view as it would seem that Mr Churchill's demand might be considered as an attempt to dictate to the
government.'[9]

The king's reply, as written by Lascelles, was a masterclass in
the non-committal. 'I am very much obliged to you for sending
me so full an account of your talk with the Opposition leaders on
August 17th. It seems certain that when Parliament does meet on
September 12th, you will have a difficult, and even critical, debate,
the course of which the general public will, I believe, follow with
deeper interest than it has felt about any other debate in recent
years. So I hope very much it will be possible for you to get some
rest between now and then, as, so far, you cannot have had a real
holiday.'[10]

The monarch knew whereof he spoke. At the state opening
of Parliament on 6 March, he was described as looking 'cross', to
say nothing of 'middle class',[11] by Channon (who, naturally, had
regained his seat with 'a colossal majority'). He went through
the usual regal motions, sometimes with more *joie de vivre* than
at others. At one party at the late Duke of Kent's home, Coppins,
Channon was astonished to see the king, after 'several glasses of
champagne', in little less than a 'rollicking mood'. Putting his finger
to the politician's cheek - a gesture of intimacy marked by two

exclamation marks in Channon's published diaries - the monarch asked how '[he] managed to look so young' at his age. The usually loquacious Channon was lost for words. 'If only I had had some sleep I might have answered wittily, but I didn't [and] grinned like a Cheshire cat, though I talked garrulously enough with everyone else.' All the same, the king's presence met with Channon's approval. '[He] now dotes on society and parties . . . He seemed much younger than the Duke of Windsor.'[12] One can only imagine the amusement with which the monarch would have regarded that particular entry.

Yet even if he could relax and unwind with a glass or two of wine, the king's worries continued. In addition to the question of his health, and his brother's machinations, there was now the concern of his country being involved in another armed conflict, only half a decade after he and his family had stood waving on the Buckingham Palace balcony to celebrate VE Day. It was common knowledge that the Soviet Union had achieved nuclear capability - 'they had the bomb', as it was known - and the thought of mutually assured destruction triggered by either the forces of communism or even the Americans made the king feel deeply depressed. He confided to one friend that 'the incessant worries & crises through which we have to live have got me down properly'. At a time when his health, never robust, was especially fragile, he could have done without the debilitating stress he was now faced with.

He may also have thought enviously of his daughter and son-in-law, who were enjoying themselves a great deal in Malta, courtesy of Uncle Dickie, who also happened to be resident on the island at the time. Whether this was a coincidence or a typically adroit example of the ever-mounting Mountbatten ensuring that he could be in the right place at the right time, he offered them gracious hospitality at his home, Villa Guardamangia. Away from the often stuffy and inhibiting atmosphere of life in Britain, they could lead what Mountbatten's wife, Edwina, described as 'a more or less human existence'.[13] Philip's valet, John Dean, later said that 'They were so relaxed and free, coming and going as they pleased like an ordinary young married couple. I think it was their happiest time.'[14] Philip took up polo, and Elizabeth was largely spared the official demands that had been a constant part of her existence at home. She became pregnant in late 1949, and would eventually give birth to their second child, her daughter, Anne, on 15 August 1950.

Even as the revelations of Crawfie's treachery caused disquiet and horror to her mother and the wider family, the princess was able, perhaps for the first time in her adult life, to concentrate on herself. She was helped, perhaps unwittingly, by a general sense at the palace that she should not be pushed into the limelight more than necessary, but instead kept in reserve. A typical example was the suggestion that she should do a broadcast on Empire Day and address the youth of the Commonwealth. As with her other radio broadcasts, she was prepared to take on the responsibility, but Lascelles vetoed her doing so, on the grounds that, as he put it to Elizabeth's comptroller, Frederick Browning, 'the world, as a whole, is pretty surfeited with broadcasts, and the last thing we want is for the world to feel that way about royal broadcasts'.[15] A man as well read as Lascelles might have thought of Walter Bagehot's famous words on the monarchy from his 1867 book *The English Constitution*: 'Above all things our royalty is to be reverenced, and if you begin to poke about it you cannot reverence it . . . Its mystery is its life. We must not let in daylight upon magic.'

Although Dean suggested that the princess 'was a little sad at leaving Prince Charles behind',[16] she managed reasonably well without him; notably, when she did return to England in late December 1949, she dealt with her correspondence and attended the races at Hurst Park in Surrey before being reunited with him at Sandringham. Unsurprisingly, her son addressed his first word to his nanny. Appropriately enough, it was 'Nana'.

His father was reported to have commented that he wanted Charles to be 'a man's man', following in his own example. Shortly after Anne's birth, Philip assumed command of the frigate HMS *Magpie*, after receiving a promotion to the rank of lieutenant commander. At last, after spending more time than he was comfortable with stuck behind a desk, he was in his element once more: at sea, surrounded by sailors, and able to exert his will to his heart's content. Not everyone was thrilled to be commanded by the husband of the queen-to-be; one anonymous rating suggested he'd rather die than serve under the duke again. Yet beneath his habitual brusqueness and plain talking, there were complex factors at play in Philip's psyche. Many years later, when asked what his ambitions in life had been, he commented, 'I'd much rather have stayed in the Navy, frankly.'[17] He was aware that his father-in-law was fading, and that upon his death his wife would have to take on hitherto unimaginable responsibilities, which he would find himself bearing, too. Even as the queen wrote to him on 21 July to congratulate him on his new command, there was the implication that he was on borrowed time: 'we are all looking forward so <u>very</u> much to your return . . . it will be delicious to see you again and I expect that Lilibet will be overjoyed'.[18]

Beneath the usual charm, the message was clear. Return home, fulfil your responsibilities and fall into line. This most private of men would, inevitably, become a public figure. It was not a destiny he relished, and, had some of the seamen under his command known of his inner struggle, they might have exhibited greater understanding, rather than commenting, as one of them did, that 'he stamped about like a fucking tiger'.[19] Wild beasts kept in cages seldom end up tame.

Shortly after the Duke of Windsor sent his would-be withering reply to the king in June 1950, he heard from an old friend, keen as ever to promote his ideas of what the duke should be doing. Kenneth de Courcy could never be described as unambitious, and from the passive-aggressive wheedling of the opening of his letter of 10 June - 'You and the Duchess promised to stay with me this summer . . . [and] I cannot let you off that' - to the revelation of his impending marriage, 'upon [which] I fancy Your Royal Highnesses will not cease to congratulate me', he was on his usual insinuating form. Yet his greater purpose was soon made clear by his description of the response that the duke's recent *Life* articles had engendered, supposedly from his New York press office. 'This extraordinarily effectively written justification of the actions of the former King has led to a widely held view here that this is the first move towards the possible return by the Duke to Britain and a position of very high leadership in British affairs in the event of a world crisis.'

De Courcy omitted to mention that the last time there had been a world crisis, a decade before, the duke's ambiguous sympathies were felt to be so toxic to British interests that he had been exiled to the Bahamas to sit out the war, thousands of miles from where he could do any damage.* Conveniently, Edward's publicists suggested that he should give a press conference to hint at his future intentions ('it is curious that they should suggest this because I have been considering it myself and their suggestion comes to me spontaneously'), and de Courcy said, with his usual lack of ambition for his friend, 'if this whole situation is now handled very cleverly, it might well be on the road towards a betterment which is of historic importance'.[20]

If the duke was interested in de Courcy's suggestion, there is no surviving letter that indicates his acquiescence. Instead, it was left to Wallis to apologise for their being unable to attend de Courcy's wedding due to a prior engagement, before suggesting that her husband needed to spend the summer working on his book in order to have it ready for publication. She concluded, '[we] wish you and the bride-to-be all the good things of life and that you find the same happiness and contentment together that we have found'.[21] They were noble sentiments indeed, but the duchess omitted to mention that earlier that year, they had made the acquaintance of the man who, if gossip was to be believed, represented the first true threat to the harmony of their marriage: James 'Jimmy' Donahue Jr.

If F. Scott Fitzgerald had created Donahue, he could have been

---

* As luck would have it, he still managed to befriend Nazi sympathisers even there, suggesting the truth of the old adage that birds of a feather flock together.

proud of his work. The heir to the Woolworth fortune, Donahue had inherited $15 million in 1950, at the age of thirty-four, and so any work ethic he had possessed – never a strong component of his character – vanished along with any check on his behaviour. Rejoicing in the nickname 'Jeem' among the gilded circles in which he moved, he led a recklessly self-indulgent existence, in which his debauched antics had led his family to have a lawyer on hand twenty-four hours a day to keep him out of the papers and the cells alike.

He combined superficial charm with remarkable viciousness when he was crossed or felt that he was disrespected; whether or not one believes the story about how on one occasion he and a friend tried firstly to rape and then castrate a waiter at the Waldorf Towers,* Ziegler's contemptuous description of him as 'the American millionaire socialite and pederast'[22] seems all too accurate. He was, in other words, the latest in a long line of thorough rotters that the duke and duchess had encountered, and with their usual dismal judgement in such matters, they insisted on taking him up immediately.

In Murphy's pithy description, before he had met the Windsors, Donahue had been 'a court jester in search of a court'.[23] Now, apparently captivated by the pair – but especially the duchess – he ingratiated himself with them both. When they headed back to France in the summer of 1950, they were accompanied by the flamboyant jester, now firmly ensconced in their lives as an apparent fixture. Donahue offered them several things that had previously been missing from their existence. He was witty, in a bitchy, unpleasant way; ostentatiously open-handed, which removed the duke's brow-furrowing need to pay for anything when they went out; and, to the increasingly fevered hum of gossip, the constant companion of the duchess. As Murphy wrote, 'they were on display together from noon until dawn . . . [this] did not go unnoticed'.[24]

---

* There are many such stories in Charles Higham's biography of Wallis, all both revolting and factually suspect in nature: Higham suggests that Donahue was known to the duke and duchess from 1947, whereas in fact he did not meet them until 1950.

Donahue's overt homosexuality made him a safe companion for Wallis, at least theoretically. Ella Maxwell, the American gossip columnist and hostess, was a friend of both the duke and duchess, and was driven to ask him, 'Don't you get jealous letting the Duchess go out every night with Jimmy?' Edward was said to have roared with laughter and, 'in his special semi-Cockney' accent, replied, 'She's safe as houses with *him!*'[25] Yet the gossip around Donahue and Wallis continued to circulate.

It remains uncertain to this day whether their relationship ever had a sexual component. Ziegler believes that the duke's confidence that their friendship was purely platonic was accurate, but others, from Mountbatten's daughter, Pamela Hicks, to the duke's secretary, Anne Seagrim, have suggested that it was a considerably deeper relationship, whatever took place between the two. Given that there has been much speculation as to the sexual dynamic between Wallis and Edward, it would be unwise to categorise Donahue and the duchess's *tendresse* as simply the appropriate respect paid by a younger man to an older woman. Yet Donahue was indubitably, in the immortal words of Flanders and Swann, base, bad and mean. Like Charles Bedaux, the Nazi sympathiser who owned the chateau where the duke and duchess married in 1937, he was happy to pick up the bills, but all the while, greater expenses mounted up.

An additional complication for the duke was the knowledge that he was under contract to finish a book that was due to be published the next year. Its creation had proved a gruelling process. Murphy remarked to Monckton on 6 April, while sending him the extracts intended for *Life* magazine, that 'these four instalments represent the King's story as he wishes to tell it. There are many places in it where, if I had my way, the story would have taken a different form. And much is lacking that would have given breadth and depth to his life. But this, after all, is the Duke's story; there comes at every stage a point beyond which he cannot be taken, and there, always, the narrative stops.'

The ghostwriter was most dismissive of Edward's belief that

the book was ultimately a romance. 'It is, as no one knows better than you, a love story not out of royal folklore but out of life - and for that reason it suffers somewhat for want of the timeless virtues.' The only praise he could summon for it was faint - 'the tale is told simply and with a minimum of platitudes' - and his truer judgement on the book and its author could be ascertained from his judgement that 'if occasionally it suddenly splinters off into a startling naivete, that too is in character'.[26]

Murphy had long since wearied of dealing with the duke. In his later account of working with him, he wrote, '[I] tried to tie him to a schedule, however light; and the Duke, moved as much by consideration of the handsome royalties at stake as by his contractual obligations, attempted to discipline himself and cut short his partying and nightclubbing.'[27] As the duchess was driven ever further into Donahue's embrace, it became clear that the duke was not in a position to deliver a finished manuscript for publication in 1950, as had originally been hoped for. Murphy was offered the chance to return to New York, where, in his words, 'more stimulating assignments awaited',[28] but he stayed, either because of his dedication to seeing the job through or because he feared that if the project collapsed without his involvement, he would lose out on what promised to be a lucrative payday.

He found support from an unexpected quarter. In between assignations with Donahue, Wallis told her husband that it was his duty to finish the book, even if she was bound to return to New York in the autumn of 1950 for a round of social engagements. She eventually left, and work continued. In Murphy's words, the duke, 'rubbing his hands', now announced that 'There'll be no distractions. We should wind up the job in a month or six weeks.' Unsurprisingly, they did not. In Wallis's absence, Edward was driven to a virtual breakdown, unable to cope without her.

Eventually, he decided that he had to return to New York, citing his belief that war with Russia was imminent, and that it would be a dereliction of his uxorious duty not to be by Wallis's side 'as I was in the last war' if bombs fell in Central Park. Eventually Murphy had to 'finish the book with only fitful help from the Duke',[29] with sections all but missing and others barely sketched. The duke's reaction to being asked to provide the unfinished material was an unhelpful one. 'I don't want to waste time on things that happened so long ago.' Murphy did not make the obvious rejoinder that such was the point of a memoir. Eventually, however, *A King's Story* was bashed into shape, and left to await its commercial and critical fate upon publication the following year.

Few who had known the duke in Britain looked forward to its appearance with any anticipation. Monckton groaned to Lascelles on 5 May that he and Allen had worked together with Murphy and consequently 'once again all we have succeeded in doing, by the most drastic attacks, has been to make what was horrible [a] little less so'.[30] Churchill, meanwhile, commented to his friend and acolyte Brendan Bracken on 1 August that 'I am sure it would not be in accordance with HRH's character or reputation for him to publish reports of private conversations which he had with me, and still less to impute to me political motives and I request and hope that these may be cut out.'[31] He was to be disappointed; the book was published with these details intact. Although it made no difference to his re-election hopes the following year, it was still an embarrassing reminder that he had taken the losing side in this particular conflict, for motives that have been debated ever since.

Although no letters detailing the king or queen's thoughts on the book's publication exist, it is a safe assumption that their opinion did not stray far from that of Lascelles. The private secretary hinted as much when he wrote to Monckton on 10 May 1950 to thank him for his near-superhuman efforts. 'Allen & you have done all that mortal men could to make this wretched publication as decent as possible, and you may be sure that all here are deeply grateful to you.' He described the task that they had accomplished as 'very disagreeable and exasperating'.[32]

Lascelles reserved his greatest scorn for his former employer. He responded to a colleague forwarding a horrified letter about the forthcoming memoirs with typical vigour. 'You are quite right in thinking that we get many communications similar to this. All of them express disgust at a former King of England selling for money his recollections of his family life, in a form that is indecent and for a motive that is squalid. But none of them has yet suggested any machinery whereby such a sale can be prevented.' He then unburdened himself of decades of contempt towards Edward. 'The only remedy that has ever occurred to me is that somebody should awake in the author the instincts of a gentleman; but as I devoted the eight best years of my life to this end with signal ill-success, I fear I am not the man to make any constructive suggestion.'[33]

Murphy estimated that the duke earned close to a million dollars from *A King's Story*, a book that Edward soon convinced himself he was solely responsible for.* Its publication would become a cause célèbre, and would give him the financial security he had always desired, even as it estranged him from his family for ever. If it was revenge for all the insults and snubs levelled towards him and Wallis, it was a peculiarly specific kind of vengeance, one that would cause embarrassment and hurt in equal measure.

---

* Although he supposedly remarked to one journalist, who praised it as 'a fascinating tale and very well written', that '[I] didn't write it myself.'

Chapter Fifteen

'It May Be That This Is the End'

At the start of 1951, Britain needed cheering up. The years of post-war austerity, bleakness and general belt-tightening meant that the national atmosphere was one of virtually unrelieved misery, as it had been since the VE Day celebrations in 1945. Labour had won the election shortly after that on a platform of rebuilding the country, but their much-reduced majority in the 1950 poll was testament to their qualified success - at best - in such an endeavour. Therefore, with limited funds at their disposal and Attlee's increasing, and justified, belief that his time as premier was limited, there was only one sure-fire means of increasing the gaiety of the nation: throwing a party.

The Festival of Britain, as it was known, was not a spontaneous occurrence. Herbert Morrison had first come up with the idea in 1947. The initial concept was to celebrate the centenary of the Great Exhibition of 1851, but Morrison soon realised that there could be a wider and broader purpose at hand: ostensibly promoting British endeavour in everything from the arts and sciences to design and architecture, with a distinguished council that included such luminaries as T. S. Eliot and John Gielgud as advisers. That it would also double as a celebration of the Labour Party's achievements in office was a welcome by-product. In Morrison's words, it would be 'something jolly . . . something to give Britain a lift'.[1] The theme decided upon was 'new Britain springing from the battered fabric of the old', and the site earmarked was on London's South Bank, close to both Waterloo station and the Houses of Parliament.

The Conservatives, naturally, decried the festival from its inception. Churchill sneeringly described it as Morrison's 'fun fair'[2] and openly criticised its operation at a time of international crisis, writing to his former scientific adviser Lord Cherwell that 'I feel increasing doubts about the Festival of Britain now that the United States have declared and are taking vast emergency measures.'[3] He may or may not have described the festival as 'three-dimensional Socialist propaganda',* but he certainly joined his colleagues in voting down Morrison's proposal to open the site on Sundays, which was dismissed on 28 November 1950. As Channon put it, 'the saints triumphed over the sinners . . . and by an enormous margin defeated the government's proposal to open the Fun-Fayre of the Festival of Britain on Sundays'. His own motivation for voting was not to keep the Sabbath holy, but 'to slap Morrison and to catch the nonconformist vote in [his constituency of] Southend'.[4]

For all the Conservative cavilling about the festival – the author Michael Frayn wrote in 1963 that its opponents could be summarised as 'the readers of the *Daily Express*; the Evelyn Waughs; the cast of the Directory of Directors – the members of the upper- and middle-classes who believe that if God had not wished them to prey on all smaller and weaker creatures without scruple he would not have made them as they are'[5] – it was clear that it was a popular endeavour in the true sense of the term, and one of broad appeal to the entire nation.

It was appropriate that it would be opened by the king, on 3 May, in a ceremony on the steps of St Paul's Cathedral. Unfortunately, when the monarch was seen in public – on one of his increasingly infrequent appearances – his declining health was now obvious to shocked onlookers. Channon was able to comment at the end of the month, accurately, that the king 'is more ill than was announced',[6] although he was typically mean-spirited about

---

* The phrase seems likely to be one of the many sayings that have been optimistically ascribed to Churchill rather than having actually been said by him.

the cause. 'It is not overwork as the newspapers suggest but "over-pleasure"; he is killing himself as we all know, but the secret is kept.' The so-called secret was the king's heavy smoking, something Channon described as a 'harmless pleasure'[7] but that had probably caused the lung cancer that was now rapidly leading to his terminal decline.

The tenor of many of Queen Elizabeth's letters between late 1950 and the summer of 1951 could be described as either optimistic or delusional. She may have genuinely believed, as she wrote to Queen Mary on 15 October 1950, that George 'is really better I think ... it is a great and blessed relief to see him stronger and more able to cope with the many worries & difficulties of life nowadays',[8] but complaints about his declining health now permeated her correspondence. On 12 December, he had 'a painful attack of lumbago, or something like it, but is better now',[9] and on 7 April 1951, Princess Elizabeth was informed that while he was, again, much better, 'that flu got him very down, & he took a long time to shake it off'.[10] It was the epitome of the uncomplaining stoicism she had manifested throughout the war, and it had worked beautifully then. Now, however, her husband was facing a far more implacable foe than even Nazi bombs: his own mortality.

Shortly after the ceremony at St Paul's Cathedral, the king appeared at Westminster Abbey, on 24 May, to install his brother, the Duke of Gloucester, as Great Master of the Order of the Bath. By now, it was obvious that his illness was more serious than either flu or a chest infection. A few days later, he took to his bed to try to, as he put it, 'chuck out the bug', but his condition had moved far beyond bed rest. Although he wrote to his mother two days later, in an attempt to reassure her, that 'the doctors can find nothing wrong with my chest so rest & quiet is the only thing for it',[11] it was clear that simply removing himself from the stresses of everyday life was insufficient. He was examined repeatedly by doctors, and X-rays indicated that there was a shadow on his left lung. Yet out of complacency, ignorance or a misguided attempt at *noblesse oblige*, the seriousness of his illness was played down.

Instead, he was told that he had pneumonitis, a less threatening cousin of pneumonia: he informed Queen Mary that 'at last doctors have found the cause of the temperature. I have a condition on the left lung known as pneumonitis. It is not pneumonia though if left it might become it.' Although he had been informed about the presence of the ominous shadow, he was prescribed daily injections of penicillin for a week, and wrote blithely that 'this condition has only been on the lung for a few days at the most so it should resolve itself with treatment . . . everyone is very relieved at this revelation & the doctors are happier about me tonight than they have been'.[12]

This optimism did not last. Despite the penicillin, the king was unable to recover his strength over the summer of 1951, and continued to remain an invalid, missing several events such as the Trooping of the Colour parade in June; Princess Elizabeth deputised for him on that occasion, and her presence reminded spectators, as if it needed to, both that her father's ill health was as much a public concern as it was a family one, and that the date of her accession to the throne was drawing ever closer. Yet few would have believed that George's illness was terminal; after all, he had been assured by his doctors that it was merely a passing period of poor health, one that could be managed and would resolve itself naturally in time.

He underwent a further battery of tests on 10 July, and then headed to Balmoral for the summer. Here, he seemed to rally slightly, as he went out grouse shooting. One of his beaters said of him that he was 'still the same laird, alert to every detail, eager for sporting news, pertinacious and critical'.[13] Yet even as he said of himself that he was 'stronger every day', he caught a chill at the end of the month, and the queen insisted that his doctors head to Scotland to examine him. They, in turn, asked that the reluctant king return to London to undergo a biopsy on his left lung, something he wished to keep secret; he informed his mother on 11 September that 'I am telling no one about this new development.'[14] With mordant humour, as he left Balmoral he sang a couple of lines from a comic song that was popular at the time: 'It may be that this is the end. Well, it is . . .'[15]

In an attempt to preserve normality, he insisted his wife remain in Scotland, but her presence at Balmoral was anything but relaxing. She wrote to Queen Mary on 17 September without her previous optimism, acknowledging that 'it is very worrying about Bertie, and I feel miserable being up here, and feel most cut off'. Acknowledging that her husband would not want her to be alarmist – 'he had a faint hope of returning here, and . . . did not want to agitate people too much', she nonetheless spelled out the situation. 'I have been dreadfully worried all the time up here, as Bertie was really very unwell with a bad cough & so unfortunately caught a bad cold, & tho' he really was feeling much better last week, he was far from well.' She concluded that 'I do pray that the doctors will be able to find something to help the lung recover.'[16]

By the time his wife was confiding her anxieties to her mother-in-law, the king had been seen by several specialists, and it was clear to them that he was suffering from a tumour on his lung. Yet to avoid worrying or distressing him, the word 'cancer' was never used; instead, the euphemism 'structural changes' was deployed with an obituarist's skill. Those around him, however, were under no such illusions. Lascelles informed Churchill, without the king's knowledge, of the growth in the organ and the consequent inevitability of a major operation. It was believed that the entirety of his lung would have to be removed to have any chance of saving his life. Even as Churchill was preparing for the increasing likelihood of a snap election, which would eventually take place on 25 October and return him and the Conservatives to power once again, he was overcome with sympathy. He remarked, 'Poor fellow, he does not know what it means',[17] and replied to Lascelles that 'I am deeply grieved to receive your letter and I share to the full the anxiety which you feel.'[18]

The king was told that the cause of his illness was an obstruction in one of his bronchial tubes, which would require a 'resection' of the lung. Given the graveness of the situation, there was little time for delay, and Sunday 23 September was the date selected for the operation, to be performed at Buckingham Palace by Clement

Price Thomas, a leading chest surgeon. The king was miserable at
the idea, commenting, 'if it's going to help me get well again I don't
mind but the very idea of the surgeon's knife again is hell'. There
were numerous complications and concerns. It became clear on
the day of the operation that there was a risk of permanent damage
to the king's larynx, meaning he might never speak above a whisper again. Given his lifelong difficulties with his speech, this was
an especially cruel piece of irony. There was also the risk, after a
major piece of invasive surgery such as this, either of thrombosis
taking place, or the monarch bleeding to death through uncontrol-
lable haemorrhaging.

The procedure was a success, as far as it could be. In the early
afternoon, Queen Elizabeth wrote to the anxious Queen Mary to
state that 'I have just seen the surgeon, and he is very satisfied with
the operation, which is a <u>marvellous</u> relief. Bertie stood it very well
- about 3 hours of it, and if he goes on as he is now, the doctors
will be pleased. He said that we must be anxious for 2 or 3 days,
because of reaction & shock etc, but his blood pressure is steady, &
his heart good.' She tried to be as positive as she could, observing,
'It does seem hard that he should have to go through so much,
someone as good as darling Bertie who always thinks of others -
but if this operation is successful, he may be much stronger in the
future.'[19]

She struck a different, more religious note to Lascelles later that
day. Allowing that the last few weeks had been 'pure hell', and acknowledging that it would now be necessary to convene a council
of state, which would allow the queen, her daughters, the Duke of
Gloucester and the Princess Royal to take on monarchical responsibilities of everyday necessity, she nonetheless hoped that there
could be some salvation at this time for her husband. 'I am sure that
today the King was utterly surrounded by a great circle of prayer,
and that he has been sustained by the faith of millions. There must
be great strength in such an uprising of spiritual forces.'[20]

One man to whom she did not hold out any such Christian
forgiveness was currently in Britain, preparing for what would

eventually be the abortive launch event for his new book. Although the Duke of Windsor had written to his brother with – for him – warmth and compassion, commiserating about the 'recurrence of that damned lung trouble – it's too bad and I am sorry indeed'[21] and suggesting a meeting between the two,* his sister-in-law had no desire to see him. She indicated to Lascelles that 'You can imagine that I do not want to see the Duke of Windsor', who she described as 'the part author of the King's troubles';[22] the contempt she had felt for him since the abdication crisis, usually couched in euphemism, here saw its full expression.

Public reaction to the procedure was one of deep and sincere sympathy. A crowd of thousands gathered outside Buckingham Palace, waiting for news of the king's condition. None was forthcoming until five p.m. that day, when a terse bulletin was posted outside the building: 'The King underwent an operation for lung resection this morning. Whilst anxiety must remain for some days, His Majesty's immediate post-operative condition is satisfactory.'

Yet many people remained sceptical about any long-term improvement in his health. Nicolson, who wrote in his diary on 24 September that 'the King pretty bad. Nobody can talk about anything else – and the election is forgotten',[23] saw Churchill's personal physician, Lord Moran, at a party at the London Library the day after the operation. In response to his unspoken enquiry, the doctor shook his head gravely. Even as Lascelles informed Churchill on 27 September that 'I saw the King for two minutes this morning. He was in full possession of all his faculties, and my brief talk with him was reassuring',[24] the monarch was clearly desperately unwell. It was little wonder that on 10 October, a formal meeting was held, with Lascelles and others present, to discuss the arrangements for what would happen in the event of the 'demise of the Crown'; the matter had swiftly moved beyond the theoretical by now.

---

* The duke also wrote to his brother the day after the operation, saying, 'I know you've had a tough time – it's too bad. Later in the week if you feel like seeing anyone I will await word from you – but it is important that you take it easy the next few days.'

In the aftermath of the king's operation, all his public commitments were postponed or called off, including his long-delayed trip to Australia and New Zealand, which was formally cancelled on 9 October. Two days previously, Princess Elizabeth and Prince Philip had headed off to Canada by air, something Churchill had initially opposed due to the risk of the plane crashing. Philip took a certain wry satisfaction in reminding the politician that he had undertaken considerably more hazardous journeys during the war, when he was prime minister. The trip was ostensibly a successful and enjoyable one, echoing her parents' visit to Canada and the United States shortly before the outbreak of war in 1939, but Elizabeth's concern about her father's health overshadowed her diplomatic functions, despite her husband's bonhomie and energy. She was much criticised by the media for looking anxious and drawn, even if she snapped, at one stressful point, 'My face is aching with smiling.' That her private secretary, Martin Charteris, was travelling with the documents for her accession to the throne in the event of her father's sudden death did not improve her mood.

Nonetheless, there were happier moments. At the end of the formal trip, a short visit to Washington was added, so that the princess could meet President Truman. All were aware that in the increasingly likely event that her father died while Truman continued in office, good relations between the future queen and the president were a prerequisite. While Truman and George VI had got on well enough during their brief encounter in 1945,[*] the president was positively enraptured by the princess; Charteris even went as far as to say that 'he fell in love with her'.[25] Not only did he declare publicly that 'Never before have we had such a wonderful couple, that so completely captured the hearts of all of us', but he remarked to the *Washington Evening Star*, shortly after Elizabeth and Philip's departure, that 'when I was a little boy, I read about a fairy princess, and there she is'.[26]

---

[*] After George VI's death, Truman privately remarked that 'he was worth two of his brother Ed'.

When her father saw Truman's glowing words, he must have felt both proud of his daughter and envious that he was confined to his home as a virtual invalid. The election on 25 October returned Churchill and the Conservatives with a majority of seventeen; this was not quite the hung parliament territory that Attlee had been in the previous year, but it was hardly robust. Nonetheless, despite the amity and trust that had developed between the Labour premier and the king,* the return of his long-standing friend to 10 Downing Street was undeniably a much-needed morale boost. Eleven years earlier, when Churchill had replaced Chamberlain as prime minister, the relationship between monarch and politician had been initially strained and awkward, with both men struggling to impose their wishes. Now, Churchill's presence offered continuity and, it was hoped, stability.

The court circular of 26 October was laconic. After offering the details of Attlee's resignation, it noted that 'the King subsequently received in audience the Right Honourable Winston Spencer-Churchill and requested him to form a new Administration. The Right Honourable Winston Spencer-Churchill accepted His Majesty's offer, and kissed hands upon his appointment as Prime Minister and First Lord of the Treasury.' Yet if it was hoped that the partnership between the two could recapture the spirit of 1940-45, this was an optimistic ambition. Churchill was an aged figure, elderly at seventy-six and recovering from the first of his strokes; the king, meanwhile, coped as best he could, all the while plagued by the spectre of his own declining health. Nonetheless, his residual stubbornness still demonstrated itself. When Churchill drew up his first Cabinet, the king vetoed Anthony Eden's title of deputy prime minister, arguing that in the event of Churchill's death or incapacity, it remained his constitutional right to choose his next premier, rather than having one foisted upon him via the back door. Churchill acquiesced.

---

* Sufficiently so for Attlee to be awarded the Order of Merit on 5 November 1951.

It was hoped, in the aftermath of the king's operation, that it had been successful. The queen reported to Princess Elizabeth on 15 October that 'I really think that Papa is getting stronger . . . and he is today sitting in the audience room for lunch and tea.' Although she reported that his voice was still 'very hoarse' and that his recovery was inevitably slow, she was able to observe that 'he is beginning to take an interest in things again, and once he makes a start, he will, I am sure, get on quicker . . . the doctors are pleased, & he is a little more cheerful'.[27] Certainly, when his daughter and son-in-law returned from their travels, he made a concerted effort to seem more his old self. On 14 November, a photograph was taken of him and his grandson, Prince Charles, sitting side by side to mark the boy's third birthday, and a general – if premature – belief that the worst was past meant that a day of national thanksgiving was declared on 2 December.

The king headed to Sandringham for Christmas that year, and pre-recorded his broadcast to the nation; his stamina would not have allowed him to read it live, as he had the previous year. Tidings of his health dominated the address, as he praised those around him, and suggested that he had recovered. 'I myself have every cause for deep thankfulness, for not only – by the grace of God and through the faithful skill of my doctors, surgeons and nurses – have I come through my illness, but I have learned once again that it is in bad times that we value most highly the support and sympathy of our friends.' He expressed gratitude for his subjects' prayers and good wishes, reiterated his disappointment at not being able to visit Australia and New Zealand, and praised the spirit of his worldwide well-wishers, saying, 'We are living in an age which is often hard and cruel, and if there is anything that we can offer to the world today, perhaps it is the example of tolerance and understanding that runs like a golden thread through the great and diverse family of the British Commonwealth of Nations.'[28]

The sentiments were uplifting and positive, but recording the broadcast proved taxing. Robert Wood, the BBC engineer, who had worked on the king's speeches before, later observed that the two-hour recording session was prolonged by the monarch only managing to say a few words at a time before being overcome by exhaustion. He observed that 'it was very, very distressing for him, and the Queen, and for me, because I admired him so much and wished I could do more to help'. Wood noted that the king's voice, never his greatest feature, was now 'husky, hoarse [and] wheezing as if he had a heavy cold audible between phrases'.[29] Had the speech been broadcast live, it would have been disastrous.

Yet in other regards, his health seemed to have stabilised, if not improved. He was well enough to go shooting at Sandringham, and to involve himself in world affairs, albeit in a low-key way; he wrote to both Truman and his former comrade-in-arms Eisenhower to emphasise his hope that, with the continuing uncertainty of the world situation, they might work closely with Churchill to attempt to resolve matters in Korea and beyond. He decided that he was due a holiday, and so made plans to head to South Africa on 10 March, for what would be pure relaxation; his fragile health would not have allowed any affairs of state to be considered. Yet the king believed that he was on the way to recovery. When he returned to London in late January, he saw his doctors, who were said to be 'very well satisfied' with his progress, and on 30 January, he saw *South Pacific* with his daughters at Drury Lane, his first public appearance in a considerable time.

As it was considered impossible for the king to head to Australia, Princess Elizabeth instead undertook the trip, and left for Kenya on 31 January, along with Prince Philip. Ignoring any suggestion that he should conserve his strength, the king headed to London Airport to bid farewell to his daughter, joined by Churchill. The pictures that exist of him that day, hat in hand and looking gaunt and unwell, are marked by a rare intensity in his eyes; he had considered it all-important to be at the airport, whatever its cost. Churchill later observed that although his monarch was superficially 'gay and even jaunty', and drank a glass of champagne, 'I think he knew he had not long to live'.[30] He returned to Sandringham afterwards, and his final days were happy and contented ones, taken up with everything from shooting hares and rabbits to viewing new pictures by the artist Edward Seago. His wife was sufficiently confident of his continued recovery to write to Princess Elizabeth on 2 February that 'Papa seems pretty well, & I do hope that a good soaking from the sun will do him good. But he does hate being away from his responsibilities and interests - & I don't expect we shall stay long!'[31] After a pleasant family dinner with Princess Margaret on 5 February, the king headed to bed in jolly spirits. It would be the last time anyone saw him alive.

In an emotional letter to Queen Mary* the following day, the queen briefly summarised what had happened. 'This morning, only a few hours ago, I was sent a message that his servant couldn't waken him. I flew to his room, & thought that he was in a deep sleep, he looked so peaceful - and then I realised what had happened.' He had died not of cancer, but of a coronary thrombosis; the blood clots that had begun to afflict him so grievously in 1948 had finally done their worst. His wife had spent years fearing for his health, and now, at the age of fifty-one, she found herself a widow. Acknowledging that it was 'impossible to grasp' what had happened to him, she wrote, 'he was my whole life, and one can only be deeply thankful for the utterly happy years we had together'.[32]

Shortly after he was discovered, Edward Ford, the assistant private secretary to the monarch, was deputed to tell Churchill what had occurred, using the codeword 'Hyde Park Corner'. When Ford arrived at Downing Street, all he could say was 'I've got bad news, Prime Minister. The King died last night.' Churchill, intensely affected, replied, 'Bad news? The worst', and burst into tears. When his private secretary, Jock Colville,† arrived, the prime minister was sitting alone weeping, unable to concentrate on either his official papers or the newspapers. As Colville observed, 'I had not realised

---

* When his mother learnt of her son's death, she was only able to say, 'What a shock!' Never one for expressing her emotions, she was nevertheless hit hard by the news.

† He had left Princess Elizabeth's service to return to Churchill's side in 1951.

how much the King meant to him.' He attempted to reassure Churchill by stressing the competence and dutiful nature of the new queen, whom he had served as private secretary between 1947 and 1949, but a grief-stricken prime minister could only respond, 'I do not know her. She is only a child.'[33]

When Churchill recovered from the initial shock of the king's death, he knew that he would have to rise to the occasion with a public broadcast that would require all his rhetorical skill, which he delivered on 7 February. He was speaking to a nation poleaxed by grief. When the news was announced, people spontaneously stopped their cars in the street, stepped out and saluted. Tears became the common expression of a shared loss. The king had been a great unifying figure for the nation during the war and beyond. A matter of two months earlier, there had been a belief that he was on the road to recovery. And now he was gone, replaced by a twenty-five-year-old woman who was hurriedly returning from Africa as soon as she was informed of her father's death.

The prime minister was addressing at least some sceptics. Channon, the eternal cynic, wrote in his diary on 6 February that 'life suddenly stopped', and at a lunch party that day, he stated his belief that 'His late Majesty committed a form of suicide: with only one lung, and a generally debilitated condition, it was foolish to spend the weeks of recovery at damp Sandringham.' Warming to his denunciation, he suggested that 'he rarely worked . . . he wore himself out by fidgeting and doing nothing'. Channon blamed the queen, naturally, for being 'limited and insular' and refusing to allow her husband to go abroad, before offering his final judgement on his sovereign. Although he admitted that 'he could, on occasion, be kind', his attitude was deeply sceptical and heartless. 'His death is regrettable; it is a pity it couldn't have been postponed for a while – but it is not a disaster at all. He was cross, uninteresting, lightly nervous and often disagreeable.'[34]

Churchill, then, was faced with a difficult task. He had to memorialise his friend and console the nation, but also implicitly rebuke the naysayers, who had always muttered about the king being ill-suited to the role he had occupied for the past decade and a half. It was inevitable, perhaps, that he began his broadcast by observing the 'deep and solemn note in our lives, which, as it resounded far and wide, stilled the clatter of twentieth-century life in many lands and made countless millions of human beings pause and look around them'. He then segued elegantly from the universal to the personal. He praised the king for his stoicism, his bravery and his commitment to his country, both in the wartime years and during his illness, and went on, in words that have justly become famous even if they employed more than a little dramatic licence:

> The last few months of King George's life, with all the pain and physical stresses that he endured – his life hanging by a thread from day to day, and he all the time cheerful and undaunted, stricken in body but quite undisturbed and even unaffected in spirit – these have made a profound and an enduring impression and should be a help to all.
>
> He was sustained not only by his natural buoyancy, but by the sincerity of his Christian faith. During these last months the King walked with death as if death were a companion, an acquaintance whom he recognized and did not fear. In the end death came as a friend, and after a happy day of sunshine and sport, and after 'good night' to those who loved him best, he fell asleep as every man or woman who strives to fear God and nothing else in the world may hope to do.
>
> The nearer one stood to him the more these facts were apparent. But the newspapers and photographs of modern times have made vast numbers of his subjects able to watch with emotion the last months of his pilgrimage. We all saw him approach his journey's end. In this period of mourning and meditation, amid our cares and toils, every home in all the realms joined together under the Crown may draw comfort for tonight and strength for the future from his bearing and his fortitude.

He ended the broadcast by looking not to the past, but to the future. For all the scorn he had expressed to Colville in the depths of his grief, he was aware that it was now his role to offer succour and optimism to the nation, and he spoke with all the cheer he could summon about what was now upon them: the second Elizabethan age. As he declared, 'Famous have been the reigns of our queens. Some of the greatest periods in our history have unfolded under their sceptre. Now that we have the second Queen Elizabeth, also ascending the Throne in her twenty-sixth year, our thoughts are carried back nearly four hundred years to the magnificent figure who presided over and, in many ways, embodied and inspired the grandeur and genius of the Elizabethan age.'

He acknowledged that the sudden advent of Elizabeth's reign was a shock, but reminded his listeners of her popularity both in her native country and abroad; countering his own comments of the previous day, he said, 'already we know her well'. He then built up to a suitably stirring peroration. 'Tomorrow, the proclamation of her sovereignty will command the loyalty of her native land and of all other parts of the British Commonwealth and Empire. I, whose youth was passed in the august, unchallenged and tranquil glories of the Victorian era, may well feel a thrill in invoking once more the prayer and the anthem, "God save the Queen!"'

The king was dead. Long live the queen. Yet at a time of personal loss and unimaginable responsibility, Elizabeth had to deal with a range of complex and unprecedented difficulties. And one of these, inevitably, was none other than her uncle, who had been waiting for such an occasion ever since the day of his abdication.

Chapter Sixteen

'And They Lived Happily Ever After'

As fears for the king's health had grown in the latter part of 1951, the Duke of Windsor had paid lip service to national concerns, but also kept a close watch on his book sales. The reaction in Britain to *A King's Story* was cooler than it had been in the United States, although not without enthusiasm for both its historical and literary qualities.* The *Times Literary Supplement* talked of how 'it is the Duke's own book . . . his own personality, his likes and strong dislikes, spring to life as well as his keen sense of humour'. Had they known of the extent of Murphy's involvement, the praise may have been less warm.

One of these strong dislikes was especially obvious to British readers. The duke's vitriolic portrayal of Stanley Baldwin, even in toned-down form, came in for both public and private criticism – the Earl of Athlone's reaction that 'you were a bit too strong about Baldwin, who was really very fond of you'[1] was typical – and some of the press reviews were less glowing about the duke's own self-presentation. The *Observer* sighed, 'the wisdom of publication is arguable . . . the hero emerges as rather a pathetic figure', while in the *Spectator*, Wilson Harris wrote, of Edward's adulterous relationship with Wallis, that 'on the Duke's resolve to drag every detail of this old unhappy affair to light again when it had been well forgotten some judgement is called for . . . it must be unreservedly adverse'.[2]

---

* Even Lascelles, a man implacably opposed to both the duke and his works, grudgingly allowed that his nemesis had 'written a good book'.

Yet even these criticisms could not harm the book's sales, which were considerable: eighty thousand copies were sold in Britain in the first month of sale.

It had received greater acclaim on its publication in the United States earlier in the year, on 14 April; Stephen Spender's review in the *New York Times* the next day went so far as to compare Edward's downfall to that of Byron and Wilde, and suggested that in his 'important and highly interesting book', the duke had redeemed himself in the public eye, even if the saga remained 'on the level of serious comedy rather than tragedy'. Spender, perhaps not entirely au fait with the wider circumstances of the duke's relationship with his family, wrote that the abdication crisis - 'a situation pregnant with disaster' - had, in the end, 'ended with comparative happiness all round'.[3]

Edward's private secretary, Anne Seagrim, wrote that 'HRH [is] in terrific form . . . very happy about the book, which has had a wonderful reception, and the reviews have been too marvellous . . . He spends most of the day signing his name.'[4] A more critical observer may have remarked that the duke's most famous - and worthwhile - signature was that with which he had sealed the deed of abdication on 11 December 1936. Yet the warmth of the public response meant that as the duke and Seagrim were packing up his office, he gave her 'a look that meant a thousand things', and suggested that, given the success of *A King's Story*, he was considering writing a sequel that would explore his post-abdication life. He added, 'with a repetition of the confidential look', 'I dare say it will be a great deal more interesting than this one . . .'[5] It sounded like a threat as much as a promise.

However, despite the vast publicity that *A King's Story* had engendered, the expensive tastes of the duke and duchess meant that sums of money that would have kept most people happy for years were spent in a matter of a few months. They wished to purchase a property using their new income, rather than being perpetual renters, and Wallis had written to her Aunt Bessie on 4 November to suggest that 'we cannot find the one unit near Paris, and the

Duke must have the country. So now we are looking for a small house or flat in Paris and something small in the country for week-ends.'[6]

Edward occupied a strange and unsatisfactory position in public life at this time. His memoir had once again thrown him back into the spotlight, but the news of his brother's ill health had meant that its British publication was overshadowed by far graver matters. He had seen Lascelles on 27 September, during one of his increasingly frequent visits to Britain, and the private secretary reported to Churchill that 'The Duke of Windsor was with me for the best part of an hour this morning. His Royal Highness, without mentioning that he had had a letter from you on the subject, asked me for my advice with regard to his projected attendance at this Publishers' Dinner tomorrow. I gave it. As a result, His Royal Highness was good enough to say that he would, for the present at any rate, cancel his appearance at the dinner.'[7]

This thwarted desire stemmed from an invitation that the duke had accepted to address the Book Publishers' Representatives' Association at their annual dinner at the Connaught Rooms in London on 28 September 1951. This was a major, if unglamorous, event that would nevertheless have presented the duke as an *homme des lettres*, in addition to being the former king; his publisher, Desmond Flower, suggested that 'your gracious presence at the dinner would give your book the finest possible send off throughout the trade'.[8]

Additionally, it would have allowed him to make his first high-profile speech in Britain in fifteen years. Not since his abdication broadcast of 1936 had Edward given any kind of public statement in his home country. The major exception to this, a global broadcast that he made from Verdun on 8 May 1939, was not transmitted by the BBC for fear that the former monarch might rile his country-men, despite his being in France. Tellingly, the Verdun recording in the BBC archives remains marked 'not for broadcast'; the duke's activities were off limits as far as the national broadcaster was concerned.

Had Edward made a more conventionally high-profile appearance - for instance, an 'in conversation' at the Royal Albert Hall
with a literary friend or admirer such as the Scottish novelist and
biographer Compton Mackenzie* or Nicolson - he would immediately have been accused of showboating on the grandest scale. He
was caught between the considerable demands of his own ego (and
the attendant boost that his publisher, Cassell & Co., would have
received from such an event and its concomitant publicity) and the
knowledge that his family's horror at his having written the book
at all would be magnified a hundredfold if he took to the stage to
present himself no longer as a regal figure, but, of all unbecoming
things, a *writer*.

Therefore, his acceptance of the invitation to address the BPRA
seemed like a compromise that his family would have to accept,
however reluctantly. Yet when it became clear that the duke would
be appearing in public, his friends and intimates intervened to frustrate his plan. Rowland Baring, 2nd Earl of Cromer and a former
Lord Chamberlain of the royal household, had already written to
Edward in August in the warmest terms. He praised *A King's Story*
for its 'literary qualities and tactful choice of words that elevate
this pathos-laden story to such a high and dignified plane', as well
as saying that the book boasted 'verity, sincerity and graciousness
of style . . . it cannot but command respect in the hearts of all
the fair-minded'.[9] Yet a month later, on 19 September, just over a
week before the dinner, he wrote to the duke and urged him not
to attend, on the grounds that his presence would have been too
closely associated with commercialism.

Given that by this stage Edward seldom saw a money-making
opportunity he was prepared to turn down, it is likely that he
would have ignored Lord Cromer's words, on the spurious
grounds that it would be harsh to disappoint the good men - and

---

* Who was also notable for being one of the few high-profile members of the
Octavians, a society founded with the aim of restoring the Duke of Windsor to
the British throne.

they would exclusively have been men – of the BPRA. Churchill, however, made a more apposite intervention on 26 September, the eve of the book's publication, to remind him of his brother's grave ill health and the necessity of remaining out of the public eye until the monarch was recovered, suggesting, 'it is so important that the first time you address the British public [you] should have the most cordial welcome'.[10]

Reluctantly, the duke cancelled his appearance at the dinner. He was replaced at the last moment by Max Aitken, Lord Beaverbrook's son; hardly the high-profile figure the former monarch was. The assembled company rose 'as one man' to drink the duke's health in absentia at the Connaught Rooms in London, but this did little to assuage his displeasure. It did not help his ill temper that the young princesses were seen enjoying themselves at Ascot the day that he should have been giving his speech; he grumbled to Ulick Alexander that their presence at the races when he was himself stabled was 'pretty blatant discrimination'.[11]

He wrote miserably to the BPRA's president, Kenneth H. Smith to say, 'I know you will understand the sad circumstances which have led me to cancel my long-standing engagement to be the guest of honour . . . to the great relief of all his loyal subjects, the King's recovery from his serious operation is making satisfactory progress. On the other hand there must be continued anxiety for some days to come.' He referred to his keen disappointment over 'not being able to be with you all [at the dinner] . . . to which I have been so long looking forward to attending'.[12]

If no copy of the duke's undelivered speech existed, it would be tempting to wonder what was in it. Petty grumbling? Statesmanlike oratory that he would no doubt have delivered with gravitas? Bland self-promotion that might have been received well enough over the large brandies and cigars but is deadening to read today? All are possibilities. Thankfully, in the Monckton papers in the Balliol College archives, there is a surviving copy. The speech is extraordinary. If he had been allowed to make it, it would have caused reverberations that would have echoed far beyond the function rooms of the BPRA.*

From its opening, Edward's intention was to make far wider political and social points than simply to thank a publishers' trade association for selling huge quantities of his book. He would have started by reminding his audience that 'this is the first speech - if my few remarks to you this evening can be so classified - that I have made to Great Britain since I went away almost 15 years ago'. Acknowledging that the book had already been a bestseller in the United States since its publication there in April - 'it has been generously received by the reading public of that great country' - he would also have sought to counter any criticism that he had abandoned Britain entirely.

The speech continues, 'I have of course been looking forward to the day when my book would become available to the people of the United Kingdom, where I was born, where I was raised, where I worked and played' - one imagines at this point a knowing pause, perhaps some smutty laughter from the more red-faced members of the BPRA - 'where I reigned even if only briefly, and where so many episodes and incidents recorded in my story took place.'

It would not have been a modest speech. It took as its central thesis an unusual new identity for its speaker. The Duke of Windsor had been, in his life thus far, prince, king, exiled duke and much else besides. Now he was attempting to claim another mantle for himself: that of author. In true after-dinner style, he would have professed that 'from considerable experience in public speaking I find it hard to believe those who claim that this, one of the most difficult of human accomplishments, holds for them no terrors', and flattered his 'very critical audience', whose time was spent 'reading through material that is submitted for your approval in the hope that with your assistance it may obtain the dignity of

---

* He also visited Broadcasting House and recorded the speech on 26 September; it was never broadcast. The news item reporting it stated, 'The Duke of Windsor went to Broadcasting House yesterday and used a BBC microphone for the first time since his abdication in 1936.'

print'. He acknowledged his fear that this material 'finds its way into the limbo of forgotten things', and then praised the dignity of his listeners. 'It is inevitable that the attitude of a publisher towards an author must differ from his attitude towards the rest of the world . . . for the rest of the world consists of people to whom you are anxious to sell something, while the wretched author is someone who wants to sell something to you.'

Edward may have called himself wretched, but his intentions were anything but. Acknowledging his appearance via the medium of paradox ('publishers are the servants of the public but authors are the servants of the publishers'), he would have said, with an arch dig at his family and their courtiers, 'Yes, I have written a book, and it seems in the eyes of some that in doing so I have done something very terrible.' Then the speech segues into a routine that would not have disgraced a cabaret performer, and indicates a hitherto unsuspected degree of humour and wit on the part of the duke, especially when it came to literary matters. 'It was Job I think who in the depth of his misery exclaimed that he wished his enemy had written a book.* I used to find it difficult to understand why he wished such a peculiar thing. Now, I know. Gentlemen, Job was dead right. He knew what he was talking about. If you've got a grudge against anybody, and want to do him a bad turn, all you have to do is persuade him to write a book.'

The duke then would have offered a meta-commentary on his own situation, not least his family's fears - and his hosts' hopes - that he might yet produce a sequel to *A King's Story*. 'It's the first one that gets you into trouble. After a man has written two or more books, people get used to it. They say "Oh, he's written another book, has he? Well, he's always doing it. It's too late to stop him" . . . with the first book it's different. "Why on earth should <u>he</u> write a book?"' With tongue firmly in cheek, Edward's speech suggests the

---

* The precise quote, from Job 31:35, is as follows: 'Oh that one would hear me! Behold, my desire is, that the Almighty would answer me, and that mine adversary had written a book.'

likely reactions to his authorial ambitions. 'He of all people. I never thought he'd do <u>that</u>. How very unwise, how quite unnecessary, how indiscreet, how unfair, how wrong. What a bad book it must be. I certainly shan't read it.'

He then chose to make his own status explicit, in case, for some unfathomable reason, a refreshed member of his audience was confused as to who this 'Duke Windsor' character was - 'I suppose that it follows in the minds of people who feel this way that when someone who has been a King writes a book it makes the crime even worse' - and began to advance a justification for what he had done, not least by appealing to posterity. 'Few people I believe know that previous occupants of the British throne have written books before me. Even if no monarch ever had, that would not have prevented me from writing one, for I cannot think of a worse reason for not doing so than the fact that no ancestor has done it before.'

He made no claim to be a pioneer in this regard - 'Henry VIII wrote a book, and it was a very successful book - I cannot give you the figures of its circulation, but I can tell you that the Pope was so pleased with it that he conferred upon Henry the title of Defender of the Faith' - and then compared himself to another king forced from the throne before his time, Charles I, who he described as 'an unfortunate monarch but a very good man', and implicitly compared *A King's Story* to Charles's *Eikon Basilike*, 'all his most intimate thoughts and feelings'. Anyone in the audience listening to this speech may now have realised that there was an agenda at play rather than the speaker merely cracking a few jokes, made even more explicit by the next segment. 'My great grandmother was also a writer. Queen Victoria did not think it beneath her dignity in what we regard as the extremely conventional period in which we lived to write and publish details of her most private life.'

With this appeal to the 'eminent precedents' he had followed, the duke modestly played down his own intentions. '[I did not write] *A King's Story* in any spirit of emulation of my illustrious predecessors. I wrote it because I had something I wanted to say.

Can there be a better reason for writing? As a man who having lived a life of infinite variety and become involved in perhaps more than his share of controversy, I felt impelled to tell my own story in order that it remains the final record.' He did not mention that everyone from Churchill to Beaverbrook had given him similar advice, nor that the creation of his book had been fraught because of his continual disagreements with his ghostwriter. This was glossed over by his comment 'On the whole I enjoyed writing my book, a difficult and exacting task as it was', and he expressed his hopes for its commercial success and its wider purpose. 'I hope that many people will read my book. I hope so not only because I do not want my publishers to lose money but because I want as many people as possible to realise that there are two sides to every story.'

He acknowledged that such 'fair' criticism as the book had received had been directed 'more towards the principle of my writing it at all than towards the material', but in typical self-aggrandising fashion commented that 'approval of my undertaking has been gratifyingly generous'. 'At the risk of being accused of self-glorification', he would then have read out a tribute from 'an old and trusted friend of my family who served my father for many years and then me during my short reign, in one of the most distinguished posts at Court'.

This statement* announced that 'Always outspoken in my relations with my sovereign I am led to say now, Sir, how glad I am you have recorded your "King's Story" for the peoples of this and other lands to learn at first hand. Both for personal and historical reasons it had to be told and there was little point in unduly delaying its telling.' The puffer praised the book's 'variety, sincerity and graciousness of style', and concluded that 'it cannot but command respect in the hearts of all the fair minded'. One can only imagine the smirk on the duke's face as he might have delivered such an encomium to himself.

---

* The man was, of course, Lord Cromer.

The undelivered speech remains one of the great 'what-ifs' of the royal family's history of this period. Its provocations and innuendo would not have escaped the attentions of the media and his family alike, and Churchill and Cromer's advice for him not to give his address - presumably with the text sight-unseen - was savvy foresight when it came to the most mercurial and unreliable member of the monarchy. Over the previous decade, he had been caught up in everything from an intrigue with pro-Nazi forces, perhaps even the Nazis themselves, to toying with assuming a regency if ill health forced his brother from the throne. Now he was promoting a book, and doing so in typically inimitable fashion.

In his address to the BPRA, he showed an even more mischievous - some would say reckless - side. With his brother gravely ill, his niece facing the impending burden of monarchy that her uncle had so calmly given up, his former country crippled by debt and national despair, and discontent running riot, the nation of which he said, 'I always remember with pride that . . . [my native land's welfare] is ever near to my heart' was being brought to its knees. It was therefore unorthodox for the duke to suggest that his book was 'as far as its last chapters are concerned' a romance, and that the 'lovely and wonderful lady to whom the book is dedicated' was its subject. And now such a story was being dangled in front of the hungry association of publishers as the golden goose, for their - and his - enrichment.

The duke would have gazed out over the audience on 28 September and privately derided them as the little people, as he had everyone else he had come into contact with throughout his life. Yet they were there to lap up his wisdom, and he had a last piece of brilliance - 'one final thought' - to bestow on them: 'For myself - I only wish that I had thought to add the old familiar ending of all romances - "And they lived happily ever after."'[13]

If he could have said such a thing without a grin, then he was a master of deadpan. With Britain on the edge of existential disaster, the idea of a happy ending for anyone seemed remote.

*

When Edward was not seething with frustration at his thwarted opportunities for self-promotion, he continued to rail against the left-wing menace that he saw as society's greatest threat, and the weakness of the British government in combating it. Congratulating Monckton on his appointment to the Cabinet as Minister for Labour and National Service, the duke stated, 'it's too bad that the electorate did not give Winston a proper mandate. It's proof of how evenly divided the British nation still is between sanity and bedlam. Between those who realise that you can't have everything for nothing, and those who do not . . . I'm afraid, therefore, that it's going to be very difficult for your party to bring about all the necessary reforms to save the country from further ruin with so slender a majority. However, if in the next year you can convince more people of the follies of socialism by correcting their economic blunders, then a change of political thinking might well follow, and the Conservatives be re-elected for a full and effective term of office.'[14]

Yet just as the country was distracted from the election with the news of the king's indisposition, so Edward was unable to pursue his own desired agenda while he remained in his brother's shadow. He still wished Wallis to be granted the coveted HRH title, but he knew such a thing was impossible while his brother was gravely ill. Therefore, writing to the king on 12 November, he not only expressed his relief at 'the change of "His Majesty's Servants" to use the old constitutional expression when referring to the Cabinet',* but also said, 'I have been delighted and relieved to read of the steady progress you have been making since your operation', as he suggested visiting the king between 21 and 23 November, when he was in the country once more. Concluding, 'I hope that you really are feeling better after so many wretched months of sickness',[15] the

---

* Elsewhere in the letter, he railed against 'the appalling and dangerous mess in which the Socialists have left the country after six years of crazy experimentation based on class hatred'.

letter seemed the model of fraternal amity, following their former disagreement and rancour.

The two men met around the dates Edward had suggested, and the duke later reported to Sir Oliver Franks, the British ambassador to the United States, that 'I have just returned from London where I saw the King for the first time since his serious operation. I am glad to be able to report that he is making a wonderful recovery and looks better and more robust than I have seen him in some years.'[16] It was a welcome step towards reconciliation. Had it continued, both men might have found the common ground that had eluded them since the abdication. But the king died shortly afterwards, and the drama moved into its next phase.

On 7 February 1952, the duke, bound for Britain from New York, gave a semi-impromptu press conference on board the *Queen Mary*. He made a statement in which he said, 'This voyage, upon which I am embarking on the *Queen Mary* tonight, is indeed sad - and is indeed all the sadder for me because I am undertaking it alone. The Duchess is remaining here to await my return. I am sailing for Great Britain, for the funeral of a dear brother, and to comfort Her Majesty, my mother, in the overwhelming sorrow which has overtaken my family and the commonwealth of British nations.'

He told some white lies about his relationship with his brother - 'the late King and I were very close, and the outstanding qualities of kingship he possessed made easier for me the passing on of the interrupted succession to the throne of the United Kingdom' - and then there was a hint that his visit was not an entirely selfless one. 'But Queen Elizabeth is only twenty-five - how young to assume the responsibilities of a great throne in these precarious times?' Backing away from the clear implication, he concluded, 'But she has the good wishes and support of us all.'[17]

There had, after all, been no question of his not attending the event, despite Channon's musing on 9 February, 'One wonders what the Duke of Windsor will do at the funeral? And how he will be received? It is natural but tactless of him to come.'[18] However, his motives were ambiguous. When de Courcy stated in 1949 that the duke should return to Britain and prepare himself for a de facto regency in the event of his brother's continued ill health, no letter exists in reply to the suggestion. Yet with the king dead and an inexperienced young woman on the throne, the apparent vacuum created an opportunity. Even as the duke spoke, probably accurately, of his 'profound shock' at his brother's demise, it was clear that he and Wallis had discussed the likelihood that they stood to gain preferment if they played their cards right. The question remained who held the king, and who the joker.

Over the course of a correspondence that began as soon as the *Queen Mary* set sail, and continued until the duke returned to the United States, Wallis outlined her Machiavellian belief that this represented a God-sent opportunity. After first describing her misery at their being parted – 'I hate, hate having you go away alone – but you are not really alone because I am so much a part of you' – she then got down to business. On 7 February, she advised caution with some of the participants ('Be canny with Dickie [Mountbatten] – we do not want favours through the young Prince Consort because he doesn't know how *nice* we are');[19] three days later, she was alternately sneering ('the papers and radio talk of nothing but Bertie and the girl – very, very sentimental') and exhorting: 'I hope everything won't be too hard and that for once a few decent things will come your way after the long, sad journey and the difficult relationships. You have jumped many obstacles in life and this is just one more.'[20]

The duke was unable to reply with the loquacity he usually reserved for his letters to his wife, and the only surviving correspondence from his side is a brief telegram, sent on 11 February, that stated, 'Smooth voyage is giving good if lonely rest. Hope digglets [*sic*] better. All love your D.' Yet it was clear that they both had the same intent in mind, as could be discerned by Wallis's reply of 12 February. 'I am really scared to breathe . . . I hope you can make some headway with Cookie and Mrs Temple Jr.'[21] The couple had come up with the insulting sobriquets 'Cookie' or 'Mrs Temple Sr' for the queen mother, and 'Mrs Temple Jr' or 'Shirley' for the new queen; she was given her title after the popular film star Shirley Temple, to whom Edward and Wallis fancied she bore a likeness. The king, while he had been alive, had been known simply as 'Mr Temple'.

It remains unclear which, if any, works from Temple Jr's oeuvre the couple were familiar with. Perhaps if they had seen 1935's *The Littlest Rebel* or 1945's *Kiss and Tell*, the films might have given them ideas. Yet when the duke arrived at Southampton on 13 February, private irritation had to be replaced with statesmanlike dignity. He issued another statement upon his embarkation, repeating many of the same phrases he had uttered on leaving New York, but now he took care to offer an olive branch of sorts to the queen mother and Queen Elizabeth.

Alluding to his abdication broadcast of December 1936, he said, 'My brother drew strength in his heavy responsibilities from what I once described as "a matchless blessing . . . a happy home with a wife and children". So as we mourn a much beloved monarch our hearts go out to the widowed Queen Mother and her two daughters in their grief.' He concluded with an encomium to the new monarch. 'The eldest, Elizabeth, has by God's will been called upon to succeed her father. His well known attributes will I am sure descend to the young princess.'[22]

If the duke's public statement had the intent of offering an implicit reconciliation to his semi-estranged family, it had the desired effect. Shortly after he arrived in Britain, he headed for tea at Buckingham Palace, where he was received by the new queen, Prince Philip and the queen mother.* His presence there may have been assisted by a letter that Queen Mary had written to her daughter-in-law on 10 February, saying, '[I] beg & beseech of you & the girls to see him & to bury the hatchet after 15 whole years . . . I gather

---

* Elizabeth formally adopted the title of 'Queen Elizabeth, the Queen Mother' shortly after the funeral in February 1952, although privately she denigrated it as a 'horrible name'.

D is awfully upset as in old days the 2 brothers were devoted to each other before that dreadful rift came.' She acknowledged that 'I feel grieved to have to add this extra burden on you 3 just at the moment', but she lived up to her acknowledged role as the matriarch of 'the Firm' when she suggested, 'I feel that you are so kind hearted that you will help me over what is to me a most worrying moment in the midst of the suffering we are going through just now.'[23]

Underneath the Christian sentiments, the tone of command was clear. And despite the queen mother's reluctance, the reception duly took place. That the duke believed he had been reconciled with his family seems clear from a draft of a letter he wrote to the duchess immediately afterwards, stating, 'officially and on the surface my treatment within the family has been entirely correct and dignified ... but gosh they move slowly within these palace confines & the intrigues & manoeuvrings backstage must be filling books'.[24] Wallis's reaction to the news was straightforward, even as she counselled, 'I hope you will not leave [this] around the room for all and sundry to read.' She wrote, 'I am so glad that things for once have been done properly regarding you ... Now that the door has been opened a crack try and get your foot in, in the hope of making it even wider in the future because that is the best for WE.'*

Alluding to a hurtful missive that the duke had at some point written to Queen Mary, Wallis advised, 'I suggest that you see the widow and tell her a little of your feelings that made you write the offending letter. After all, there are two sides to every story.' Money was, as usual, at the forefront of her mind - 'I should also say how difficult things have been for us and that also we have gone out of our way to keep our way of life dignified which has not been easy due to the expense of running a correct house in keeping with your position as a brother of the King of England'

---

* An expression that Edward and Wallis used to denote their unbreakable love for one another.

- but she also knew what could and could not be broached. She did not attach as much significance to the matter of her HRH title as her husband did, hence her advice to 'leave it there ... *do not mention or ask for anything regarding recognition of me*'. Suggesting that the duke attempt to ingratiate himself with the new queen and her husband, the duchess added that 'I know how you hate being there but this is a golden opportunity and it may only knock but once.' She concluded, with her own hint of command, 'Do try to do what I suggest.'[25]

George VI's funeral took place on 15 February 1952. Wallis was anxious about her husband's status there, fearing that he would neither be allowed to wear his military uniform nor walk immediately behind his brother's coffin, as was his right. Her concern was needless; he took his place alongside his younger brother, the Duke of Gloucester, Prince Philip, and the sixteen-year-old Duke of Kent, the son of his late brother. It was, inevitably, a solemn and sombre occasion. Nonetheless, the Duke of Windsor's behaviour on the day attracted adverse comment. Channon described him as 'jaunty', and mused, 'What must be his thoughts and regrets?'[26] One observer, writing to the photographer Cecil Beaton, remarked on his 'swaggering' manner, and how the duke was 'talking and looking around, gesticulating and almost waving to the huge and completely silent crowd'.[27]

If one wished to be fair to the Duke of Windsor, his inappropriately cheery, even showboating, behaviour might be explained by his remaining in a state of shock and confusion, caused by the stress of a long boat journey and a continuing uncertainty as to his place in the newly reshuffled royal family. It did not help his mood that shortly before the funeral, he discovered that the £10,000 he had been receiving as an allowance since his abdication was to be stopped, as the amount had been purely in his brother's gift. Although the original agreement had been considered binding for the remainder of the former monarch's life, rather than as long as George VI lived, it was a blunt reminder that the duke's apparent reconciliation with his family was at best conditional, at worst an impossibility.

On the morning of the funeral, the duchess wrote angrily to her husband to say, 'I can hardly believe that this can go on at this time. I hope you have not taken the expensive trip to lose the £10,000 and to be insulted.' She concluded, 'love, love and fight for WE'.[28]

The day after the funeral, depression and exhaustion over-whelmed the duke. After he spoke to Wallis on the telephone, she was driven to write to him on 17 February to say, 'I did feel so distressed hearing your voice last night . . . You sounded so sunk and discouraged.' She described his family as 'beasts to continue to treat you the way they do', and suggested, 'do the best you can my darling, but I am afraid Mrs Temple Sr will never give in – all due to that letter which your mother should have kept to herself'*. Musing on his options, and offering her sorrow for her husband having 'such a hurting time', the duchess suggested, 'I am afraid Mrs T Senior won't see you as she may feel she would lose the stand she has taken . . . Naturally you can't storm the Palace, [but] you will however be able to work on some of the girl's advisers I imagine.'[29] As Lascelles remained the new queen's private secre-tary, this was a fanciful idea.

The duke lingered in Britain after the funeral, struggling to make sense of what his new role would be. He might have hoped to be received once more into the heart of the Firm, even to take on an informal counsellor role of sorts for his niece, but the loss of a substantial annual pension and the family's continued cool-ness towards him meant that any longed-for reconciliation seemed impossible. He wrote to the queen mother on 18 February to ask for a private appointment, saying, 'I can well understand your not wanting to be bothered by people at this terribly sad moment in your life. But I would very much like to have a talk with you alone before I return to America . . . I feel for you so very deeply and would like to say so in person.'[30]

---

* It remains uncertain as to which letter this refers to. Most of the duke's surviving correspondence with his mother is of a friendly, if somewhat detached, nature, which suggests that a more explosive letter of this kind was disposed of in horror.

This was untrue. He expressed his actual feelings to Wallis the same day by telegram – 'have asked to see Cookie but general atmosphere frustrating . . . am growing long grey beard in snowstorm so can't wait here too long' – and a few days later, he took stock of the situation while staying with his mother at Marlborough House. Describing his dissatisfaction at the 'difficult, painful and discouraging trip', he railed against the apparent hypocrisy of his family. 'Cookie was sugar as I've told you and [Mountbatten] and other relations and the Court officials correct and friendly on the surface. But gee the crust is hard and only granite below.' He sighed that the likely reason for his pension not to be continued was 'the fine excuse of national economy', and, in the most damning and furious statement he had made about his family to date, complained, 'it's hell to be even this much dependent on these ice-veined bitches, important for WE as it is'.*[31]

During his various interviews and appointments, the duke kept a series of notes about his reception and experiences. They make dispiriting and cynical reading. Noting that 'nobody cried in my presence . . . only Winston as usual', he christened the prime minister 'Cry Baby', and was scathing about the family's reaction to the king's death. 'Cookie & Margaret feel most . . . Mama hard as nails but failing. When Queens fail they make less sense than others in the same state.' His appointment with the queen mother was unproductive – 'Cookie listened without comment & closed on the note that it was nice to be able to talk about Bertie with somebody who had known him so well' – and he remained suspicious about the power structure that now existed. 'Economy is the slogan in G.B. . . . I don't believe the Civil List will be cut but they are all talking poor which is bad.' As for Mountbatten, his one-time friend

---

* He remained conscious about popular reaction to his presence. 'There has of course been no adverse comment over my walking in uniform in the funeral procession. On the contrary, my huge British fan mail of close on 1000 letters has been very favourable.' If this reminds the reader of a certain recent American president with a penchant for boastfulness, it is surely only a coincidence.

and supporter, the duke was dismissive. 'One can't pin much on him but he's very bossy & never stops talking. All are suspicious & watching his influence on Philip.' The only people he was warm about were the new queen and her husband; he noted that 'Clarence House [their residence] was informal & friendly. Brave New World. Full of self-confidence & seem to take job in their stride.'[32]

Edward's presence in Britain had not been wholly welcome. Channon wrote in his diary of 19 February that 'Queen Mary complained about the Duke of Windsor and particularly of his growing garrulousness - she can never get in a word!' Although Channon acknowledged that 'he has now seen all the Queens and officially at least has re-established some relations with his family', he criticised the duke as 'an advanced chatterbox'.[33] Nor did matters improve as his stay continued. Channon, damning his late king on 24 February in his diary - '"Bertie" is forgotten and nobody except his daughters really liked him' - was able to remark that 'the Duke of Windsor, too, seems out of the picture and apparently bores and irritates his mother'.[34] Two days later, the well-informed politician disclosed that '[Edward] made a poor impression on his niece and goddaughter'[35] when he finally met the queen and Prince Philip in an effort to bring them to his side over the vexed question of money. He failed.

Edward returned to the United States in early March, miserable and disappointed. Even as his mother wrote of her son's presence that it had been 'nice but a bit disturbing',[36] and expressed relief that the feud between the duke and the rest of his family appeared to be over, he was angered both by their continued refusal to acknowledge his wife and now by the withdrawal of his much-desired £10,000 a year. The Duchess of Gloucester may have felt that 'it was particularly moving listening to the Duke, because he was obviously so pleased to be talking with his own family again',[37] but his actual thoughts on them all were considerably less generous. He was angry, frustrated and lashed out whenever he could: *plus ça change.*

He returned to Britain repeatedly throughout 1952, ostensibly to see his mother and sister-in-law and to enquire about his family's well-being, but his intentions were more mercenary in nature. He was received with politeness but little more; there was no renewal of his allowance. He poured out his feelings to Queen Mary about this on 9 October, after commiserating with her about her ill health. He wrote, 'our situation is further aggravated by the fact that I have just suffered the loss of £10,000 per annum through the payment of the voluntary allowance I had from poor Bertie being stopped at his tragic death. This serious loss of income has come at a most inopportune time and will necessitate a complete revision of the style of living we have maintained ever since our marriage as befits the position of a son of a sovereign.'[38]

His entreaties were unsuccessful. Had he known of the queen mother's continued antipathy towards him, he may have been unsurprised at their poor reception. She wrote to Lascelles on 29 November, musing on the difficulties of kingship and wishing that her husband had been allowed 'a few years of <u>comparative</u> peace'. Yet she also reserved continued contempt for the man she blamed, at least in part, for George VI's tribulations. '[There was] the abdication & all the agony of mind - I doubt if people realise how horrible it all was to the King & me - to feel unwanted, & to undertake such a job for such a dreadful reason, it was a terrible experience.'[39] Sixteen years after the abdication, she showed no signs of softening towards the duke, and any support he might have hoped for from her was not forthcoming.

Greater humiliation lay at hand. After a largely terrible year in which he suffered a severe attack of food poisoning in August, the duke turned his thoughts to his niece's coronation, which was planned for 2 June 1953. If he was invited - with or without Wallis - it would prove that he had been truly reconciled with the family towards whom he alternately expressed contempt and indifference. He soon discovered, via the Duke of Norfolk giving a press conference, that his presence would be unwelcome. It was made clear that although Edward, as a royal duke, could not be barred from the ceremony, his wife could be excluded, and Norfolk not only stated that he did not believe the duke would attend, but publicly asked that he make a statement saying that he would not be present, 'to ease the situation from every point of view'.[40]

The situation was not as clear-cut as might have been imagined. The duke wished to attend, and had gone so far as to ask his solicitor, A. G. Allen, to intervene on his behalf, but Lascelles was adamant that the former king could have no place at the ceremony. He described his attending with Wallis as something that would be condemned as 'a shocking breach of taste', and that given that Edward was unable to attend his own coronation, 'however good his reasons', his presence at his niece's 'would strike a distressing and discordant note'. Even as Allen weakly attempted to suggest that the events of the abdication were now ancient history and that there was no purpose or benefit from prolonging hostilities, Lascelles, a noted scholar of the past, soon corrected him. 'Have you or I, for example, forgotten the Somme?'[41]

Had the new queen wished for her uncle to be present, such a consideration would have overruled all other matters of intention or protocol. But although relations between the two of them remained cordial - a letter exists in which she invites the duke for lunch on Tuesday 20 November 1952, and sympathises with him about Queen Mary's failing health - she, whether influenced by her mother or not, did not wish him to attend the coronation. After a discussion between Geoffrey Fisher, the Archbishop of Canterbury,* and the new monarch, both decided that it would be both inappropriate and undesirable for the duke to be present. Fisher even went so far as to write in his notes of their conversation that 'the Queen would be less willing than any one to have him there'.[42]

Around the time of the duke's lunch with Elizabeth, it was made clear to him by Churchill that his presence at the coronation, with or without his wife, would be nothing but a distraction. Edward,

---

* The feeling of contempt was mutual. In a letter to Wallis of 27 March, Edward described Fisher as 'an unctuous hypocrite like all the rest', and, most damningly of all, compared him to his nemesis Cosmo Lang, the former Archbishop of Canterbury, saying 'he reminded me of Auld Lang Swine'.

unhappily, ceded. He wrote to the prime minister on 23 November
to say of the 'delicate matter' that it stemmed from 'my family's
uncompromising attitude towards the Duchess and I which causes
the rekindling of this controversial subject as headline news with
each and every Royal public occasion'. Mindful of the desire to
avoid 'unpleasant publicity', he asked that a statement be issued
that explained that no former monarch would be invited to the ceremony, thereby placing him in the same category as such figures as
Leopold of the Belgians and Peter of Yugoslavia.

The wording he suggested was 'The Duke of Windsor will not
be present at the Coronation service in Westminster Abbey on June
2 1953 because it would not be in accordance with constitutional
usage for the Coronation of a King or Queen of England to be attended by the Sovereign or former Sovereign of any State.'[43] The
prime minister demurred, replying to the duke on 5 December to
assure him that while no former monarch would attend the coronation, 'I feel that the statement which you suggest will come with
force and dignity from Your Royal Highness personally, in reply to
any questions which may be addressed to you.'[44] For all the courtesy with which Churchill treated the duke, the implication was
clear: this is a private matter, and no longer one of state concern.

'Mama died at 10.15. All love and more.' So the duke informed Wallis
of Queen Mary's death on 24 March 1953. Just over a year after
his brother's death, his mother, who had been unwell for some
considerable time, finally succumbed to her illness. Her eldest son
was by her side, reluctantly leaving the duchess in New York on 6
March to seek a final audience with the last member of his family
who had been, after a fashion, supportive of him. Yet after the
disappointments and humiliations of the previous year, he was all
but indifferent to the affairs of the Firm. He may have informed
his friend Lord Dudley on 6 April that 'it was terrible when her
end came . . . her passing has left a great void for our generation,
and a last great personal link with our past has gone',[45] but this
was merely another of his public platitudes at times of grief, albeit

delivered privately. Privately, he felt little but contempt.

The duke had planned on joking in his undelivered speech to the BPRA in September 1951 that 'After a man has written two or more books, people get used to it . . .' It was with this in mind that he agreed to write a short, topical follow-up to *A King's Story*, this time entitled *The Crown and the People*, which would be an account of the monarchy over the past half-century and published to coincide with the coronation. As a work of history and memoir, it is unexceptional, with only the expression of the duke's increasingly conservative social and political views of any note amid the usual self-justification; many might have cavilled at his brief description of George VI's 'constant strain' at his responsibilities coming so soon after his death, even if the duke acknowledged that 'I am not insensible to the fact that through a decision of mine he was projected into sovereign responsibilities that may at first have weighed heavily upon him.'[46]

However, the main, if not the sole, purpose of *The Crown and the People* was to make money, and, in part, replace the £10,000 that showed no signs of being returned to the duke. He and his wife had recently purchased a property, a dilapidated mill named the Moulin de la Tuilerie, at Gif-sur-Yvette, a short distance from Paris, and the refurbishment of the building would be expensive and time-consuming. Yet even as Wallis complained to her aunt Bessie that 'I wish the world and particularly the US press would forget the Windsors',[47] both she and the duke were aware that their financial stability depended wholly on their not being forgotten. It was partly with this in mind that the duke boarded the *Queen Elizabeth* from New York to see a woman who was now describing herself as 'an old crock', and whose existence, after years of decline, could no longer continue for more than a matter of weeks.

He wrote a series of letters to Wallis while they were apart, which summarise the bitterness and anger he felt towards his family by then. On 9 March, he stated that 'fate certainly can be tough taking me away from you after two weeks of separation with my nose to the grindstone to repair the loss of income my very wealthy niece withholds ... What I think of having to make this ridiculous and costly trip instead of our being together in Palm Beach is nobody's business.' He reserved little but contempt for his dying mother - 'ice in place of blood in the veins must be a fine preservative'[48] - and upon his arrival in Britain, he wrote about her with cold detachment. 'She is very sick indeed and it's just a question of how long she will last ... She repeats herself a lot and has one or two theme songs upon which she harps all the time.' Given his own constancy on certain matters, mainly financial, this was an inherited family trait.

Acknowledging that it was 'hellish' for 'poor Mama',[49] he nevertheless occupied himself alternately with asking the advice of the likes of Monckton and Nicolson on the merits of *The Crown and the People*, and complaining that his mother's final decline was lasting too long. He wrote to Wallis on 21 March that 'it's one of the most trying situations I've ever found myself in and hanging around someone who has been so mean and vile to you my sweetheart is getting me down'.

He intended to return to New York on 1 April, informing the duchess that 'I just can't take this hanging around any longer and anyway as I have no part in the Royal Family beyond Burke's Peerage or Who's Who and don't stand to benefit from Mama's will I'm off back to *you* my beloved where I belong.'[50] Wallis urged her husband to eat properly; the stress and uncertainty of the situation had triggered the eating disorder he had had most of his life, and both his mental and physical state were at a low point.

His mother's death, when it came, was something of a relief. He wrote to Wallis that 'I couldn't have taken it for much longer, for her sake or mine.' He missed the actual moment of her demise, but at least he was not half-cut like the Duke of Gloucester; he sneered to Wallis that 'I found [him], glass of scotch in hand and feeling no pain* ... I guess it was emotion.' He reflected, after he saw his mother for the final time the next day, that 'my sadness

---

* A euphemism for drunkenness that both Edward and Wallis used.

was mixed with incredulity that any mother could have been so hard and cruel towards her eldest son for so many years and yet so demanding at the end without relenting a scrap . . . I'm afraid the fluids in her veins have always been as icy cold as they now are in death.' And then it was back to discussing renovations for the mill and how much he was going to be paid for *The Crown and the People*; 'I believe the price may go up to £15,000!'[51]

The funeral took place on 31 March, and the duke departed as soon as he could afterwards. He was under no illusions that he had any further place within the Firm, commenting to the duchess the previous week that 'I'm so excited to think that I'm going to be with you again so soon and that this agony is all over with . . . Thank God this is the last of these Royal Family passings that I'll ever have to leave you and cross the ocean for.' He was, naturally, keen to get his hands on his mother's possessions ('I also told my niece I wanted some nice things'), but his removal from the scene meant that, as he put it, 'I'll be at a disadvantage being away when the division is made and the "vultures" will have first pick.'

If he ever considered how his behaviour over the past two decades had estranged him from his family, and how merited his treatment had been, he showed no signs of it. Although he allowed that his sister, Mary, had been 'quite sweet' and that the Duke of Gloucester, who he sardonically called 'the Unknown Soldier', and his wife had been amicable hosts, it was with anger that he hissed to Wallis that 'what a smug stinking lot my relations are and you've never seen such a seedy worn-out bunch of old hags most of them have become'. His fury stemmed, as so often, from their refusal to accept his wife: 'of course they don't talk our language and never will and I've been boiling mad the whole time that you haven't been here in your rightful place as a daughter-in-law at my side'.

That Wallis was never regarded as a daughter-in-law, or remotely acceptable in any social sphere, was not a truth to be borne at this point. After years of trying to ingratiate himself with the royal family and the establishment at large, the duke had finally admitted defeat. He could only take some consolation from the knowledge that with his mother and brother dead, and his niece the new monarch, he was free to live his life as he saw fit, estranged from his family but also with all responsibility or expectation removed from him. He revelled in this second abdication of sorts, as he declared to the duchess, 'let us skip this rude interlude and enjoy our lovely full life together far removed from the boredom, the restrictions and the intrigues of the Royal Family and the Court . . . God bless WE.'[52] Yet as he abandoned the final trappings of his inheritance, it would be left to others to pick up where he had so gleefully left off.

Chapter Seventeen

'The Hopes of the Future'

For the woman who became the longest-serving monarch in British history, the circumstances in which Queen Elizabeth II discovered her new destiny were hardly propitious. As Harold Nicolson quipped, 'She became Queen while perched in a tree in Africa watching the rhinoceros come down to the pool to drink.'[1] This was an exaggeration, but it was true that when the king died in the early hours of 6 February 1952, the heir to the throne was one of the last members of the immediate circle to know, because of the intrinsic difficulties of contacting her in Kenya. Not only were she, Philip and their entourage staying at the isolated Tree-tops Hotel in Aberdare National Park, but the mixture of grief and panic that had greeted the news of the king's death in Britain was only exacerbated by the knowledge that telling his daughter - the new monarch - was a far harder undertaking than it ever should have been.

The news reached Philip's equerry, Mike Parker, from Martin Charteris, who had heard the tidings from a journalist as a news flash. At quarter to three in the afternoon, Parker informed the prince, who looked 'absolutely flattened' at his father-in-law's death and the realisation of the responsibilities that would now overwhelm both his wife and him; Parker later recalled that 'I never felt so sorry for anyone in my life.'[2] Philip then broke the news to Elizabeth, and they walked up and down the garden for a few moments. When they returned, the new queen was composed and calm, and said to the assembled ladies-in-waiting and other staff,

'I'm so sorry. It means we're all going to have to go back home.'[3]

Leaving aside the shock and grief that any young woman would inevitably feel at the sudden death of a parent, the queen now returned to a country she had only left a matter of a few days before, but that had altered existentially. Although she managed to remain businesslike, she summoned Charteris on the return flight and asked simply, 'What's going to happen when we get home?' Had her private secretary been honest, he might have replied, 'Your life will change beyond recognition, Your Majesty.' Instead, he simply offered her what comfort he could, as the plane came in to land and she was greeted by the solemn phalanx of Churchill, Attlee, Eden and other political worthies. Philip followed behind her once she was on the ground, as was now expected of him. While her father had lived, these people had meant little more to her personally than they did to most of the country. Now they would become men – exclusively men – she would have to deal with on a daily basis.

The queen's first official task was to attend the Accession Council, which took place on 8 February. Lascelles had written a speech for her back in September 1951, and it was with the assurance that had typified her previous public utterances that she now spoke. She alluded to her grief, and declared that 'at this time of deep sorrow, it is a very great consolation to me to have an assurance of the sympathy which you and all my peoples feel towards me, to my mother, and my sister, and to the other members of my family. He was its revered and beloved head, as he was of the wider family of his subjects; the grief which his loss brings is shared among us all.'

Yet it was her concentration on the idea of duty that would be of greater relevance to her reign. She stated, in an abbreviated version of the prepared text, that 'My heart is too full for me to say more to you today than that I shall always work as my father did throughout his reign.' In the original version, she would have gone on to promise 'to uphold constitutional government and to further the happiness and prosperity of my peoples everywhere ... I know that in my determination to follow his shining example of selfless service and tireless devotion, I shall be given strength by the loyalty and affection of those whose Queen I have been called to be, and by the wisdom of their elected Parliaments . . . I pray that God will guide me to discharge worthily this heavy task that has been laid upon me thus early in my life.'[4] Yet it was not the time to do so.

Her speech, which she delivered with considerably more confidence than her father had at the same point in his reign, was a success, and reassured anyone who might have doubted the young woman's ability to handle the public responsibilities that were concomitant with her new title, even if she did later weep in the car that took her back to St James's Palace. Yet as her biographer, Ben Pimlott, later wrote, 'there was also a peculiarity about the prostration of old gentlemen before a twenty-five-year-old Queen who had no choice but to accept the part she was asked to play'.[5]

Queen Victoria had been just eighteen when she had inherited the throne in 1836, avoiding the need for a regency by a month, but she had been beset by counsellors both welcome and unwelcome from the beginning of her reign, jostling for position and influence. The next queen had no ambitious John Conroy* to fear – the Duke of Windsor's musings on a quasi-regency would have been given short shrift indeed by Philip if they had ever been known – but nor did she have a Lord Melbourne on hand to guide her. Instead, she had the now seventy-seven-year-old Churchill, whom she barely knew and now had to rely on as a guide through the Byzantine paths of political skulduggery. He was not, perhaps, the man she would have chosen in this situation.

For his part, the prime minister was open about his distaste for her husband. Colville recorded Churchill saying that while he did not actively wish Philip ill, he neither liked nor trusted him and only hoped he would not do the country any harm. When he discovered that Mountbatten had proposed a toast to the newly

---

* Sir John Conroy was comptroller to both the Princess Victoria and her mother, the Duchess of Kent, and tried to force the young queen to his will; the historian Christopher Hibbert commented scathingly of how he was 'imposing, vain, clever, unscrupulous, plausible and of limitless ambition'.

royal house that – in theory – bore his name at his country home of Broadlands on 7 February, he 'went through the roof', according to Colville, and regarded Dickie's nephew with even greater distrust. The comments were relayed to Queen Mary by one guest, and the ailing queen, who had been the first to kiss the new monarch's hand the same day, was 'greatly disturbed' by the implication that the House of Mountbatten would supplant the House of Windsor as the country's ruling family. Something would have to be done.

Before it could be, the queen mother broadcast to the nation on 18 February. After thanking her listeners for their sympathy and affection 'throughout these dark days', she emphasised a theme of continuity rather than change. She began by saying that 'through-out our married life, we have tried, the King and I, to fulfil with all our hearts and all our strength the great task of service that was laid upon us ... my only wish now is that I may be allowed to continue the work we sought to do together', and then looked to the new queen. 'I commend to you our dear daughter: give her your loyalty and devotion: though blessed in her husband and children she will need your protection and your love in the great and lonely station to which she has been called.'[6] Her speech was intended to reassure, but there was another implication, too: the former queen, still only fifty-one, was not going anywhere. For all her public and private proclamations that she was now taking on a supporting role, she remained a powerful figure, and one not ready to shuffle off into her dotage.

The first indication that she was prepared to flash steel came shortly after her broadcast, at the end of the month. Philip was reluctant to move his family from Clarence House to Buckingham Palace, having spent a considerable amount of time and money re-furbishing the residence to his specifications; he argued that with Buckingham Palace either a five-minute walk or a minute-long car journey away, there was no need for the expense and bother of uprooting the new royal family. He was soon put in his place by both Churchill and the wider infrastructure of courtiers. One member of the household later commented that 'Prince Philip didn't want to go to Buckingham Palace, but all the old codgers like Lascelles said "you must go".[7] The prime minister reminded Philip that every monarch since Queen Victoria had lived at the palace - even, briefly, Edward VIII, who hated it but accurately remarked, 'I had a feeling that I might not be there very long'[8] - and that there was no reason why precedent should be altered to suit the young family. After all, the monarchy was a far greater institution than four people.

This necessitated the queen mother's departure from the place that had been her home, which she regarded with mixed feelings. Nobody believed more strongly in upholding protocol than her, but a letter she wrote to her daughter in late February suggested that she was still coming to terms with her altered status. 'I have been feeling very unhappy all today, and I suppose that talking about leaving Buckingham Palace just finished me off . . . naturally you must move back to B.P. in the Spring . . . I expect that the best plan would be for you & Philip to move into the Belgian rooms, because you are quite independent there . . . That would give me time to move my things without any ghastly hurry, and I could be quite self contained upstairs, meals etc.' Poignantly, she stated, 'you would hardly know I was there'.[9]

Yet before any move could happen, the question of the name of the family who would be taking up residence needed to be resolved. After Queen Mary's alarm at the idea that the House of Mountbatten would reign, Colville stepped in and not only assured her that the Windsor name should be the only one attached to the ruling family, but that it would be supported by the government. He was correct; not only were the Cabinet 'strongly of the opinion that the family name of Windsor should be retained', but Churchill was invited 'to take a suitable opportunity of making their views known to Her Majesty'. The premier, unsurprisingly, concurred - no doubt relishing the opportunity to frustrate the ambitions of both Philip and his uncle, against whom he held a lingering grudge for his apparent sacrifice of India - and on 20 February, he informed the Cabinet that 'it was the Queen's pleasure that she and their descendants should continue to bear the family name of Windsor'.[10]

This went down exceptionally badly with Philip, who shouted, 'I am nothing but an amoeba – a bloody amoeba', and stated, 'I am the only man in the country not allowed to give his name to his own children.' He might have walked behind his wife publicly, but he was not prepared to suffer the slight without a fight. Following a huge row, he wrote what Colville described with some understatement as 'an ably but strongly worded memorandum', in which he conveyed his feelings of anger at length, concluding with the suggested compromise that the royal family could henceforth be known as the House of Edinburgh. Churchill was vexed by his recalcitrance, and asked Colville to draft a 'firm, negative answer', in association with the Lord Chancellor, the Home Secretary, the Leader of the House of Commons and the Lord Privy Seal.

In due course, on 7 April, the Lord Chancellor was able to assert that 'it cannot be doubted that by His Proclamation of 1917 King George V intended that, so long as there was a member of His House to ascend the Throne, the name of the House should be Windsor'.[11] It therefore became inevitable that a new proclamation would be issued on 9 April, stating, 'The Queen today declared in Council her Will and Pleasure that She and Her Children shall be styled and known as the House and Family of Windsor, and that Her descendants other than female descendants who marry and their descendants shall bear the name of Windsor.' Had Philip been a more conciliatory – or tactical – man, he might have arranged a compromise, so that his children might have come to be known as the 'Mountbatten-Windsors'* or something similar. But his energy and focus, which could be so useful in practical and military contexts, now butted up against carefully orchestrated protocol, and could only come off second.

Parker later described how Philip 'was deeply wounded', and one confidant of the prince said, 'it was a terrible blow. It upset

* The name the queen was said to be in favour of.

him very deeply and left him feeling unsettled and unhappy for a long while.'[12] Even as the ailing Queen Mary remarked disapprovingly, 'what the devil does that damned fool Edinburgh think that the family name has got to do with him',[13] he contracted jaundice, possibly because of the stress he was under, and was miserably bedridden for several weeks.

His wife, meanwhile, was discovering confidence in adversity. She commented to one friend that 'I no longer feel anxious or worried . . . I don't know what it is - but I have lost all my timidity somehow becoming the sovereign and having to receive the Prime Minister.'[14] These receptions became increasingly friendly and personal in nature. Had her husband known that he had a rival for his wife's affections in the unlikely form of a seventy-seven-year-old Old Harrovian with some military and authorial experience, he may have been less than sanguine about their weekly meetings, conducted à deux and without any record of their discussions.

Yet the wholly platonic relationship between Elizabeth and Churchill would be crucial to the early months and years of her reign. He had enjoyed a warm friendship with her father, but it had been tempered by a certain degree of wariness on both men's parts, with each of them acknowledging the other's desired primacy during wartime. George VI's final illness meant that the first few months of Churchill's second premiership did not register as strongly as either man would have wished. Yet the man whom the Duke of Windsor had so contemptuously dubbed 'Cry Baby' was anything but po-faced or humourless.

Although the queen initially described him as 'very obstinate',[15] there was another issue at hand: was Churchill up to the job? His physical health was fading, and although he was still sharp and witty, it was whispered that he lacked the necessary powers of concentration to cope with the demands of the premiership. He had been re-elected by his country in a symbolic act of contrition for allowing Labour to win in 1945, and the sentimental hope that he would once again lead the country to greatness in its hour of need. But peacetime prime ministers face very different challenges to wartime leaders, and it seemed inevitable that Elizabeth's first premier would not last long in his post.

However, having coveted a return to 10 Downing Street since the day he was ejected from it, Churchill would not leave willingly. Therefore, it was hinted that the queen should offer him the chance to retire at a time of his own choosing - an honourable departure, with laurels bound around his noble brow, but nonetheless a departure. Lascelles, however, scorned the idea. When it was put to him on 22 February, he remarked, 'If she said her part, [Churchill] would say charmingly "It's very good of you, Ma'am, to think of it" - and then he would politely brush it aside.' There was the possibility that George VI might have been robust about the matter, but as Lascelles remarked, 'he is gone'.[16] Churchill himself let it be known that he wished to remain in office at least until the coronation of the new queen, and even as his personal doctor Lord Moran suggested that his departure would be 'best for the Monarch, the country and his successor', to say nothing of being regarded as a 'noble gesture', the prime minister responded with typical sangfroid, remarking to Moran, 'I don't want you to worry. You really needn't. One has to die some time.'[17]

He was at the Trooping the Colour ceremony in the first week of June, watching the queen parade. Channon said of it that 'the presence of the youthful Queen added excitement . . . she seemed perfectly self-possessed, and a tiny bit cross but she is a competent horsewoman'.[18] Churchill described to the Press Association, at their annual luncheon on 11 June, how the event made him feel. 'As I watched our young Queen riding at the head of her Guards, I thought of the history of the past and the hopes of the future. Not only of the distant past - it is barely ten years since we upheld on our strong, unyielding shoulders the symbols, the honour and perhaps even the life of the free world. Certainly no one of British race could contemplate such a spectacle without pride. But no thinking man or woman could escape the terrible question: on what does it all stand?'[19]

Just as Attlee had inherited a country in chaos and turmoil, and had only been partially successful in his efforts to rebuild the war-ravaged state, so Churchill now faced an uncertain and unresolved situation. Britain was no longer Great, it seemed. Its king was dead, and Russia was in the ascendant. Another world war - this time nuclear - was something he had warned about while he was out of power, but now fine words and inspirational speechifying had to contend with fears of impending Armageddon. Less than a week later, Colville wrote in his diary that Churchill no longer saw himself as being up to the job; 'the Prime Minister is depressed and bewildered . . . [and] said to me this evening: "the zest is diminished". I think it is more that he cannot see the light at the end of the tunnel. Nor can I.'[20]

It was fortunate, then, that in the final hour of his political life, Churchill found himself falling in love again. As Charteris told Gyles Brandreth, 'Churchill was nearly eighty, and the Queen was no more than twenty-five, but it was not simply her youth and beauty that entranced him. He was impressed by her. She was conscientious, she was well-informed, she was serious-minded. Within days of her Accession she was receiving prime ministers and presidents, ambassadors and High Commissioners . . . and doing so faultlessly. She had authority and dignity as well as grace.'*[21] There are those who will find Churchill's comment to Moran - 'all the film people in the world, if they had scoured the globe, could not have found anyone so suited to the part'[22] - breathless and syrupy, the distasteful expression of an old man's panting over a much younger woman. And then there are others who will find it a gesture of the deep affection the prime minister came to feel for his monarch.

A pattern soon developed in their weekly audiences. The 'rather obstinate' prime minister would arrive at Buckingham Palace formally attired in frock coat and top hat - as he might have done half

---

* Charteris went further to the constitutional historian Peter Hennessy in 1994, remarking, 'I think she had him around her little finger. I think he was absolutely crazy in love with her.'

a century before - looking as if he was off for a day at the races rather than an appointment with the queen. Onlookers noticed that he had a gleam in his eye, and seemed younger, somehow, as if he was rejuvenated by his meetings. Once the premier and the monarch were ensconced together, they would not be interrupted for the length of their session, which often stretched well beyond the allotted hour. Courtiers were surprised to hear that these usually solemn occasions were punctuated by the sound of hearty laughter from both participants. Colville, after one such audience, figuratively caught the prime minister by his lapel and asked, 'What do you talk about?' Churchill smiled and said, 'Oh, mostly racing.'

Throughout 1952, the relationship between the two deepened and strengthened. It may have helped that, as Channon noted on 26 February, the queen was 'openly, assuredly, dangerously Tory'[23] - in contrast to her more progressive husband - but Churchill began to act around her as if he were both an *ami de maison* and a watchful guardian. In October, the queen commissioned a bust of the prime minister, to be sculpted by Oscar Nemon, who frequently sculpted both royalty and politicians. Churchill sat for him over a dozen times, but he could be a quixotic subject. Nemon later wrote to the royal librarian, Owen Morshead, to say, 'the progress of my work depends on this most unpredictable sitter. On Sunday for instance I moved to Chequers where I had a very pleasant contact in a relaxed setting.' Upon its completion, the bust was placed in the Queen's Guard Chamber at Windsor Castle: a conspicuous mark of favour, and one never extended to any other living prime minister.

Whether Churchill was praising the queen's charm in conversation with the US president-elect, Dwight Eisenhower, in January 1953, or cheerfully batting away an intrusive journalist's question about how Britain could justify the expense of the coronation when the country was in such dire financial straits with the reply 'Everybody likes to wear a flower when he goes to see his girl', there was little doubt that he was smitten. Yet it was not simply the doting affection of an older man for a younger woman, but a genuine belief that the queen offered Britain the same hope for the future that he himself had done nearly a decade and a half previously. Then, he had said to an exhausted and frightened country that 'I have nothing to offer but blood, toil, tears and sweat.' Now, his country needed a different kind of inspiration. Grandstanding and rhetoric had their place, but the young woman who, seven and a half years earlier, he had stood next to on the Buckingham Palace balcony as they celebrated VE Day represented modernity and progress.

A few months before that occasion, the prime minister had been offered the Order of the Garter by her father, in recognition of his services during the war. Although he described himself as 'touched and honoured' by the recognition, he turned it down, as he considered it inappropriate to accept such an award while he continued to serve as premier. Although the king was greatly disappointed by this, saying, 'I feel that the country will expect me to give you a high honour which it will acclaim as a fitting tribute for all your arduous work in this war, and one which will still enable you to remain in the House of Commons',[24] he did not press the issue, especially as Churchill conceded that, were he to be nominated by a future premier on his retirement, he would be prepared to reconsider accepting the award.

Lascelles now suggested to Colville that in view of the changed circumstances, the queen was keen to offer Churchill the Garter once more, but wanted to discreetly sound out the chances of his acceptance. When Colville dined with the prime minister and his wife, he was pleasantly surprised to discover that Churchill was open to the idea; he wrote in his diary, 'Mr Churchill said that he always felt that it had been discourteous of him to refuse the Garter . . . and what is more, as the 1st Duke of Marlborough's father had been Sir Winston Churchill, he felt that he himself would not mind being Sir Winston . . . In the end, he said he thought that if he were offered it he might well reconsider his view.'[25]

Shortly before the coronation, Churchill remarked to Moran, 'I will tell you a secret. You mustn't tell anyone. The Queen wants me to accept the Garter.' He went on to say that he had refused it before, 'but the Prime Minister had a say in it. Now only the Queen decides.' And when he finally accepted it, he took great pride in telling his well-wishers why he had changed his mind. He wrote to his friend Pamela Lytton on 3 May 1953 to say, 'I took it because it was the Queen's wish. I think she is splendid.'[26]

Meanwhile, Philip – the de facto rival for Elizabeth's attentions – was shaking off his frustrations over dynastic nomenclature by throwing himself into energetic pursuits. When he and the rest of his family had moved into Buckingham Palace, he marched from room to room, asking everyone he met who they were and what their purpose was. Ever the naval man, he called this his 'organisation and methods review', and his straight-talking, fast-walking manner offended some of the older and stuffier courtiers, who were unable to keep up with him, figuratively or literally. Nor did he have time for sycophancy. One overawed woman was rebuked when she referred to him as 'Your Highness'; he brusquely responded, 'I don't like to be "Highnessed". Just call me "sir". This is the 20th century. You're not at King Arthur's court, you know!'[27]

He occupied himself with everything from flying lessons to helping to plan his wife's coronation, taking the role of chairman of the coronation committee. One courtier described him to Churchill as 'insupportable when idle',[28] and Channon wrote on 21 May that Philip was 'desperately bored with his three womenfolk, the two Queens and Princess Margaret'.[29] If he felt frustrated, or belittled, or redundant, he made his feelings and opinions plain, but this did little to harm public opinion of him. When the *Daily Mirror* asked in February 1953 whether Philip should take a virtually equal role by his wife's side at the coronation, or if it should centre entirely on her, 42,680 readers took the former stance; a mere 432 disagreed. The paper's editorial was staunchly pro-duke. 'These figures show overwhelmingly Britain's affection and high regard for Philip. The people think he is a fine man doing a fine job. The *Daily Mirror* agrees.'[30] Channon remained entranced, saying breathlessly on 10 January 1953, '[he was] as always perfect . . . he is an enchantment'.[31]

Yet for all the *haut ton*'s admiration for the royal couple, the combined stress of Queen Mary's death and preparing for the coronation told on them. Channon wrote of how, on 6 April, Philip was 'white and ill - "almost dying"'.[32] There were lengthy arguments about whether the coronation should be televised; George VI's in 1937 had not been, but this was partly because broadcast technology was in its infancy, and partly because his nervousness and discomfort with public speaking might have turned the event into a disastrous and embarrassing spectacle.

The queen, perhaps surprisingly, was against it, and so Colville, informed of her opinion via Philip, sent a memo to Churchill in which he stated, 'the Committee was almost unanimous in considering that television of the actual ceremony should not be allowed'. He justified this by adding, 'whereas film of the ceremony can be cut appropriately, live television would not only add considerably to the strain on the Queen (who does not herself want TV) but would mean that any mistakes, unintentional incidents or undignified behaviour by spectators would be seen by millions of people'.[33] That there might yet be a greater good in televising it did not seem to occur to anyone involved in its organisation.

Initially, it seemed as if the government would simply support the royal wishes. The Cabinet noted that due to 'the importance of avoiding unnecessary strain for Her Majesty and upholding the sanctity of the ceremony', they concurred with the committee's decision. However, this was not the end of the matter. The public desired to see their young, attractive monarch being crowned, and if they could not be present at Westminster Abbey themselves, they wanted the next best thing: to be able to watch the ceremony on television. So overwhelming and consistent was the outcry, ably communicated to their elected representatives, that in October 1952, it was stated that in view of the 'serious public disappointment', the sacred event would indeed be broadcast live. According to Colville, the decision was not only accepted by the queen, but almost encouraged, with her agreeing that 'all her subjects should have an opportunity of seeing [the Coronation]'.[34]

As the event approached, there were rehearsals of near-unimaginable length and complexity, which the queen claimed to enjoy, and Churchill had to be allowed his moment of grandstanding. On 17 May, in the queen's presence, he delivered a speech at Westminster Hall on the theme of monarchy, in which he declared that 'I have served your Majesty's great-great grandmother, great-grandfather, grandfather, father and now yourself.' Ignoring the obvious riposte that it was unclear whether he was her premier or Old Father Time, he went on to remind her that the crown was as much a burden as it was a symbol of majesty, but stated that it was also a unifying symbol; he called it 'the central link in all our modern changing life, the one which above all others claims our allegiance to death'.[35]

It was an imposing, even awesome weight that was placed upon her, and the coronation on 2 June threatened to overwhelm the young queen. It is testament, then, to her calm that she was able to maintain a sense of humour. 'You must be feeling nervous, ma'am', a lady-in-waiting said to her, with an attempt at woman-to-woman compassion. The monarch replied, deadpan, with an allusion to one of her favourite activities: horse racing. 'Of course I am, but I really do think Aureole will win.'[36] In the event, her horse came second in the 1953 Derby, but he never faltered in the attempt, and would subsequently go on to triumph.

Chapter Eighteen

'God Save the Queen'

'Well, George, we knocked the bastard off.' Those were the words of the thirty-four-year-old explorer and mountaineer Edmund Hillary to his fellow mountaineer, George Lowe, upon his successful ascent of Mount Everest on 29 May 1953. The New Zealander and his Nepalese Sherpa Tenzing Norgay had achieved something widely believed to be impossible: they had scaled the highest mountain in the world, overcoming weather conditions, a lack of bottled oxygen, and health fears occasioned by the height of the altitude, to write themselves into history. Their names, deservedly, would live for ever.

Yet the immediate challenge upon their return from the peak of Everest was how to inform the rest of the world. That challenge fell to James - later Jan - Morris, then a reporter for *The Times* and the only journalist who had been attached to the expedition. Everest was over four and a half thousand miles away from London, and Morris sent a coded message to the newspaper on 30 May via the British embassy in Kathmandu, reading, 'Snow conditions bad stop advanced base abandoned yesterday stop awaiting improvement.' The message - innocuous to the uncomprehending - announced that the summit had been reached ('snow conditions bad'), and that those who had done so were Hillary ('advanced base abandoned') and Norgay ('awaiting improvement'). The news took two days to reach Britain, where - by pure, serendipitous coincidence - the story led the newspapers on 2 June 1953: the day of the coronation.

Had Elizabeth had a moment to glance at the headlines that

morning, she would undoubtedly have been delighted at the way
the ascent of Everest was conflated with her sacred duties that day.
The *Daily Mail* called Hillary's achievement 'The Crowning Glory',
and the *Daily Express*, above the headline 'All This - and Everest
Too!' - declared, 'Be Proud of Britain on This Day, Coronation
Day'. Despite the errors of fact (Hillary was a New Zealand citizen,
not the Briton the paper claimed, but he was, at least, a member of
the Commonwealth, as well as the '20th Century Elizabethan' he
was described as), the fortunate tidings gave the country a much-
needed morale boost amid the miserable wet weather that had
threatened to mar the coronation celebrations.

In the event, the downpour could not dampen the spirits of
those who had thronged the streets, desperate to catch a glimpse
of the young queen on her way to the ceremony. The *Express*'s reporter, R. M. MacColl, wrote, with a touch of colour, that 'Despite
the rain, defying the rain, singing in the rain, the people surged into
London all day yesterday and equably sat or lay down in its streets.'
Just as there had been on VE Day, nearly eight years earlier to the
day, there were spontaneous public singalongs; MacColl observed
that the most popular tune appeared to be 'It's a Long, Long Way to
Coronation' sung to the tune of 'It's a Long Way to Tipperary', and
wrote with wry indulgence that 'Near the Admiralty Arch a High-
land reel was started by some youths wearing tartan bonnets. In no
time a great section of the crowd was bobbing up and down with
them and when a couple of good-humoured policemen moved up
their arms were raised and they too for a few moments appeared
to be swaying to the rhythm.'[1]

Amid the noise and celebrations and good humour, the queen
prepared for the day. There had been a gradual build-up of excitement over the previous ten days, culminating in a Buckingham
Palace garden party on 29 May with a cast of characters that ranged
from foreign royalty to English bishops, all brought together with
one aim: to see the coronation, and to watch the young monarch
succeed. Even the usually straight-faced Colville, not a man given
to hyperbole or unnecessary excitement, wrote in his diary, 'Never

has there been such excitement . . . never has a monarch received such adulation.'[2] The rehearsals, masterminded by Prince Philip and the Duke of Norfolk, had gone well, although the queen had one unorthodox request: the Bishop of Durham, Michael Ramsey, who was graced with suitably dramatic eyebrows, had to be asked during one rehearsal to keep his brows still, on the grounds, in the words of Ramsey's biographer, Owen Chadwick, that 'they made her smile and she did not wish to smile in the wrong place'.[3]

On the day itself, the weather remained atrocious and inauspicious, both grey and wet, it was enough to lower the spirits of all but the most ardent royalists. Which on that day seemed to comprise virtually the entire country, not least the half-million who lined the streets to cheer the dignitaries, foreign and domestic alike, who began arriving at Westminster Abbey from eight o'clock in the morning. One of them, Queen Salote of Tonga, occasioned one of Noël Coward's greatest apocryphal quips: the queen was statuesque, to say the least, and accompanied by the minuscule Sultan of Kelantan, they made an incongruous duo in their open carriage, visible to the cheering crowds. When a friend of Coward's asked, 'Who's that?' as they sat watching the ceremony on television, Coward reportedly said, 'Her lunch.'[4]

Churchill, as at the royal wedding six years earlier, attracted cheers and excitement that practically rivalled the monarch's welcome for giddy approval. He was, appropriately, clad in the robes of the Order of the Garter that he had recently received, and, fearing exhaustion, had spent the previous night at Downing Street, a short carriage ride from the abbey. A few days earlier, he had addressed the queen and Prince Philip at a lunch reception for the Commonwealth Parliamentary Association, and had hinted at what she might expect from the events of the coronation and beyond, saying, 'in our island, by trial and error, and by perseverance across the centuries, we have found out a very good plan . . . the Queen can do no wrong. But advisers can be changed as often as the people like to use their rights for that purpose. A great battle is lost: Parliament turns out this Government. A great battle is won

- crowds cheer the Queen.' He called this 'a very commanding and durable doctrine', and offered a paradox designed to indicate the immortal, unchanging nature of the Crown: 'what goes wrong passes away with the politicians responsible . . . what goes right is laid on the altar of our united Commonwealth and Empire'.[5]

One of the queen's maids of honour, Anne Glenconner, had arrived at the abbey early that morning. She described London as 'an extraordinary sight, the streets full of tremendously cheerful people sitting or standing in the pouring rain', and remarked that 'after the doom and gloom of the post-war years, it was an especially incredible sight to behold'.[6] She knew the precise timings of the day: the journey from Buckingham Palace to Westminster Abbey would take nineteen minutes, and so the (notoriously uncomfortable) Gold State Coach that was bearing the queen and Prince Philip had to leave at 10.26 a.m. in order to convey the monarch to the Great West Door of the abbey, from where she would enter to begin the coronation. Perhaps as Glenconner glanced around at the guests, she would have seen Channon, sitting opposite the peeresses' benches; he pronounced the long wait 'enthralling' for people-watching, although, ever sharp, he wrote in his diary that 'Queen Mum was OK but compared badly with Queen Mary's entry last time'.[7]

When the queen and Philip arrived, he was not allowed to enter with her - a decision made by Lascelles - but instead joined the procession, something that Charteris later commented 'looked *awful* . . . when they shouted "Vivat! Vivat Regina!" she was on her own. It was not calculated to make him feel cheerful.'[8] It had also been made clear to him that during the ceremony he would be expected to kneel before his wife and declare, 'I, Philip, Duke of Edinburgh, do become your liege man of life and limb and of earthly worship, and faith and truth I will bear unto you, to live and die against all manner of folks. So help me God.'[9] The keenest-eyed viewer might have detected the hint of a wry smile on his face as he delivered these lines, all bound up with the suspicion of several courtiers and dignitaries that he was not taking the sacred ceremony as seriously as they were,* but was instead prepared to demonstrate what the day's official photographer Cecil Beaton described as 'a rather ragging attitude towards proceedings'.[10]

The duke's comparative irreverence may or may not have made the queen feel more comfortable as she stood among her ladies-in-waiting, hearing the great swell of trumpets and the abbey's organ, and preparing to enter for the ceremony. She was attired in a Norman Hartnell dress of ivory silk, embroidered with roses, thistles and the emblems of the British Isles and the Commonwealth, and she wore a long crimson velvet train over it, as was customary. As she waited for the moment that would define the rest of her life, she was calm. If she had any nerves, they were invisible to those around her. Sixteen years earlier, aged eleven, she had been present for her father's coronation; five and a half years earlier, she had married at Westminster Abbey. It was not a building that held any fear for her.

She remembered the timings that had been so painstakingly worked out over the previous weeks. There was a fifteen-minute pause between her arrival and entrance, and it would take fifty-five seconds for her to walk into the Gothic arch of the abbey, at which point the trumpet fanfares would begin and she would proceed down the central aisle, watched by as many as three hundred and fifty million people round the world. It was estimated that the ceremony that she and her courtiers had been so reluctant to have televised would be viewed by around twenty-seven million people in Britain. Given that the population of the country was thirty-six million, this meant that three quarters of her subjects were able to watch every moment of proceedings.

As she prepared to enter, she may have thought of the broadcast she would deliver that evening. In it, she would declare that

---

* Nonetheless, as Anne Glenconner wrote, he was 'rushing around all of us, checking that everything was in order and generally being very fussy'. His intentions may have been benign – 'I think he wanted it to be the most perfect day for the Queen' – but as she said, 'we knew exactly what to do and his frantic behaviour only added to the tension'.

'Throughout this memorable day I have been uplifted and sustained by the knowledge that your thoughts and prayers were with
me', and, recognising the millions who had watched the event, 'It is
hard for me to find words in which to tell you of the strength which
this knowledge has given me.' Yet most important was the renewed
compact that she now made with the British people and the rest
of her audience. On her twenty-first birthday, in her Cape Town
broadcast, she said that 'I declare before you all that my whole life
whether it be long or short shall be devoted to your service and
the service of our great imperial family to which we all belong.'
Now, just over six years later, with the burden of monarchy thrust
upon her, she could say, 'I have in sincerity pledged myself to your
service, as so many of you are pledged to mine. Throughout all my
life and with all my heart I shall strive to be worthy of your trust.'[11]

As she glanced around her, with the drizzle falling on her
garments, she would have seen the anxious, excited faces of her
ladies-in-waiting, as well as the sterner expression of the Duke of
Norfolk. When her father had been crowned on 12 May 1937, he
had overcome his near-crippling nerves with a sense of religious
deliverance; he had remarked afterwards to the Archbishop of
Canterbury that 'he felt throughout that Some One Else was with
him'. Now, sixteen years later, as his daughter prepared to take up
the mantle of majesty, it was not fanciful to imagine that she was
accompanied, on some level, by her father's spirit. He had incul-
cated a sense of duty in her, but also a compassion and a humility
that meant that she had the potential to take the institution of the
Crown in directions unimagined by any monarch since Victoria.

Her uncle had been an appalling, selfish king; her father a dutiful and serviceable one, who had found his true mettle in wartime.
But Elizabeth II was someone quite different. The new Elizabethan era would be one of change, of evolution and of hope. She
would establish herself as the longest-serving monarch in British
history, and in many regards the greatest. Her reign would not be
without controversy, incident or upset, but never would she be
regarded by her loyal and adoring subjects as anything other than

an inspiration to them all, right up until her death in September 2022. In the words of Handel's coronation anthem, which would sound out so triumphantly during the anointing ceremony:

> Zadok the priest
> And Nathan the prophet
> Anointed Solomon king
> And all the people
> Rejoiced, rejoiced, rejoiced

The music grew to its climax. It was time for the queen to embrace her destiny. She looked around at her ladies-in-waiting and smiled reassuringly. 'Ready, girls?' Then they stepped forward into the abbey and processed into immortality. As the anthem that would be sung so enthusiastically by millions that day, and for decades afterwards, declared:

> God save our gracious Queen!
> Long live our noble Queen!
> God save the Queen!

Acknowledgements

It is with regret that I must now conclude my 'Windsors trilogy', but as ever, there are many people to thank, without whom neither this book nor the preceding two would exist. The team at Weidenfeld & Nicolson has been consistently superb, including my brilliant editor Ed Lake, my excellent project editor Sarah Fortune, my copy-editor Jane Selley, my picture editor (and highly accomplished photographer) Natalie Dawkins and the painstaking campaigns director Elizabeth Allen. It has been a pleasure to work with them all once again.

It has also been a privilege to be published by St Martin's Press in the United States, and I would like to thank the peerless Michael Flamini, editor par excellence, as well as his assistant editor Hannah Phillips, my publicist Sophia Lauriello, and SMP's marketing manager Michelle Cashman; it has been an honour to continue our professional association with this book.

My literary agent and good friend Ed Wilson has been a continued source of inspiration, wine and advice throughout the creation and editing of *Power and Glory*, and his insights are always eagerly awaited by me - as I'm sure they are by all his clients. My former editor Alan Samson, meanwhile, remains my first port of call for any discussion of matters literary or historical, and so it has proved here; his insights into the subject, from proposal stage onwards, have been invaluable.

As with *The Crown in Crisis* and *The Windsors at War*, there are many distinguished historians and authors whose advice, counsel and insights have been invaluable. I was fortunate enough to talk with the late Philip Ziegler as I researched *The Crown in Crisis*, but so wide-ranging was our conversation that I continue to use his insights to this day. His erudition and generosity were enormously helpful to me as a young(er) historian and biographer. I am also grateful to Anne Sebba (as ever), Andrew Roberts, Walter Monckton's late daughter-in-law Marianna, Richard Aldrich and Rory Cormac, Ben Pimlott, Sarah Bradford, William Shawcross and Michael Bloch, whose contributions, directly or through their published works, have been invaluable.

Public and private archival collections are crucial to any writer's research, and a few of the people who have made the greatest contribution include Bethany Hamblen at the Balliol College Archives, Julie Crocker at the Royal Archives, and Hannah Carson at the Bodleian Library's Special Collections department. I should like to thank the Master and Fellows of Balliol College for permission to quote from the Walter Monckton archive. Additionally, I am grateful to the staff of the National Archives, the Hoover Library at Stanford, the Oxford Union, the Parliamentary Archive and, in particular, the ever-excellent London Library. And, of course, I would like to thank His Majesty King Charles III for his kind permission to quote from letters and documents in the Royal Archives.

I owe deep gratitude to many friends and fellow writers, including Sophie Buchan, Dan Jones, Gustav Temple, Amanda Craig, William Boyd, David Taylor, Daisy Dunn, Oliver Soden, Dominic Green, Michael Bhaskar, Philip Womack, Simon Sebag Montefiore, Brice Stratford, Thomas Grant, Ben Schott, Catherine Bray, Emrys Jones, Mark Atherton, Toby White, Sophie Dunn, Sean Herdman-Low, 'Boothby' Renshaw, James Douglass, Raymond Stephenson and many others besides.

Six books in, my wife Nancy has yet to murder me in understandable frustration at having her husband taken away from her through his research and writing, so I must thank her for that, as well as the countless other kindnesses she shows me each and every day. However, it is to the dedicatee of this book, our wonderful daughter Rose, that I must offer my greatest thanks and love. *Power and Glory* is nothing if not a paean to a father's love for his daughter, and you, my wonderful girl, are the very finest, kindest and most rewarding child I could ever have hoped to have.

Bibliography

Aldrich, Richard J., and Cormac, Rory, *The Secret Royals*, Atlantic, 2021

Alexandra of Yugoslavia, *For A King's Love,* Odhams, 1956

Alsop, Susan Mary, *To Marietta from Paris*, Weidenfeld & Nicolson, 1976

Aronson, Theo, *The Royal Family at War*, John Murray, 1993

Balfour, John, *Not too Correct an Aureole*, Salisbury, 1983

Barrow, Andrew, *Gossip: A History of High Society 1920-1970*, Hamish Hamilton, 1978

Beaton, Cecil, *The Strenuous Year: Diaries 1948-55*, Weidenfeld & Nicolson, 1973

Beckett, Francis, *Clem Attlee*, Richard Cohen, 1997

Bew, John, *Citizen Clem*, Riverrun, 2016

Birkenhead, Lord, *Walter Monckton*, Weidenfeld & Nicolson, 1969

——*The Life of Lord Halifax*, Hamish Hamilton, 1965

Blackledge, Catherine, *The Story of V: Opening Pandora's Box*, Weidenfeld & Nicolson, 2003

Bloch, Michael, *The Secret File of the Duke of Windsor*, Bantam, 1988

——*The Reign & Abdication of Edward VIII*, Bantam, 1990

——*The Duchess of Windsor*, Weidenfeld & Nicolson, 1996

Boothroyd, Basil, *Philip: An Informal Biography*, Longman, 1971

Bradford, Sarah, *King George VI*, Weidenfeld & Nicolson, 1989

——*Elizabeth: A Biography of Britain's Queen*, Heinemann, 1996

Brandreth, Gyles, *Philip and Elizabeth: Portrait of a Marriage*, Century, 2004

Bryan III, J., and Murphy, Charles, *The Windsor Story*, Granada, 1979

Chadwick, Owen, *Michael Ramsey: A Life*, Oxford, 1990

Churchill, Winston, *The Second World War: The Gathering Storm*, Cassell 1948

——*The Second World War: Their Finest Hour*, Cassell, 1949

——*The Second World War: The Grand Alliance*, Cassell, 1950

——*The Second World War: The Hinge of Fate*, Cassell, 1950

——*The Second World War: Closing the Ring*, Cassell, 1951

——*The Second World War: Triumph and Tragedy*, Cassell, 1953

Clark, Mark, *Calculated Risk*, Harrap, 1951

Colville, Jock, *The Fringes of Power: Downing Street Diaries 1939-1955*, Hodder & Stoughton, 1989

Cooper, Diana, *Autobiography*, Michael Russell, 1979

——*The Light of Common Day*, Hart-Davis, 1959

Crawford, Marion, *The Little Princesses*, Cassell, 1950

Dean, John, *HRH Prince Philip, A Portrait by his Valet*, Robert Hale, 1954

Donaldson, Frances, *King Edward VIII*, Weidenfeld & Nicolson, 1974

Donoghue, Bernard, and Jones, G. W., *Herbert Morrison: Portrait of a Politician*, Weidenfeld & Nicolson, 1973

Dunlop, Tessa, *Elizabeth and Philip*, Headline, 2022

Eade, Philip, *Young Prince Philip*, HarperPress, 2011

Eisenhower, Dwight, *Crusade in Europe*, Doubleday, 1948

Farrell, Brian, ed., *Churchill and the Lion City*, NUS Press, 2011

Frankland, Noble, *Prince Henry, Duke of Gloucester*, Weidenfeld & Nicolson, 1980

Gilbert, Martin, *Prophet of Truth*, Heinemann, 1976

——*Never Despair: Winston S. Churchill 1945-1965*, Heinemann, 1988

Glenconner, Anne, *Lady in Waiting*, Hodder & Stoughton, 2019

Gloucester, Alice, Duchess of, *The Memoirs of Princess Alice, Duchess of Gloucester*, HarperCollins, 1981

Grimes, Frank, *Sundry Times*, John Murray, 1986

Guedalla, Philip, *The Hundredth Year*, Hodder & Stoughton, 1939

Heald, Tim, *The Duke*, Hodder & Stoughton, 1990

Heffer, Simon, ed., *Henry 'Chips' Channon: The Diaries 1943-1957*,

Hutchinson, 2022

Higham, Charles, *Mrs Simpson: Secret Lives of the Duchess of Windsor*, Sidgwick & Jackson, 1998

Hoare, Philip, *Noël Coward*, Mandarin, 1996

Hyde, H. Montgomery, *Walter Monckton*, Sinclair-Stevenson, 1991

Jenkins, Roy, *Churchill*, Macmillan, 2001

Kinross, Lord, *The Windsor Years,* Collins, 1967

Larman, Alexander, *The Crown in Crisis*, Weidenfeld & Nicolson, 2020

——*The Windsors at War*, Weidenfeld & Nicolson, 2023

Lascelles, Alan, *King's Counsellor: Abdication and War*, Weidenfeld & Nicolson, 2006

Laura, Duchess of Marlborough, *Laughter From a Cloud,* Weidenfeld & Nicolson, 1980

Lees-Milne, James, *Harold Nicolson*, Chatto & Windus, 1981

Longford, Elizabeth, *The Queen: The Life of Elizabeth II,* Knopf 1984

Lownie, Andrew, *The Mountbattens*, Blink, 2019

MacDonald, Malcolm, *People and Places*, Collins, 1969

Maxwell, Elsa, *I Married the World*, Heinemann, 1955

McCullough, David, *Truman*, Simon & Schuster, 1992

Moran, Lord, *Winston Churchill: The Struggle for Survival 1940-1965,* Constable, 1965

Morrison, Herbert, *An Autobiography*, Odhams, 1960

Penelope Mortimer, *Queen Elizabeth: A Life of the Queen Mother,* Viking, 1986

Morton, Andrew, *The Queen*, Michael O'Mara, 2022

Nicolson, Nigel, ed., *Harold Nicolson Diaries and Letters 1945-1962,* William Collins, 1968

Norwich, John Julius, ed., *The Duff Cooper Diaries: 1915-1951,* Weidenfeld & Nicolson, 2005

Ogilvy, Mabell, *Thatched with Gold*, Hutchinson, 1962

Pasternak, Anna, *Untitled: The Real Wallis Simpson, Duchess of Windsor*, William Collins, 2019

Payn, Graham, and Morley, Sheridan, ed., *The Noël Coward Diaries*, Weidenfeld & Nicolson, 1982

Pimlott, Ben, *The Queen: Elizabeth II and the Monarchy*, HarperCollins, 2001

——ed., *The Political Diary of Hugh Dalton*, Jonathan Cape, 1986

Powell, Ted, *Edward VIII: An American Life*, OUP, 2018

Pye, Michael, *The King Over the Water*, Holt Reinhart & Winston, 1981

Raphael, Frederic, *Growing Up*, Robson Press, 2015

Rhodes James, Robert, *A Spirit Undaunted*, Little Brown, 1998

Roberts, Andrew, *Churchill*, Allen Lane, 2018

——*Eminent Churchillians*, Weidenfeld & Nicolson, 1994

Rose, Kenneth, *Kings, Queens and Courtiers*, Weidenfeld & Nicolson, 1985

Sebba, Anne, *That Woman*, Weidenfeld & Nicolson, 2011

Shawcross, William, *Queen Elizabeth: The Queen Mother*, Macmillan, 2009

——ed., *Counting One's Blessings: The Selected Letters of Queen Elizabeth, the Queen Mother*, Macmillan, 2012

Sissons, Michael, and French, Philip, ed., *Age of Austerity 1945–51*, Hodder & Stoughton, 1963

Sitwell, Osbert, *Queen Mary and Others*, Michael Joseph, 1974

Smith, Amanda, ed., *Hostage to Fortune: The Letters of Joseph P. Kennedy*, Penguin, 2001

Spoto, Donald, *Dynasty: The Turbulent Saga of the Royal Family from Victoria to Diana*, Simon & Schuster, 1995

Stuart, Charles, ed., *The Reith Diaries*, Collins, 1975

Taylor, A. J. P., *Beaverbrook*, Hamish Hamilton, 1972

Templewood, Viscount, *Nine Troubled Years*, Collins, 1954

Townsend, Peter, *Time and Chance*, Collins, 1978

Turner, Graham, *Elizabeth: The Woman and the Queen*, Macmillan, 2002

Vickers, Hugo, *Behind Closed Doors*, Hutchinson, 2011

——*Elizabeth: the Queen Mother*, Hutchinson, 2011

Vincent, John, ed., *The Crawford Papers*, Manchester University Press, 1984

Warwick, Christopher, *George and Marina: The Duke and Duchess of*

Kent, Weidenfeld & Nicolson, 1988

Watson, Sophia, *Marina: The Story of A Princess*, Weidenfeld & Nicolson, 1994

Wheeler-Bennett, John W., *King George VI: His Life and Reign*, Macmillan, 1958

Wheen, Francis, *Tom Driberg: His Life and Indiscretions*, Chatto & Windus, 1990

Williams, Kate, *Young Elizabeth*, Weidenfeld & Nicolson, 2012

Williams, Susan, *The People's King*, Allen Lane, 2003

Windsor, Duke of, *A King's Story*, Cassell, 1951

——*The Crown and the People*, Cassell, 1953

Windsor, Wallis, *The Heart Has Its Reasons*, Michael Joseph, 1956

Ziegler, Philip, *King Edward VIII*, Collins, 1990

——*Diana Cooper*, Hamish Hamilton, 1981

——*Crown and People*, Collins, 1978

——*Mountbatten*, HarperCollins, 1985

Notes

Prologue: 'My Whole Life Shall Be Devoted to Your Service'
1 Morton, p.86
2 Alan Lascelles to Dermot Morrah, 10 March 1947, in Morton, p.86
3 Dunlop, p.89
4 Princess Elizabeth Commonwealth broadcast, 21 April 1947
5 Lascelles diary, 30 April 1947, in *King's Counsellor*
6 Morton, p.87

Chapter One: 'The Most Terrible Thing Ever Discovered'
1 George VI diary, 8 May 1945, Royal Archives, GVI/PRIV/DIARY/WAR
2 Kate Williams, p.196
3 Crawford, p.90
4 Kate Williams, p.196
5 Ibid.
6 Henry 'Chips' Channon diary, 9 May 1945, in Heffer, p.277
7 Channon diary, 13 May 1945
8 Channon diary, 17 May 1945
9 George VI diary, 22 May 1945
10 Ibid., 28 May 1945
11 Bradford, *George VI*, p.499
12 George VI diary, 20 June 1945
13 Ibid.
14 Beckett, p.198
15 Ibid.
16 Ibid.
17 Ibid.
18 George VI diary, 26 July 1945
19 Ibid.
20 Rhodes James, p.275
21 George VI diary, 26 July 1945

22 Lascelles diary, 27 July 1945
23 See Larman, *The Windsors at War*, Chapter Five, for further details
24 McCullough, *Truman*, p.436
25 Hugh Dalton diary, 28 July 1945, in Pimlott, ed.
26 Lascelles diary, 2 August 1945
27 Bradford, *George VI*, p.502
28 George VI diary, 2 August 1945
29 Lascelles diary, 2 August 1945
30 Winston Churchill statement, 6 August 1945
31 Harold Nicolson diary, 6 August 1945, in Nicolson, p.31
32 Nicolson diary, 7 August 1945
33 Lascelles diary, 7 August 1945
34 Ibid., 8 August 1945
35 Channon diary, 15 August 1945
36 Lascelles diary, 15 August 1945
37 George VI to House of Commons, 15 August 1945, from Hansard, HL Deb 15 August 1945 vol 137 cc8-129
38 George VI VJ Day broadcast, 15 August 1945
39 Lascelles diary, 15 August 1945
40 Queen Elizabeth to Lady Helen Graham, 15 August 1945, Royal Archives, RA/QEQM/OUT/GRAHAM/117, in Shawcross, p.387

Chapter Two: 'I Never Saw a Man So Bored'

1 Bryan and Murphy, p.455
2 Grimes, p.72
3 Balfour, p.108
4 Ziegler, *King Edward VIII*, p 497
5 Kinross, p.231
6 Duke of Windsor to Duncan Stewart, 24 July 1945, Royal Archives, RA/DW/5891, in Ziegler, *King Edward VIII*, p.497
7 Oliver Harvey to Jock Colville, 29 June 1945, National Archives, FO 800/521
8 Duke of Windsor to Clement Attlee, 3 August 1945, National Archives, FO 800/521
9 Duke of Windsor to George Allen, 30 July 1945, Royal Archives, RA/EDW/PRIV/MAIN/5899
10 Bryan and Murphy, p.455
11 Lascelles diary, 12 August 1945

12 George VI to Duke of Windsor, 23 August 1945, National Archives, FO 800/521

13 Lascelles to John Martin, 21 December 1944, Chartwell Papers, in Ziegler, *King Edward VIII*, p.499

14 George VI to Queen Mary, 23 September 1945, Royal Archives, RA/GV/CC/13/135, ibid., p.500

15 Lascelles diary, 26 September 1945

16 George VI diary, 5 October 1945

17 Channon diary, 16 October 1945

18 Queen Elizabeth to Queen Mary, 18 September 1945, Royal Archives, RA/QM/PRIV/CC13/133, in Shawcross, *Counting One's Blessings*, p.386

19 Channon diary, 16 October 1945

20 Owen Morshead, notes on conversation with Queen Mary, 18 February 1946, Royal Archives, RA/AEC/GG/12/0S/2, in Shawcross, *Queen Elizabeth*, p.600

21 Lascelles diary, 11 October 1945

22 Duke of Windsor to Queen Mary, 13 October 1945, Royal Archives, RA/EDW/PRIV/MAIN/6001

23 Queen Mary to Duke of Windsor, 17 October 1945, Royal Archives, RA/EDW/PRIV/MAIN/6009

24 Bryan and Murphy, p.456

25 Duke of Windsor to George VI, 18 October 1945, Royal Archives, GVI/PRIV/01/02/20

26 George VI diary, 24 October 1945

27 George VI to Duke of Windsor, 10 November 1945, Royal Archives, RA/EDW/PRIV/MAIN/6042

28 Duchess of Windsor to Bessie Merriman, 5 December 1945, in Bloch, *Secret File*, p.264

29 Duke of Windsor to Winston Churchill, 15 November 1945, ibid., pp.261-2

30 Duke of Windsor to George VI, 15 November 1945, Royal Archives, GVI/PRIV/01/O2/21

31 Ibid.

32 Edward Holman to Oliver Harvey, 24 September 1945, National Archives, FO 800/521

33 Bryan and Murphy, p.456

34 Duke of Windsor to Queen Mary, 18 June 1946, Royal Archives, RA/QM/PRIV/CC9

35 Alsop, p.55

36 Bryan and Murphy, p.457

37 Lascelles diary, 8 November 1945

38 Ibid., 9 November 1945

39 Ibid., 30 November 1945

40 Ibid., 6 December 1945

41 George VI diary, 6 December 1945

42 Duke of Windsor to Walter Monckton, 9 December 1945, Royal Archives, RA/DW/6083, in Ziegler, *King Edward VIII*, p.506

43 Duchess of Windsor to Bessie Merriman, 3 January 1946, in Bloch, *Secret File*, p.265

44 Lascelles diary, 20 December 1945

45 Hon. David Bowes-Lyons to Rachel Bowes-Lyon, 1 January 1946, Bowes-Lyon Papers, in Shawcross, *Queen Elizabeth*, p.600

46 Lascelles diary, 31 December 1945

Chapter Three: 'I Believe She Loves and Will Marry Him'

1 Queen Elizabeth to Sir D'Arcy Osborne, 1 January 1946, Royal Archives, RA/QEQM/OUT/OSBORNE, in Shawcross, *Counting One's Blessings*, p.389

2 Crawford, p.96

3 Ibid., p.33

4 Heald, p.30

5 Ibid., p.32

6 Ibid., p.37

7 Ziegler, *Mountbatten*, p.101

8 Heald, p.59

9 Pimlott, *The Queen*, p.85

10 Bradford, *George VI*, p.301

11 Ziegler, *Mountbatten*, p.102

12 Crawford, p.98

13 Channon diary, 11 January 1942

14 Alexandra of Yugoslavia, pp.68–9

15 Eade, p.143

16 Queen Elizabeth to Queen Mary, 12 December 1943, Royal Archives, RA/QM/PRIV/CC13/76, in Shawcross, *Queen Elizabeth*, p.578

17 Princess Elizabeth to Marion Crawford, 1 January 1944, Royal Archives, RA/QEII/OUT/BUTHLAY, ibid.

18 Lascelles diary, 1 January 1944

19 Eade, p.154

20 Crawford, p.85

21 Prince Philip to Queen Elizabeth, 31 December 1943, Royal Archives, RA/QEQM/PRIV/RF

22 Pimlott, *The Queen*, p.95

23 Channon diary, 16 February 1944

24 Ibid., 21 January 1944

25 Queen Mary to King George VI, 6 March 1944, Royal Archives, RA/GVI/PRIV/RF/11, in Shawcross, *Queen Elizabeth*, p.578

26 Eade, p.155

27 King George VI to Victoria Milford Haven, 31 October 1941, in Eade, p.143

28 King George VI to Queen Mary, 17 March 1944, Royal Archives, RA/QM/PRIV/CC13/84, in Shawcross, *Queen Elizabeth*, p.579

29 Eade, p.155

30 Pimlott, *The Queen*, p.96

31 Louis Mountbatten to King George VI, 20 February 1944, Royal Archives, RA GVI/PRIV/RF/24/084, in Lownie, p.185

32 Louis Mountbatten to King George VI, 10 May 1944, Royal Archives, RA/GVI/PRIV/RF/24/088, ibid., pp.185-6

33 King George VI to Louis Mountbatten, 10 August 1944, in Ziegler, *Mountbatten*, p.308

34 Louis Mountbatten to Princess Victoria of Hesse, 28 August 1944, ibid.

35 Louis Mountbatten to Princess Alice, 9 February 1945, ibid.

36 Prince Philip to Louis Mountbatten, 6 September 1945, ibid., pp.308-9

37 Alan Lascelles to R. A. Strutt, 2 March 1945, Royal Archives, RA/GVI/270/01, in Pimlott, *The Queen*, p.97

38 Lascelles diary, 7 August 1945, ibid.

39 Alexander Maxwell to Lascelles, 26 October 1945, ibid., p.98

40 Heald, p.69

41 Crawford, p.92

42 Ibid., p.99

43 Prince Philip to Queen Elizabeth, 14 September 1946, Royal Archives, RA QEQM/PRIV/RF, in Shawcross, *Queen Elizabeth*, p.625

44 Crawford, p.99

45 Ibid.

46 Ibid., pp.99-100

47 Ibid., p.99

48 Ibid., p.101

49 Kate Williams, p.202

50 Eade, p.175

Chapter Four: 'This Poor Battered World'

1 Lascelles, p.xii
2 Ibid.
3 Duchess of Windsor to Bessie Merriman, 3 January 1946, in Bloch, *Secret File*, p.266
4 George VI to Lascelles, December 1945, in Rhodes James, p.291
5 Lascelles diary, 8 January 1946
6 Ibid., 9 January 1946
7 George VI diary, 8 January 1946
8 Duchess of Windsor to Bessie Merriman, 25 January 1946, in Bloch, *Secret File*, p.267
9 Duke of Windsor to Alan Lascelles, 28 January 1946, ibid.
10 Duke of Windsor to George VI, 2 February 1946, Royal Archives, GVI/PRIV/O1/02/25
11 Alan Lascelles to Sir Pierson Dixon, 5 February 1946, National Archives, FO 800/521
12 Ernest Bevin to Archibald Clark Kerr, 10/11 February 1946, ibid.
13 Archibald Clark Kerr to Ernest Bevin, 12 February 1946, ibid.
14 Sir Pierson Dixon to Ernest Bevin, 19 February 1946, ibid.
15 Ernest Bevin to Lord Halifax, February 1946, ibid.
16 Lord Halifax to Ernest Bevin, 5 March 1946, ibid.
17 Sir Pierson Dixon to Ernest Bevin, 5 March 1946, ibid.
18 George VI to Duke of Windsor, Royal Archives, RA/EDW/PRIV/MAIN/6227
19 Duke of Windsor to George VI, 21 March 1946, Royal Archives, GVI/PRIV/01/02/26
20 Channon diary, 2 February 1946
21 Queen Elizabeth to Eleanor Roosevelt, 6 January 1946, in Shawcross, *Counting One's Blessings,* p.389
22 George VI message of support to the United Nations, 10 October 1945, Royal Archives, RA/PS/PSO/GVI/PS/MAIN/7880
23 Morrison, p.248
24 King George VI diary, 20 November 1945
25 Lascelles diary, 26 February 1946
26 George VI diary, 24 August 1946
27 Crawford, p.97
28 Ibid., p.91
29 Lascelles diary, 15 March 1946
30 Larman, *The Crown in Crisis,* p.251

31 Winston Churchill to Duke of Windsor, 15 December 1945, Royal Archives, RA/EDW/PRIV/MAIN/6088

32 'Churchill's Call for World Domination', *Chicago Sun*, 6 March 1946

33 Winston Churchill to *Chicago Sun*, 7 March 1946, in Gilbert, *Never Despair*, p.204

34 George VI diary, 12 March 1946

35 Duke of Windsor to Winston Churchill, 5 May 1946, Royal Archives, RA/EDW/PRIV/MAIN/6274

36 Ibid.

Chapter Five: 'Nothing Ventured, Nothing Gained'

1 Brandreth, p.138

2 Boothroyd, p.89

3 Brandreth, p.167

4 Ibid., p.168

5 Ibid., p.182

6 Kate Williams, p.203

7 Shawcross, *Queen Elizabeth*, p.624

8 Barrow, p.100

9 Prince Philip to Queen Elizabeth, 12 June 1946, Royal Archives, RA QEQM/PRIV/RF, in Shawcross, *Queen Elizabeth*, p.624

10 Crawford, p.101

11 Prince Philip to Queen Elizabeth, 14 September 1946, Royal Archives, QEQM/PRIV/RF, in Shawcross, *Queen Elizabeth*, p.625

12 George VI diary, 8 August 1946

13 Turner, p.23

14 Ibid.

15 Crawford, p.102

16 George VI diary, 14 October 1946

17 Pimlott, *The Queen*, p.99

18 Ziegler, *Mountbatten*, p.341

19 Lord Mountbatten to Tom Driberg, 14 August 1946, in Wheen, p.212

20 Ibid.

21 *News Chronicle*, 10 December 1946

22 Rhodes James, p.297

Chapter Six: 'The Old Values Have Disappeared'

1 Duff Cooper to Foreign Office, 5 July 1946, National Archives, FO 371/60757

2 Winston Churchill to Duke of Windsor, 19 May 1946, Royal Archives, RA/EDW/PRIV/MAIN/6285

3 Duke of Windsor to Walter Monckton, 31 May 1946, Dep. Monckton Trustees 20

4 Winston Churchill to Duke of Windsor, 19 May 1946, Royal Archives, RA/EDW/PRIV/MAIN/6285

5 Duchess of Windsor to Bessie Merriman, 24 April 1946, in Bloch, *Secret File,* pp.271-2

6 Kenneth de Courcy note, 10 December 1936, Kenneth Hugh de Courcy papers, reel 3, box 3, folder 4, Hoover Institution Library & Archives

7 Kenneth de Courcy to Duke of Windsor, 21 February 1946, ibid., reel 2, box 2, folder 9

8 Kenneth de Courcy to Duke of Windsor, 14 March 1946, ibid.

9 Duke of Windsor to Kenneth de Courcy, 19 March 1946, ibid.

10 Kenneth de Courcy to Duke of Windsor, 17 July 1946, ibid.

11 Duchess of Windsor to Bessie Merriman, 12 July 1946, in Bloch, *Secret File,* pp.273-4

12 Kenneth de Courcy to Duke of Windsor, 26 July 1946, Kenneth Hugh de Courcy papers, reel 2, box 2, folder 9, Hoover Institution Library & Archives

13 Duke of Windsor to Kenneth de Courcy, 3 October 1946, ibid.

14 Kenneth de Courcy to Anthony Rumbold, 15 November 1946, ibid.

15 George VI diary, 16 October 1946

16 Laura, Duchess of Marlborough, pp.104-5

17 Ibid.

18 Duke of Windsor press statement, 18 October 1946

19 Kathleen Kennedy Hartington to Joseph P. Kennedy, 27 October 1946, in Smith, p.632

20 Duke of Windsor to Robert Young, 18 October 1946, Royal Archives, RA/EDW/PRIV/MAIN/6505

21 Laura Peek, 'Retired in Bognor, the prime suspect in the case of missing £13m gems', *The Times,* 2 February 2004

22 Higham, pp.324-5

23 Duke of Windsor to George VI, 10 November 1946, Royal Archives, GVI/PRIV/01/02/31

24 Duke of Windsor to Lord Portal, 9 November 1946, Royal Archives, RA/DW/7336, in Ziegler, *King Edward VIII,* p.513

Chapter Seven: 'The Loneliest Man in the World'

1 Lascelles to Joan Lascelles, 7 February 1947, in *King's Counsellor*, p.397

2 Ibid., pp.102–3

3 Ibid., p.103

4 Wheeler-Bennett, p.416

5 Crawford, p.104

6 Pimlott, *The Queen*, p.112

7 Crawford, p.104

8 Ibid.

9 George VI diary, 28 January 1947. His diary came to an end shortly afterwards, with the final entry on 30 January

10 Queen Elizabeth to Queen Mary, 1 February 1947, Royal Archives, RA/QM/PRIV/CC13/162, in Shawcross, *Counting One's Blessings*, p.394

11 Bradford, *George VI*, p.515

12 Shawcross, *Queen Elizabeth*, p.611

13 Lascelles to Joan Lascelles, 7 February 1947, in *King's Counsellor*, p.397

14 Lascelles to Joan Lascelles, 12 February 1947, ibid., p.398

15 Pimlott, *The Queen*, p.113

16 Townsend, p.169

17 Princess Elizabeth to Marion Crawford, 15 February 1947, Royal Archives, RA/QEII/OUT/BUTHLAY, in Shawcross, *Queen Elizabeth*, p.612

18 Princess Elizabeth to Queen Mary, 16 February 1947, Royal Archives, RA/QM/PRIV/CC14/148, ibid., p.612

19 Crawford, p.104

20 Bradford, *George VI*, p.516

21 Lascelles to Joan Lascelles, 18 February 1947, in *King's Counsellor*, p.399

22 Lascelles to Joan Lascelles, 22 February 1947, ibid.

23 Queen Elizabeth to Queen Mary, 21 February 1947, Royal Archives, RA/QM/PRIV/CC13/169, in Shawcross, *Counting One's Blessings*, p.395

24 Lascelles to Joan Lascelles, 22 February 1947, in *King's Counsellor*, p.399

25 Ibid.

26 Mortimer, p.213

27 Queen Elizabeth to Queen Mary, 16 April 1947, Royal Archives, RA/QM/PRIV/CC13/176, in Shawcross, *Counting One's Blessings*, p.398

28 Shawcross, *Queen Elizabeth*, p.619

29 Ibid.

30 Bradford, *George VI*, pp.517–18

31 Ibid., p.518

32 Townsend, p.177

33 Ibid., pp.177–8

34 Queen Elizabeth to May Elphinstone, 26 April 1947, Royal Archives, RA/QEQM/OUT/ELPHINSTONE, in Shawcross, *Counting One's Blessings*, p.399

35 Ibid.

36 Lascelles to Joan Lascelles, 1 April 1947, in *King's Counsellor*, p.403

37 Lascelles to Joan Lascelles, 30 April 1947, ibid., pp.404–6

38 George VI to Duke of Windsor, 19 April 1947, Royal Archives, RA/EDW/PRIV/MAIN/A/6783

Chapter Eight: 'Don't You Recognise an Old Friend?'

1 Larman, *The Crown in Crisis,* p.97

2 Duke of Windsor to Queen Mary, 15 December 1946, Royal Archives, RA/QM/PRIV/CC9

3 Sir William Murphy to Arthur Creech Jones, 30 December 1946, National Archives, CO 537/2250

4 Ernest Bevin memorandum, 1 January 1947, National Archives, CO 537/2250

5 Arthur Creech Jones to Sir William Murphy, 17 January 1947, National Archives, CO 537/2250

6 Duchess of Windsor to George Allen, February 1947, in Bloch, *The Duchess of Windsor,* p.132

7 Godfrey Thomas memo, 8 October 1947, in Ziegler, *King Edward VIII*, p.521

8 Duke of Windsor to Queen Mary, 16 October 1947, Royal Archives, RA/QM/PRIV/CC9

9 Duchess of Windsor to Bessie Merriman, 19 July 1947, in Bloch, *Secret File,* p.278

10 Nicolson diary, 29 May 1947

11 Ibid.

12 Ernest Bevin to Clement Attlee, 13 August 1945, National Archives, FO 800/521

13 Larman, *The Windsors at War,* p.352

14 Anthony Eden to Winston Churchill memorandum, 7 May 1953, National Archives, FO 800/847

15 Ernest Bevin to Clement Attlee, 30 June 1947, National Archives, PREM 8/1578

16 Ernest Bevin to Clement Attlee, 31 July 1947, National Archives, PREM 8/1578

17 George Marshall to Dean Acheson, 15 March 1947, US National Archives, Diplomatic Branch 841.001/3-1547

18 Godfrey Thomas memo, 10 July 1947, in Ziegler, *King Edward VIII*, p.550

19 Bryan and Murphy, p.462

20 Ibid.

21 Duke of Windsor to Queen Mary, 8 March 1948, Royal Archives, RA/QM/PRIV/CC9

22 Duke of Windsor to Queen Mary, 16 October 1947, Royal Archives, RA/QM/PRIV/CC9

23 John Gordon to George Allen, 17 February 1948, Royal Archives, RA/PRIV/QM/CC9

Chapter Nine: 'I Felt That I Had Lost Something Very Precious'

1 Alan Lascelles to Joan Lascelles, 30 April 1947, in *King's Counsellor*, p.406

2 Crawford, pp.105-6

3 Ibid.

4 Queen Elizabeth to May Elphinstone, 7 July 1947, Royal Archives, RA/QEQM/OUT/ELPHINSTONE, in Shawcross, *Counting One's Blessings*, p.400

5 Crawford, pp.107-9

6 *Daily Express*, 10 July 1947

7 Eade, p.193

8 Pimlott, *The Queen*, p.123

9 Robert Coe to George Marshall, 14 July 1947, file 841.0011/7-1047, 1945-49 Central Decimal File, RG 59: General Records of the Department of State

10 Queen Elizabeth to Sir Osbert Sitwell, 10 July 1947, Sitwell Papers, in Shawcross, *Counting One's Blessings*, p.401

11 Queen Elizabeth to Prince Philip, 9 July 1947, Duke of Edinburgh Personal Archives, Buckingham Palace, in Shawcross, *Counting One's Blessings*, p.401

12 Crawford, p.108

13 Brandreth, pp.179-80

14 Lord Mountbatten to Tom Driberg, 28 July 1947, in Wheen, pp.212-14

15 Lord Mountbatten to Tom Driberg, 3 August 1947

16 Brandreth, p.193

17 Pimlott, *The Queen*, pp.124-5

18 Kate Williams, p.217

19 Eade, p.200

20 Pimlott, *The Queen*, p.13

21 Turner, p.31

22 Channon diary, 25 October 1947

23 Ibid., 6 November 1947

24 Pimlott, *The Queen*, p.135

25 Brandreth, p.196

26 Eade, p.204

27 Channon diary, 20 November 1947

28 Winston Churchill to George VI, 16 July 1947, in Gilbert, *Never Despair,* p.341

29 Channon diary, 20 November 1947

30 Crawford, pp.115–16

31 Pimlott, *The Queen*, p.139

32 Crawford, p.117

33 Ibid., p.118

34 John Reith diary, 20 November 1947, in Stuart, p.204

35 Eade, p.207

36 George VI to Princess Elizabeth, 20 November 1947

Chapter Ten: 'The Future Is a Gloomy One'

1 Duchess of Windsor to Bessie Merriman, 11 September 1947, in Bloch, *Secret File,* p.279

2 Duke of Windsor to Queen Mary, 11 July 1947, Royal Archives, RA/EDW/PRIV/MAIN/A/6883

3 Ibid.

4 Duke of Windsor to Earl of Dudley, 16 October 1947, Royal Archives, RA/EDW/PRIV/MAIN/A/6958

5 'Three American Women' to George VI, 4 October 1947, Royal Archives, RA/EDW/PRIV/MAIN/A/6952

6 Kenneth de Courcy to Duke of Windsor, 17 November 1947, Kenneth Hugh de Courcy papers, reel 2, box 2, folder 9, Hoover Institution Library & Archives

7 F. J. Dadd to D. M. McCausland, 10 November 1947, National Archives, HO 144/23378

8 Duke of Windsor to Lord Beaverbrook, 4 November 1948, Beaverbrook papers, in Ziegler, *King Edward VIII,* p.515

9 Duke of Windsor to Queen Mary, 15 August 1947, Royal Archives, RA/QM/PRIV/CC9

10 Duke of Windsor to George VI, 8 September 1947, Royal Archives, GVI/PRIV/01/02/34

11 Duchess of Windsor to Bessie Merriman, 16 August 1948, in Bloch, *Secret File,* p.281

12 Kenneth de Courcy to Duke of Windsor, 22 July 1948, Kenneth Hugh de Courcy papers, reel 2, box 2, folder 9, Hoover Institution Library & Archives

13 Duke of Windsor to Kenneth de Courcy, 28 August 1948, ibid.

14 Dan Longwell to Duke of Windsor, 10 September 1948, Dep. Monckton Trustees 20

15 Duke of Windsor to Walter Monckton, 11 September 1948, Dep. Monckton Trustees 20

16 Walter Monckton to Alan Lascelles, 3 December 1948, Dep. Monckton Trustees 20

17 Walter Monckton to Major Gray Phillips, 17 December 1948, Dep. Monckton Trustees 2

18 Lord Beaverbrook to Duke of Windsor, July 1948, in Bloch, *Secret File,* p.286

19 Duke of Windsor to Beaverbrook, August 1948, ibid., pp.286-7

20 Bryan and Murphy, p.465

21 Ibid., p.466

22 Donaldson, p.396

23 Duchess of Windsor to Bessie Merriman 15 September 1948, in Bloch, *Secret File,* pp.281-2

24 Duchess of Windsor to Bessie Merriman, 2 October 1948, ibid.

25 Duchess of Windsor to Bessie Merriman, 20 October 1948, ibid.

26 Duchess of Windsor to Bessie Merriman, 1 December 1948, ibid.

27 Duchess of Windsor to Bessie Merriman, 18 December 1948, ibid.

Chapter Eleven: 'An Unkind Stroke of Fate'
1 Wheeler-Bennett, p.762

2 Queen Mary to Duke of Windsor, 12 February 1948, Royal Archives, RA/EDW/PRIV/MAIN/A/7042

3 Bradford, *George VI,* p.594

4 Townsend, p.182

5 Channon diary, 20 October 1948

6 Shawcross, *Queen Elizabeth,* p.637

7 Queen Elizabeth to Queen Mary, 14 November 1948, Royal Archives, RA/QM/PRIV/CC13/211, in Shawcross, *Counting One's Blessings,* p.409

8 Bradford, *George VI*, p.595

9 Channon diary, 30 November 1948

10 Princess Elizabeth to Queen Elizabeth, 22 November 1947, Royal Archives, RA/QEQM/PRIV/RF, in Eade, p.209

11 Queen Elizabeth to Princess Elizabeth, 24 November 1947, Royal Archives, RA/QEQM/PRIV/RF, in Shawcross, *Queen Elizabeth*, p.631

12 Pimlott, *The Queen*, p.144

13 Prince Philip to Queen Elizabeth, 3 December 1947, Royal Archives, RA/QEQM/RF, in Shawcross, *Queen Elizabeth*, p.631

14 Eade, p.211

15 Brandreth, p.209

16 Crawford, p.124

17 Ibid., p.125

18 Lascelles diary, 15 January 1969

19 James Chuter Ede to Alan Lascelles, 22 June 1948, Royal Archives, RA/GVI/PS/9091, in Pimlott, *The Queen*, p.153

20 Lascelles diary, 15 January 1969

21 Beaton, p.17

22 Crawford, p.127

23 Queen Elizabeth to Queen Mary, 20 November 1948, Royal Archives, RA/QM/PRIV/CC13/212, in Shawcross, *Queen Elizabeth*, p.638

24 Princess Elizabeth to May Elphinstone, 18 November 1948, Royal Archives, RA/QEQM/OUT/ELPHINSTONE, in Shawcross, *Queen Elizabeth*, p.637

25 Crawford, p.128

26 Winston Churchill to George VI, 22 November 1948, Royal Archives, PS/PSO/GVI/C/069/68

27 Duke of Windsor to George VI, 6 December 1948, Royal Archives, GVI/PRIV/01/02/35

28 Hugh Dalton diary, 14 November 1948, in Pimlott, ed.

29 Channon diary, 30 November 1948

30 Ziegler, *Crown and People*, p.84

Chapter Twelve: 'Untold Injury in Every Quarter'

1 Queen Elizabeth to Winston Churchill, 27 December 1948, Royal Archives, RA/QEQM/PRIV/OUT/MISC, in Shawcross, *Counting One's Blessings*, p.412

2 Queen Elizabeth to Marion Crawford, 1 January 1949, Royal Archives, RA/QEII/OUT/BUTHLAY, in Shawcross, *Queen Elizabeth*, p.641

3 Crawford, p.109

4 Kenneth de Courcy to Duchess of Windsor, 13 May 1949, Kenneth Hugh de Courcy papers, reel 2, box 2, folder 9, Hoover Institution Library & Archives

5 Charles Murphy to Walter Monckton, 23 April 1949, Dep. Monckton Trustees 20

6 Godfrey Thomas to Walter Monckton, 19 June 1949, ibid.

7 Walter Monckton to Alan Lascelles, 8 July 1949, ibid.

8 Walter Monckton to Charles Murphy, 8 July 1949, ibid.

9 Walter Monckton to Alan Lascelles, 8 July 1949, ibid.

10 Duke of Windsor to Walter Monckton, 13 August 1949, ibid.

11 Walter Monckton to Duke of Windsor, 22 August 1949, ibid.

12 Charles Murphy to Walter Monckton, 4 August 1949, ibid.

13 Charles Murphy to Walter Monckton, 1 September 1949, ibid.

14 A. G. Allen to Walter Monckton, 13 October 1949, ibid.

15 A. G. Allen notes on book chapters, 21 October 1949, ibid.

16 Walter Monckton notes on book chapters, September 1949, ibid.

17 Walter Monckton notes, 4 October 1949, ibid.

18 Queen Elizabeth to Marion Crawford, 4 April 1949, in Vickers, *Elizabeth*, p.283

19 Marion Crawford to Bruce Gould, 19 September 1949, ibid., p.285

20 Queen Elizabeth to Lady Astor, 19 October 1949, ibid., pp.285-6

21 Dermot Murrah to Bruce Gould, 21 November 1949, ibid., pp.287-8

22 Marion Crawford to Bruce Gould, 25 November 1949, ibid., p.288

23 Marion Crawford to Bruce Gould, 26 December 1949, ibid., p.289

24 Vera M. Brunt to Alan Lascelles, 30 December 1949, Royal Archives, PS/PSO/GVI/PS/MAIN/2870

25 Alan Lascelles to Vera M. Brunt, 5 January 1950, Royal Archives, PS/PSO/GVI/PS/MAIN/2870

26 Vickers, *Elizabeth*, p.290

27 Nancy Banks-Smith, *The Guardian,* 27 June 2000

Chapter Thirteen: 'In My Faith and Loyalty I Never More Will Falter'

1 Queen Elizabeth to Sir D'Arcy Osborne, 5 March 1949, in Shawcross, *Counting One's Blessings*, pp.415-16

2 Alan Lascelles to Lord Hardinge, 30 December 1948, in Vickers, *Elizabeth*, p.276

3 Bradford, *George VI*, p.596

4 Ibid.

5 Duke of Windsor to Queen Mary, 10 March 1949, Royal Archives, RA/ QM/PRIV/CC9

6 Queen Elizabeth to Princess Margaret, 8 May 1949, in Shawcross, *Counting One's Blessings*, p.416

7 Nicolson diary, 21 March 1949

8 Queen Elizabeth to Eleanor Roosevelt, 21 July 1949, in Shawcross, *Counting One's Blessings*, pp.417–18

9 Channon diary, 17 June 1949

10 Ibid., 31 May 1949

11 Eade, pp.230–1

12 Brandreth, p.232

13 Pimlott, *The Queen*, p.160

14 Ibid.

15 Ibid., p.161

16 Channon diary, 4 April 1949

17 Larman, *The Windsors at War*, p.25

18 Duchess of Windsor to A. G. Allen, 23 February 1948, in Bloch, *Secret File* p.109

19 Alan Lascelles to George VI, 13 November 1948, Royal Archives, RA/ PSO/GVI/C/042/325

20 George VI to Duke of Windsor draft, 13 November 1948, Royal Archives, RA/PSO/GVI/C/042/325A

21 William Jowitt to Alan Lascelles, 14 April 1949, Royal Archives, RA/ PSO/GVI/C/042/319

22 William Jowitt to Alan Lascelles (Jowitt report), Royal Archives, RA/ PSO/GVI/C/042/320

23 Alan Lascelles to George VI, 16 April 1949, Royal Archives, RA/ RA/ PSO/GVI/C/042/318

24 Duke of Windsor briefing note, 14 April 1949, in Bloch, *Secret File*, p.120

25 Clement Attlee to Duke of Windsor, 26 April 1949, Royal Archives, RA/ EDW/PRIV/MAIN/A/7497

26 Duke of Windsor to William Jowitt, 3 June 1949, in Bloch, *Secret File*, p.121

27 William Jowitt to Duke of Windsor, 13 June 1949, ibid.

28 Nicolson diary, 20 October 1949, in Bradford, *George VI*, p.592

29 Alan Lascelles to Clement Attlee, 9 December 1949, National Archives, PREM 8/1580

30 Clement Attlee to Alan Lascelles, 10 December 1949, National Archives, PREM 8/1580

31 George VI to Duke of Windsor (draft), 11 December 1949, Royal Archives, RA/PSO/GVI/C/042/030

32 Alan Lascelles to George VI, December 1949, Royal Archives, RA/PSO/GVI/C/042/031

33 George VI to Duke of Windsor (draft), *c.*16 December 1949, Royal Archives, RA/PSO/GVI/C/042/033

34 Duke of Windsor to George VI, 6 June 1950, Royal Archives, GVI/PRIV/01/02/36

Chapter Fourteen: 'The Incessant Worries and Crises'

1 Bew, p.478

2 Churchill press statement, 16 February 1950

3 Winston Churchill to Alan Lascelles, 27 February 1950, in Gilbert, *Never Despair*, p.512

4 Raphael, pp.58-9

5 Queen Elizabeth to Prince Philip, 3 March 1950, in Shawcross, *Counting One's Blessings*, p.424

6 Gilbert, *Never Despair*, p.516

7 Alan Lascelles to *The Times*, 29 April 1950

8 *Manchester Guardian*, 25 August 1950

9 Clement Attlee to George VI, 18 August 1950, Royal Archives, RA/PSO/GVI/C/350/11

10 George VI to Clement Attlee, 21 August 1950, Royal Archives, RA/PSO/GVI/C/350/13

11 Channon diary, 6 March 1950

12 Ibid., 16 June 1950

13 Eade, p.235

14 Dean, p.117

15 Alan Lascelles to Frederick Browning, 31 March 1950, in Pimlott, *The Queen*, p.166

16 Ibid., p.162

17 Eade, p.240

18 Queen Elizabeth to Prince Philip, 21 July 1950, in Shawcross, *Counting One's Blessings*, p.426

19 Boothroyd, p.144

20 Kenneth de Courcy to Duke of Windsor, 10 June 1950, Kenneth Hugh de Courcy papers, reel 2, box 2, folder 9, Hoover Institution Library & Archives

21 Duchess of Windsor to Kenneth de Courcy, 4 July 1950, ibid.

22 Ziegler, *King Edward VIII*, p.520
23 Bryan and Murphy, p.469
24 Ibid., p.470
25 Ziegler, *King Edward VIII*, p.520
26 Charles Murphy to Walter Monckton, 6 April 1950, Dep. Monckton Trustees 20
27 Bryan and Murphy, p.470
28 Ibid., p.471
29 Ibid., p.475
30 Walter Monckton to Alan Lascelles, 5 May 1950, Dep. Monckton Trustees 20
31 Winston Churchill to Brendan Bracken, 1 August 1950, ibid.
32 Alan Lascelles to Walter Monckton, 10 May 1950, ibid.
33 Alan Lascelles to D. Rickett, 18 May 1950, Royal Archives, RA/PSO/GVI/C/042/350

Chapter Fifteen: 'It May Be That This Is the End'

1 Donoghue and Jones, p.492
2 Gilbert, *Never Explain,* p.608
3 Winston Churchill to Lord Cherwell, 8 January 1951, in Ibid, p.584
4 Channon diary, 28 November 1950
5 Michael Frayn, 'Festival', from Sissons and French
6 Channon diary, 30 May 1951
7 Ibid., 4 June 1951
8 Queen Elizabeth to Queen Mary, 15 October 1950, in Shawcross, *Counting One's Blessings*, p.430
9 Queen Elizabeth to Princess Elizabeth, 12 December 1950, ibid., p.432
10 Queen Elizabeth to Princess Elizabeth, 7 April 1951, ibid., p.437
11 King George VI to Queen Mary, 26 May 1951, in Shawcross, *Queen Elizabeth*, p.645
12 King George VI to Queen Mary, 31 May 1951, in Bradford, *George VI*, pp.598–9
13 Eade, p.241
14 King George VI to Queen Mary, 11 September 1951, in Shawcross, *Queen Elizabeth*, p.647
15 Bradford, *George VI*, p.600
16 Queen Elizabeth to Queen Mary, 17 September 1951, in Shawcross, *Counting One's Blessings*, p.438
17 Bradford, *George VI*, p.601

18 Winston Churchill to Alan Lascelles, 20 September 1951, Royal Archives, RA/PS/PSO/GVI/C/343/002

19 Queen Elizabeth to Queen Mary, 23 September 1951, in Shawcross, *Counting One's Blessings*, p.439

20 Queen Elizabeth to Alan Lascelles, 23 September 1951, ibid.

21 Duke of Windsor to George VI, 13 September 1951, Royal Archives, GVI/PRIV/01/02/37

22 Queen Elizabeth to Alan Lascelles, 23 September 1951, in Shawcross, *Counting One's Blessings*, p.439

23 Harold Nicolson diary, 24 September 1951

24 Alan Lascelles to Winston Churchill, 27 September 1951, Royal Archives, RA/PSO/GVI/C/042/362

25 Pimlott, *The Queen*, p.171

26 *Washington Evening Star,* 2 November 1951

27 Queen Elizabeth to Princess Elizabeth, 15 October 1951, in Shawcross, *Counting One's Blessings*, p.440

28 George VI Christmas day broadcast, 25 December 1951

29 Bradford, *George VI*, p.605

30 Ibid., p.607

31 Queen Elizabeth to Princess Elizabeth, 2 February 1952, in Shawcross, *Counting One's Blessings*, p.443

32 Queen Elizabeth to Queen Mary, 6 February 1952, ibid., p.444

33 Colville, p.640

34 Channon diary, 6 February 1952

Chapter Sixteen: 'And They Lived Happily Ever After'

1 Lord Athlone to Duke of Windsor, 5 January 1952, Royal Archives DW/8194, in Ziegler, *King Edward VIII*, p.527

2 Wilson Harris, *The Spectator,* 5 October 1956

3 Stephen Spender, *New York Times,* 15 April 1951

4 Bloch, *Secret File,* p.301

5 Ibid.

6 Duchess of Windsor to Bessie Merriman, 4 November 1951, ibid.

7 Alan Lascelles to Winston Churchill, 27 September 1951, Royal Archives, RA/PSO/GVI/C/042/362

8 Desmond Flower to Duke of Windsor, 26 April 1951, Royal Archives, RA/EDW/PRIV/MAIN/A/7932

9 Lord Crome to Duke of Windsor, 21 August 1951, Royal Archives, RA/DW/7988, in Ziegler, *King Edward VIII*, p.526

10 Winston Churchill to Duke of Windsor, 26 September 1951, Royal Archives, RA/DW/8023, ibid.

11 Duke of Windsor to Ulick Alexander, 6 October 1951, Royal Archives, RA/DW Add 1/184

12 Duke of Windsor to Kenneth H. Smith, 28 September 1951, Royal Archives, RA/EDW/PRIV/MAIN/A/8029

13 Duke of Windsor speech notes for BPRA annual dinner, 28 September 1951, Dep. Monckton Trustees 20

14 Duke of Windsor to Walter Monckton, 5 November 1951, Royal Archives, RA/EDW/PRIV/MAIN/A/8057

15 Duke of Windsor to George VI, 12 November, Royal Archives, GVI/PRIV/01/02/39

16 Duke of Windsor to Sir Oliver Franks, 26 November 1951, Royal Archives, RA/EDW/PRIV/MAIN/A/8065

17 Duke of Windsor press conference, 7 February 1952, in Higham, pp.336-7

18 Channon diary, 9 February 1952

19 Duchess of Windsor to Duke of Windsor, 7 February 1952, in Bloch, pp.304-5

20 Duchess of Windsor to Duke of Windsor, 10 February 1952, ibid.

21 Duchess of Windsor to Duke of Windsor, 11 February 1952, ibid.

22 Ibid., pp.306-7

23 Queen Mary to Queen Elizabeth the Queen Mother, 10 February 1952, in Shawcross, *Queen Elizabeth*, p.660

24 Duke of Windsor to Duchess of Windsor, draft letter, 13 February 1952, in Bloch, *Secret File,* pp.307-8

25 Duchess of Windsor to Duke of Windsor, 14 February 1952, ibid., pp.308-9

26 Channon diary, 15 February 1952

27 Vickers, *Behind Closed Doors,* p.304

28 Duchess of Windsor to Duke of Windsor, 15 February 1952, in Bloch, *Secret File,* pp.309-10

29 Duchess of Windsor to Duke of Windsor, 17 February 1952, ibid., pp.310-11

30 Duke of Windsor to Queen Elizabeth the Queen Mother, 17 February 1952, in Shawcross, *Queen Elizabeth*, p.660

31 Duke of Windsor to Duchess of Windsor, 22 February 1952, in Bloch, *Secret File,* pp.311-12

32 Duke of Windsor notes, ibid., pp.312-13

33 Channon diary, 19 February 1952

34 Ibid., 24 February 1952

35 Ibid., 26 February 1952

36 Ziegler, *King Edward VIII*, p.537

37 Gloucester, p.174

38 Duke of Windsor to Queen Mary, 9 October 1952, Royal Archives, RA/QM/PRIV/CC9

39 Queen Elizabeth the Queen Mother to Alan Lascelles, 29 November 1952, in Shawcross, *Counting One's Blessings*, p.447

40 Bloch, *Secret File*, p.314

41 Ibid.

42 Pimlott, *The Queen*, p.208

43 Duke of Windsor to Winston Churchill, 23 November 1952, Royal Archives, RA/EDW/PRIV/MAIN/A/8394

44 Winston Churchill to Duke of Windsor, 5 December 1952, Royal Archives, RA/EDW/PRIV/MAIN/A/8403

45 Duke of Windsor to Lord Dudley, 6 April 1953, in Ziegler, *King Edward VIII*, p.538

46 Windsor, Duke of, *The Crown and the People*, p.47

47 Duchess of Windsor to Bessie Merriman, 3 October 1952, in Bloch, *Secret File*, pp.315-16

48 Duke of Windsor to Duchess of Windsor, 9 March 1953, ibid., p.319

49 Duke of Windsor to Duchess of Windsor, 14 March 1953, ibid., p.322-3

50 Duke of Windsor to Duchess of Windsor, 21 March 1953, ibid., pp.323-5

51 Duke of Windsor to Duchess of Windsor, 27 March 1953, ibid., pp.326-8

52 Duke of Windsor to Duchess of Windsor, 31 March 1953, ibid., pp.329-30

Chapter Seventeen: 'The Hopes of the Future'

1 Nicolson diary, 6 February 1952

2 Turner, p.41

3 Eade, p.254

4 Queen Elizabeth draft for Accession Council declaration (dated 22 September 1951), Royal Archives, RA/PSO/GVI/C/343/043

5 Pimlott, *The Queen*, p.180

6 Queen mother message to the nation, 18 February 1952

7 Bradford, *Elizabeth*, p.176

8 Larman, *The Crown in Crisis*, p.96
9 Queen Mother to Queen Elizabeth, undated but late February-early March 1952, in Shawcross, *Counting One's Blessings*, p.456
10 Bradford, *Elizabeth*, p.176
11 Ibid., p.178
12 Eade, p.261
13 Pimlott, *The Queen*, p.185
14 Longford, p.157
15 Eade, p.257
16 Moran, p.378
17 Gilbert, *Never Forget*, pp.711-12
18 Channon diary, 5 June 1952
19 Churchill speech, 11 June 1952
20 Colville, pp.650-1
21 Brandreth, p.251
22 Kate Williams, p.271
23 Channon diary, 26 February 1952
24 Larman, *The Windsors at War*, p.331
25 Gilbert, *Never Forget*, p.823
26 Winston Churchill to Pamela Lytton, 3 May 1953, ibid., p.824
27 Longford, p.154
28 Pimlott, *The Queen*, p.204
29 Channon diary, 21 May 1952
30 *Daily Mirror*, 28 February 1953
31 Channon diary, 10 January 1953
32 Ibid., 6 April 1953
33 Pimlott, *The Queen*, p.205
34 Ibid., p.206
35 Ibid., p.207
36 Rose, p.36

Chapter Eighteen: 'God Save the Queen'

1 R. M. MacColl, 'Crowds singing in the rain', *Daily Express*, 2 June 1953
2 Pimlott, *The Queen*, p.208
3 Chadwick, p.81
4 Hoare, p.401
5 *The Times*, 28 May 1953
6 Glenconner, p.65
7 Channon diary, 2 June 1953

8 Turner, p.43
9 Bradford, *Elizabeth*, p.176
10 Beaton, p.136
11 Elizabeth II broadcast, 2 June 1953

Illustration Credits

Page 1
Above - Jack Esten/Popperfoto via Getty Images
Left - NCJ - Topix/NCJ Archive/Mirrorpix via Getty Images

Page 2
Left - Paul Popper/Popperfoto via Getty Images
Below - Thomson Topix/Mirrorpix/Getty Images

Page 3
Above - Popperfoto via Getty Images
Right - Associated Press/Alamy

Page 4
Left - Fox Photos/Getty Images
Below left - Central Press/Getty Images
Below - PA Images/Alamy

Page 5
Above - Keystone/Hulton Archive/Getty Images
Below - Keystone-France/Gamma-Keystone via Getty Images

Page 6
Left - Ullstein bild via Getty Images
Below left - Erika Stone/Getty Images

Page 7

Left – Keystone Features/Hulton Archive/Getty Images
Right – Central Press/Hulton Archive/Getty Images
Below – Keystone/Getty Images

Page 8

Left – Hulton-Deutsch Collection/CORBIS/Corbis via Getty Images
Centre – Picture Post/Hulton Archive/Getty Images
Right – Monty Fresco/Topical Press Agency/Hulton Archive/Getty Images

Index